MW01120315

The Science of Crime Measurement

Crime statistics are ubiquitous in modern society – but how accurate are they? This book investigates the science of crime measurement by focusing on four main questions: how do we count crime? How do we calculate crime rates? Are there other measurements of crime? What are the issues surrounding crime statistics? All too often we take the measurement of crime at face value when there is, in fact, a science behind it.

This book specifically deals with issues related to spatially referenced crime data that are used to analyse crime patterns across the urban environment. The first section of the book considers alternative crime rate calculations, whilst the second section contains a thorough discussion of a measure of crime specialisation. Finally, the third section addresses a number of aggregation issues that accompany such data: crime type aggregations, temporal aggregations of crime data, the stability of crime patterns over time, and the importance of spatial scale.

This book builds on a growing body of literature about the science of crime measurement and offers a comprehensive account of this growing subfield of criminology. The book speaks to wider debates in the fields of crime analysis, environmental criminology and crime prevention and will be perfect reading for advanced level undergraduate and graduate students looking to find out more about the measurement of crime.

Martin A. Andresen is an Associate Professor in the School of Criminology and Institute for Canadian Urban Research Studies at Simon Fraser University. His research interests include crime measurement, spatial crime analysis, environmental criminology, and the geography of crime. This research has been published in leading journals on both criminology and geography including *Applied Geography*, *British Journal of Criminology*, *Environment and Planning A*, *Journal of Research in Crime and Delinquency*, and *Urban Studies*.

The Science of Crime Measurement

Issues for spatially referenced crime data

Martin A. Andresen

Routledge
Taylor & Francis Group

LONDON AND NEW YORK

First published 2013
by Routledge
2 Park Square, Milton Park, Abingdon, Oxon, OX14 4RN

Simultaneously published in the USA and Canada
by Routledge
711 Third Avenue, New York, NY 10017

Routledge is an imprint of the Taylor & Francis Group, an informa business

British Library Cataloguing in Publication Data
A catalogue record for this book is available from the British Library

Library of Congress Cataloging-in-Publication Data
A catalog record has been requested for this book

ISBN: 978-0-415-85609-6 (hbk)
ISBN: 978-0-203-72825-3 (ebk)

Typeset in Times New Roman
by Cenveo Publisher Services

For my dad

Contents

Figures

Tables

Preface

As with most books, the origins of this one began long ago, approximately 10 years ago. During graduate school, studying international economics, I was discussing research ideas with my friend and colleague, Greg W. Jenion. Greg was a graduate student in criminology and we figured there must be some way we could combine our skill sets to investigate some criminological phenomenon. After many discussions, not unlike the ones we still have today, we settled on a measurement issue and its impact on homicide trends in Canada. From that moment forward I became fascinated with the measurement of crime, particularly from a spatial perspective as my own interests shifted from economics to economic geography. The research in this book is the culmination of the ideas I have had for a number of years, and it deals with issues that have made me wonder whether my ideas have had an impact on the spatial analysis of crime. As with most academics, I had a "plan" of what I hoped to accomplish and how everything was connected. But our world, more often than not, rewards piecemeal publication, not research monographs. This book brings together the original plan plus more in order to tell the original story I was interested in. As with most works, this is not an end, but the beginning of my interests in spatial criminology.

Martin A. Andresen
School of Criminology
Institute for Canadian Urban Research Studies
Simon Fraser University
Burnaby, British Columbia
Canada

Acknowledgements

As with most quests, this one was not done alone. A number of my professors have had profound impacts on my academic trajectory. Richard G. Harris, Peter Kennedy, and Nicolas Schmitt all had significant influences on my academic career while at Simon Fraser University (SFU). I literally owe my academic career to my PhD supervisor, Trevor J. Barnes, at the Department of Geography, University of British Columbia (UBC). Spanning my academic endeavors at both SFU and UBC and someone who continues to be an influential mentor of mine is Stephen Easton. I would like to acknowledge and thank you all for the roles you have had and continue to play in my career.

Upon graduation I switched academic disciplines again and have Greg W. Jenion to thank for that. Greg has been a great friend, colleague, and co-author over the past 20 years. Like it or not, spatial criminology has Greg to thank for my presence in this field.

At the School of Criminology, SFU I have a fantastic set of colleagues with whom I teach, research, and serve. The Institute for Canadian Urban Research Studies, where almost all of my data resides, has a brilliant set of scholars with whom I have the pleasure to work. I specifically like to thank Paul and Patricia Brantingham for welcoming me into their institute. It truly is a pleasure to be a part of their research team.

Last, but certainly not least, I would like to thank Thomas Sutton and Nicola Hartley of Routledge. These two individuals not only helped me in the process of writing the original proposal and successfully convinced Routledge to publish this book, but also proved to be extremely helpful throughout the process.

Of course, the usual disclaimer regarding any remaining errors in this book applies.

1 The science of crime measurement

Introduction

Crime statistics are ubiquitous in contemporary society. In both Canada and the United States there are special government statistical bodies that solely measure criminological phenomena: the Canadian Centre for Justice Statistics and the Bureau of Justice Statistics, respectively. Whether it is through the nightly newscast, national or local papers, or discussions around the coffee machine, we are inundated with statistics regarding crime: crime is going up, crime is going down, or crime is higher/lower relative to other places in the country. Indeed, we torture our students in many introductory criminological courses by placing provinces or states in national contexts, and by placing our nations in international contexts. But how reliable is this information that we pass on to our students and colleagues? Many departments within the arts and social sciences are split between those who accept or reject the quantification of social phenomena. The rejection of this quantification, in many cases, is simply a mistrust of the data or the methods of data representation. Consequently, if we are going to use quantification we must do so critically.

But is this issue restricted to the academy? Generally, no. Despite our (unnecessary?) reliance on the quantification of social phenomena (Porter, 1996), there is a general mistrust of statistics in the public eye. Well known is the adage attributed to Benjamin Disraeli: "there are lies, damned lies and [then there are] statistics" (cited in Twain, 1906). Compounding this general mistrust of statistics are "journalists and politicians, among others, [who] often issue declarations about crime rates, … [without encouraging the public] … to think critically about what the crime rate measures really are" (Sacco and Kennedy, 2002: 92)—Pallone (1999) presents a rather scathing attack on nightly newscasts reporting on crime. This use and misuse of criminological statistics has implications for society at large because "[w]e may factor information about crime rates into our decisions about whether we will buy a home in a particular neighbourhood, vacation in a particular place, or allow our children to attend a particular school" (Sacco and Kennedy, 2002: 94).

It can be generally stated that the public and the authorities are most interested in crime rates as they pertain to both general societal risk and personal issues of safety/security. This is one possible reason why the media give crime rates so much attention (Sacco, 2000). What has become increasingly problematic over the years is when academics, politicians, and the media depart from making broad general public risk statements and move toward inferences between conventional crime rates and personal risk.

The work in this book contributes to these discussions of the proper representation of (spatially referenced) crime data. This chapter begins with a relatively brief overview of some general issues with all forms of crime data, spatially referenced or not. It concludes with a brief outline of the subject matter covered in subsequent chapters.

Official crime data

One of the most common sets of data used in criminology is official crime data. These data may be from police agencies, the criminal justice system (courts), or (sub-)national criminal justice statistical agencies. Despite these data being "official," they have a number of issues. One of the most important issues relates to the definitions of crime. This has implications for both temporal and cross-sectional analyses. If definitions change over time, any analysis of time-series crime data must account, or control, for changes in definitions; and for cross-sectional studies—just because a crime type has the same name in one place does not mean that it refers to exactly the same crime(s) in another.

The definitions of crime are all too often sociohistorical constructions such that behaviors once considered immoral or illegal became acceptable, or vice versa (LaFree, 1989). One such crime type is rape. Gender norms and patriarchal culture have dominated the response to sexual violence, more generally, in the criminal justice system (Clark and Lewis, 1977; Galvin, 1985; Estrich, 1986; Los, 1994). Historical definitions of rape are from English Common Law. In this context, women were considered the property of their fathers or husbands, such that the rape of a woman was considered a property crime, not a violent crime—the father or husband was the victim in these crimes (Clark and Lewis, 1977; Estrich, 1986; Los, 1994). Needless to say, these constructions of crime have come under much scrutiny during the past few decades. One such response in Canada was to change the definitions of sexual violence in 1983: the offenses of rape, attempted rape, indecent assault on a male, and indecent assault on a female were replaced with sexual assault (level 1), sexual assault with a weapon (level 2) and aggravated sexual assault (level 3) (Department of Justice Canada, 1990, 1992; Roberts and Grossman, 1994). These changes complicate any time series analysis of these data. Though 30 years have now passed allowing for a relatively long time-series for analysis, data on sexual violence are available at least back to 1962 in Canada. As such, 20 years of data can only be added to such an analysis with caution.

In the context of a cross-national comparison, even the crime of aggravated assault lends itself to complications. In Canada, assault, just as with sexual assault, is separated into "levels": assault (level 1), assault with weapon or causing bodily harm (level 2), and aggravated assault (level 3). However, if one wanted to compare aggravated assaults in Canada to those in the United States, the Canadian levels 1 and 2 would have to be added together to be equivalent to aggravated assault in the United States. Therefore, one must not simply assume that the same name means the same thing, even for countries that share an international border.

The most well-known, cited, and used official crime data are from the Uniform Crime Reporting (UCR) system. The UCR began in the United States in 1930— see Mosher *et al.* (2011) for a detailed history of the UCR in the United States. Nearly all of the law enforcement agencies in the United States provide data to the Federal Bureau of Investigation (FBI) that then produces a number of annual statistical publications (FBI, 2012).

In Canada, the UCR began in 1962 through what is now known as the Canadian Centre for Justice Statistics. The data in the Canadian UCR represent reported crime that has been substantiated by the police, including data on the number of criminal incidents, the clearance status of those incidents, and the person(s) charged, if any. In 1988, a new version of the Canadian UCR was created that includes data on incidents, victims, and accused, referred to as UCR2. Both the UCR1 and UCR2 are collected simultaneously—in the United States, the equivalent data are the National Incident-Based Reporting System (NIBRS), which began in 1987 (FBI, 2012; Statistics Canada, 2012). Unlike the United States, responding to the UCR survey is mandatory in Canada—very few police agencies in the United States do not respond to their UCR. More than 1,200 separate police detachments respond to the UCR survey, a total of 204 police forces (Statistics Canada, 2012).

Another form of official crime data—though this may better be considered "unofficial" official crime data—is calls for service to the police. Calls for service data have become increasing available since the late 1980s (Sherman *et al.*, 1989). Such data most often come through a computer-aided dispatch (CAD) system that processes the requests for police service made directly to the police detachment, through an (911) emergency service and allocated to the police detachment, or calls made by police officers while out on patrol. The primary advantage of calls for service data is its raw form. Unlike official crime reports, such as those filled through the UCR, calls for service data are typically not screened. As such, they are sometimes referred to as police activity data. As discussed by Sherman *et al.* (1989), some police agencies have been found to file official crime reports for as few as 66 percent of the calls for service. Another advantage of calls for service data is that they necessarily include an address for spatial analysis—the UCR2.2 in Canada, which began in 2004, includes geocoding information.

Calls for service data do have their limitations relative to UCR data. Because they are (initially) unfounded, calls for service data may include too many crimes. In addition, because of the availability of reporting locations (this is less of an issue today with mobile phones), particular places such as police stations, gas stations, and convenience stores may suffer from substantial over-reporting (Sherman *et al.*, 1989).

Despite all the benefits of (unofficial) official crime data, they suffer from a number of more general limitations. First, crime reporting is a phenomenon that will vary from police detachment to police detachment. This may be due to the history and/or culture of the population living within the police detachment, or the detachment itself which may focus on particular crime(s) because of issues with the detachment itself.

Second, as discussed in great detail in subsequent chapters, crime rates based on these official data need population figures for the calculation of crime rates. In addition to the issues discussed in subsequent chapters, the measurement of the census population is subject to significant error in most years. In most countries, the national census is conducted every 5 or 10 years. This means that population numbers and crime counts may be off by as many as 9 years. Mosher *et al.* (2011) cite an example of crime rates in 1949 using 1940 census population data, which greatly overestimated the crime rate because of the population growth in that particular decade. Of course, most countries (including Canada and the United States) use birth, death, and migration data to aid in yearly population estimates. However, with a decade between some census years, this allows for a lot of error to be generated and propagated over a span of 9 years.

Third, the crime funnel is particularly problematic. The crime funnel refers to the decreasing number of crimes that are reported as one moves through the criminal justice system: the total amount of actual crimes, the number of crimes reported to the police, the number of crimes that lead to charges, the number of crimes that actually make it to court, etc. As such, when we are working with official crime data, we are effectively working with a sample of criminal activity. The question is whether or not our samples of criminal activity are representative in a number of dimensions.

Victimization survey data

One method to address the last-mentioned limitation with official crime data, namely under-reporting, is to conduct a victimization survey. Rather than asking the police how many crimes have been committed, the researcher asks (potential) victims of crime. Victimization surveys may take a variety of forms from being rather small to quite large. Small victimization surveys, often referred to as self-report data (see Mosher *et al.*, 2011), will either lack a proper control group (non-victims of crime) or cover a relatively small geographic area. Large victimization surveys, discussed here, refer to national victimization surveys that contain information on a sample of the total population. These surveys gather data on both victims and non-victims of crime for the purposes of inference. This sampling technique alleviates the difficulties associated with not having a control group, but introduces another (geographical) difficulty—the ecological fallacy. Any activities inferred at the national level must necessarily be assumed to be representative of the local area under study if these national victimization surveys are to be used. However, if national statistical agencies wish to make inference at the sub-national level, such as with Canada, the methods of data gathering are modified appropriately.

One obvious question is: how many people to survey? Surveys are expensive. This is why most censuses are only undertaken every 10 years. However, there are statistical issues regarding how many individuals, for example, must be sampled for the results to be representative for the entire population. The choice of sample size depends, primarily, on three factors:

1. How much error can you tolerate?
2. How much confidence do you want to have with your estimates?
3. At which level do you want to be able to make inference?

For example, let us say that a victimization survey (as with the example used below) has a margin of error of plus or minus 2 percent at a 95 percent level of confidence. This simply means that if the victimization survey were conducted 100 times, the criminal victimization data would be within 2 percentage points above or below the percentage reported in 95 of the 100 surveys. In other words, Statistics Canada surveys the population and finds that 10 percent of the survey respondents were a victim of robbery in a given year. With the confidence level being 95 percent with a 2 percent margin of error, if the victimization survey were conducted 100 times, the percentage of the population who have been a victim of robbery will range between 8 and 12 percent most (95 percent) of the time.

Quite clearly, victimization surveys, and surveys in general, are better with higher degrees of confidence and lower margins of error. However, as mentioned above, these surveys are expensive and get more expensive as sample sizes increase, which is a necessity for increasing confidence and reducing the margin of error. An example is presented in Table 1.1.

A common confidence level and margin of error combination in surveys is 95 percent confidence with a 2 percent margin of error. The far right column in Table 1.1 shows the sample size needed to be representative for Canada and its various provinces and territories—the approximate populations of these administrative units are shown in column 2 for reference. Immediately obvious is that changing the base population from 33,500,000 (Canada) to 32,000 (Nunavut) has barely any impact on the size of the sample necessary to satisfy the current confidence level and margin of error. A sample of 2,401 is all that is necessary for a representative sample for Canada, but if inference is to be made at the level of the province and territory, a sample of 30,681 is necessary—coincidentally, the victimization survey undertaken by Statistics Canada uses a sample of 25,000. However, if more precision and confidence are necessary (99 percent confidence and 1 percent margin of error, for example), a much larger sample is necessary. For all of Canada, a sample of 16,580 is now necessary and if inference is to be made at the level of the provinces and territories, the sample now needs to be 212,724. This latter sample is an increase of almost seven times from what may be perceived is a small change for the confidence level and margin of error.

The Canadian victimization survey, administered as part of the General Social Survey, reveals some interesting patterns. Overall, in 2009, 31 percent of criminal victimization was reported to the police, down from 34 percent in 2004, and from 37 percent in 1999 (Perreault and Brennan, 2010). The Canadian victimization survey also covers the following individual crime types: sexual assault, robbery, physical assault, residential break and enter, motor vehicle/parts theft, theft of

Table 1.1 Example sample sizes by administrative unit, 2 percent margin of error and 95 percent confidence[a]

	Population	Sample for: confidence, 99%; margin of error, 1%	Sample for: confidence, 95%; margin of error, 2%
Canada	33,500,000	16,580	2,401
Ontario	12,850,000	16,566	2,401
Quebec	7,900,000	16,553	2,401
British Columbia	4,400,000	16,525	2,400
Alberta	3,650,000	16,513	2,400
Manitoba	1,200,000	16,362	2,397
Saskatchewan	1,000,000	16,317	2,396
Nova Scotia	920,000	16,294	2,395
New Brunswick	750,000	16,229	2,394
Newfoundland	515,000	16,070	2,390
Prince Edward Island	140,000	14,831	2,361
Northwest Territory	41,000	11,810	2,269
Yukon Territory	34,000	11,149	2,243
Nunavut	32,000	10,925	2,234
Sum of individual provinces and territories		212,724	30,681

Source: Statistics Canada (2011). Sample size calculations performed using the sample size calculator at Raosoft.com: <http://www.raosoft.com/samplesize.html>.

Note: [a]All populations are rounded for simplicity.

household property, vandalism, and theft of personal property. The percentage of self-reported victimizations reported to the police for these individual crime types are shown in Table 1.2. There is quite a variation across crime types, but property crimes have much greater levels of reporting to the police, particularly those crime types that will involve greater economic losses and require insurance such as residential break and enter and motor vehicle/parts theft. The reasons for a lack of reporting to the police range from "not important enough" (almost 70 percent) to "fear of publicity or news coverage" (approximately 5 percent).

Of course, victimization surveys are a great asset to the study of crime, but they also have their limitations. Discussed at great length in Mosher *et al.* (2011), a few of the "bigger" issues are mentioned here. First, only crimes that have a direct victim are represented in these victimization surveys. So-called victimless crimes such as drug abuse, alcohol abuse (violations), prostitution, and gambling are typically excluded. Why? One reason is that in order to put this information into the survey, one must implicate oneself of such violations.

Second, as discussed above in the context of sexual assault, defining crimes can be difficult. Property crimes tend to be easier: has your home been burgled? Has your car been stolen? Violent crimes, however, may have greater difficulty.

Table 1.2 Percentage of self-reported victimizations reported to the police

Crime type	1999	2004	2009
Total victimization	37	34	31
Sexual assault	n/a	8	n/a
Robbery	46	46	43
Physical assault	37	39	34
Total violent victimization	31	33	29
Break and enter	62	54	54
Motor vehicle/parts theft	60	49	50
Household property theft	32	29	23
Vandalism	34	31	35
Total household victimization	44	37	36
Theft of personal property	35	31	28

Source: Perreault and Brennan (2010).

Also, different cultural and social groups may define violence differently. Would a male in his early twenties say he was assaulted on such a survey in the context of a "fight" with a friend while intoxicated? Perhaps, but some may not consider such an event an assault.

Lastly, because crimes are so rare, it may be difficult to make proper inference for certain crime types or by the type of victim (age and sex, for example). In order to make proper inferences in these cases, the sample size may have to be increased substantially. If you want to be able to differentiate by sex, for example, the sample must be increase by a factor of 2.

Incidents of crime versus participations

One question that may be asked in the context of counting crime is how many times should we count each criminal incident? The obvious answer here is once, but, quite often, criminal incidents include more than one offender, that is, co-offending. The early studies of co-offending reveal that co-offending represents a substantial portion of youth offending: 82 percent of youth offences in Chicago (Shaw and McKay, 1931); 75 percent in Flint, Michigan (Gold, 1970); and 85 percent, based on a review of 11 other empirical analyses (Erickson, 1971). Recent research supports these earlier findings (Carrington, 2009; Andresen and Felson, 2010, 2012a, 2012b), but others question the magnitude of this phenomenon (Stolzenberg and D'Alessio, 2008). However, even those studies that are critical of the overwhelming magnitudes in some research still show co-offending to be a significant component of offending, more generally. As such, should we count the number of incidents, or the number of "participations" in crime? The answer, of course, is not so simple because it depends on context. In terms of resources for criminal justice systems, for example, the number of offenders in the system matters more than the number of incidents when considering time and resources: more police resources to charge two offenders than one offender, and similarly for processing more than one offender in a single incident for the courts.

In order to explain the counting issue, suppose that a *pair* of boys breaks into a car, and another (acting alone) breaks into another car. You have two *incidents*, one involving two *participations*. Thus two incidents have produced three participations. The following inequality helps keep track of the numbers:

Number of Offenders ≤ Number of Incidents ≤ Number of Participations

Thus 100 offenders might be involved in 150 incidents, and perhaps 200 participations, given that some incidents involve co-offending. Accordingly, there are more co-offending participations than co-offending events, and more co-offending events than co-offending persons. As Reiss (1988) emphasized, understanding participations requires multiple-counting of crime events. This is illustrated using the National Crime Victimization Survey in the United States.

Table 1.3 shows an example of this "crime accounting" of participations with violent crime types in the United States' National Crime Victimization Survey, 2006: column A shows the number of incidents, the number used for crime rate calculations; column B shows the number of incidents that have multiple participants (co-offending). As shown in column C, the percentage of co-offending incidence ranges from a low of just under 15 percent (rape and sexual assaults) to a high of 53 percent (completed robbery). As argued by Reiss (1988), such calculations underestimate the impact of co-offending, but these numbers still show that the co-offending phenomenon is of a magnitude that deserves the attention of those studying crime. In order to account for multiple participants, column A is multiplied by 1.5; co-offending incidents, by definition, have at least 2 offenders, but in order to prevent excessive multiple counting (one participation is included in column A), column B is only multiplied by 1.5—as such, this is an underestimate of the total number of participations. Column F shows the impact of accounting for participations. The increases in the number of participations range from 22 percent to almost 80 percent. There is no doubt that any agency that must deal with offenders, not just their incidents, is greatly affected by participations.

Repeat victimization

Co-offending participations increase the numbers for crimes through the consideration of participations, but does the counting of incidents overestimate the actual risk of victimization? It depends on who, or what, you are. Another way of framing this question is as follows: is crime as prevalent as the numbers suggest?

Over the past 20 years, a relatively large volume of research has been conducted in the area of repeat victimization. Repeat victimization is the victimization of the same target, however the target is defined, be it the same person,

Table 1.3 Violent victimization incidents and estimated violence participations taking co-offenders into account, by types of violence, United States, 2006[a]

Type of violent victimization	NCVS original violent incident estimates for the whole population			New estimated violence participations taking co-offending into account		
	(A)	*(B)*	*(C)*	*(D)*	*(E)*	*(F)*
	Violent incidents (base, N)	Multiple participation incidents	Column (B) as % of (A)	1.5 × column (B)	Sum of columns (A) and (D)	Estimated % increase, (E) over (A)
A. Total crimes of violence	5,941,650	1,207,340	20.3	1,811,010	7,752,660	**+30.5**
1. Completed violence	1,971,040	531,200	26.9	796,800	2,767,840	**+40.4**
2. Attempted, threatened	3,970,600	676,140	17.0	1,014,210	4,984,810	**+25.5**
B. Total robbery	685,850	328,990	48.0	493,485	1,179,335	**+72.0**
1. Completed robbery	458,200	242,820	53.0	364,230	822,430	**+79.5**
2. Attempted robbery	227,630	86,160	37.9	129,240	356,870	**+56.8**
C. Total assaults (excluding sexual)	4,994,850	839,820	16.8	1,259,730	6,254,580	**+25.2**
1. Aggravated assault	1,300,400	274,840	21.1	412,260	1,712,660	**+31.7**
2. Simple assault	3,694,450	564,980	15.3	847,470	4,541,920	**+22.9**
D. Rape and sexual assaults	260,920	38,520	14.8	57,780	318,700	**+22.1**

Source: Rates calculated from United State Census Bureau (2006): National Crime Victimization Survey (NCVS); Tables 38 and 44.
Note: [a] Based on offender reports of the number of offenders.

household, business, vehicle, place, etc. This research has shown that a small proportion of targets experience a vastly disproportionate amount of victimization. For example, Pease (1998) found that 1 percent of people experience 59 percent of personal crime including violence, and that 2 percent of households experience 41 percent of property crime. Needless to say, criminal victimization is hardly a random event.

Farrell and Pease (2008) outline four ways in which repeat victimization occurs: spatial repeat (same offender, same place, same offence), temporal repeat (quick repeat by same offender), crime-type repeat (same crime-type, same type of target), and tactical repeat (same tactic). Clearly, repeat victimization has a number of different forms. However, the key point is that the reporting of crime incidents that include significant proportions of repeats (such as domestic violence and burglary) overstates the risk of victimization to the average person. If these crimes are also co-offences, then counting participations aggravates this situation even further.

Issues for spatially referenced crime data

Needless to say, the measurement of crime is rather complex. Depending upon what message you wish to convey, there are going to be a number of general issues that need to be considered, even from this restricted list of issues for the measurement of crime, in general—see Mosher *et al.* (2011) for a comprehensive account of this phenomenon. In this book, however, the concern is specifically toward spatially referenced crime data, which have all the issues discussed above, but also have a number of issues specific to their form of crime data. As above, the issues covered in this book are far from exhaustive. Rather, my research over the past 10 years is brought together here with the addition of new material. Though these works appeared in, at times, disparate places, there has always been an underlying theme to my research.

In Part I, the calculation of crime rates is investigated. Much of the research that relates to crime rate calculations involves measuring the numerator, namely, crime counts—an issue that is discussed above with regard to official crime data and victimization survey data. However, as outlined by Sarah Boggs (1965) almost 50 years ago, we must consider both the numerator and the denominator in crime rate calculations if we want the number to be meaningful. Curiously, aside from the work here, and some other research I have done with colleagues, very little work has been done in this research area since. As shown below, sometimes changing the denominator has no impact on crime rate calculations and their resulting patterns, but sometimes it does. At times, the spatial shifts in patterns are subtle, but important. And the impact of changing denominators matters not only for neighborhood-level analyses, but also analyses performed at the municipal level.

In Part II, an alternative crime measure, the location quotient, is investigated. After an introduction of the location quotient, including a discussion of its alternative interpretation relative to the crime rate, it is used in the analysis of patterns at the neighborhood, municipal, and provincial levels. Not only does the location quotient provide a different and interesting interpretation, but leads to the researcher asking different questions.

Lastly, in Part III, the stability of crime patterns and various aggregation issues are investigated. The overarching result from these works is that most of the aggregations we take for granted in our crime data and analyses do not appear to be appropriate. When considering the stability of crime patterns over time, a common (though often implicit) assumption in the spatial criminology literature is ecological stability. Otherwise, much of our using historical crime data in various analyses, even if it is only a few years old, would have little practical use for criminal justice police and policing today. It is shown that this stability can only be assumed in the current context if one is using micro-spatial units of analysis such as the street segment. Moreover, in the other investigations of aggregation issues, a common finding is that micro-spatial units of analysis are less problematic than the more common larger spatial units of analysis such as the census tract. In addition, aggregating across crime types (relatively common) and across time makes yearly crime data observations (almost always done) appear to be problematic.

Part I

Crime analysis and the ambient population

The measurement of crime is a necessity for any quantitative assessment of criminological theory or policy change. This measurement is particularly useful when comparing two or more spatial units, with respect to criminal activity. Crime counts are one measure of criminal activity often used in the spatial analysis of crime. These counts are typically used in "hotspot" analysis, with hotspots generally being defined as areas with a "higher than expected level of criminal activity" (Ratcliffe and McCullagh, 2001: 331). However, high crime counts may simply be present because of the volume of people in a given area. Because crime occurs when an offender, a victim, and a law intersect in time and space, a greater number of people implies a greater number of both potential offenders and potential victims.

Given that high levels of crime may occur simply because of the high levels of people in particular places such as central business districts (Schmid, 1960a, 1960b), crime rates are commonly used to assess the risk of crime by controlling for the population at risk—this property constitutes the crime rate as one of the most common measures in crime analysis, usually employing the residential population as the control. Crime rates are an important tool in communicating messages to the public by government authorities and interest groups. However, rarely do these messages provide the surrounding context to changes in these crime rates; worse, they often infer a change in public or personal safety based upon the change in the crime rate. In the past, scholars have urged caution when using crime rates to infer risk. Prudence has been sought because crime rates often fluctuate and these fluctuations may not reflect actual changes in personal or public risk. As authorities frequently use crime rates and the media to support their policies, the constant barrage of fluctuating crime rates produces an exhausted and cynical public attitude toward statistics. This is especially true if the reporting of rates does not reflect the current perception of the public. The perception of the public is most often developed during the conscious hours of the day and not the unconscious hours, while sleeping. Worse yet, over time, if the public experiences no evidence of the changing crime rate and its relationship to public or personal safety/security, the erosion of public trust in authoritative messages begins.

In this first part of the book, the crime rate and its calculation are investigated. Specifically, the population at risk is used to calculate the crime rate.

The literature on the appropriate calculation of crime rates (populations at risk) to infer risk goes back at least 40 years. Though some research has attempted to measure the true population at risk for criminal victimization and to show the benefits of doing so for particular crimes, the acquisition of such measures may be costly—both in terms of financial and time resources.

The constant development of new technology brings about changes in the way we view the world because new information and data become available. One such set of data is a measure of the population at risk. These data, the ambient population, may be used to calculate crime rates at a spatial resolution not possible before. In the chapters that follow, the ambient population data are introduced and analyzed in the context of crime at a number of different spatial scales.

Chapter 2 introduces the ambient population data, shows the spatial impact of this different population at risk on crime rate calculations, and discusses a preliminary evaluation of the data in the local context of Vancouver, British Columbia, Canada. It is generally shown that the traditionally calculated crime rates using the resident population are vastly different from the ambient-based crime rate calculations, but also that the ambient population data are not perfect. It is argued that these data are an improvement over the traditional population at risk, the resident population, but that we need to realize that any biases present in the traditional calculations are not eliminated, but reduced.

Chapter 3 shows the impact of the different crime rate calculations on a variety of spatial crime analysis methods. Using data from different years, different (neighborhood) levels of analysis, and different spatial analytical methods, it shows that changing the population at risk can have some substantial changes in the results of an analysis.

Chapter 4 on diurnal movements is a short chapter which shows the utility of the ambient population in crime rate calculations for municipalities in a larger metropolitan region. Though there is a moderate degree of similarity between resident- and ambient-based rates, there are some significant changes in the rankings of the various municipalities within the Metro Vancouver area. Moreover, these changes are in unexpected places.

Overall, the research within the chapters of Part I shows that we cannot simply take a crime rate at face value. Many decisions have to be made before the crime rate may be calculated and each of those decisions has implications. Implications for theory, policy, and practice are all discussed in these chapters.

2 Ambient populations and the calculation of crime rates and risk

Introduction

Measuring crime has always been a key priority for criminologists. Early on, scholars realized the utility of "construct[ing] crime occurrence rates on the basis of environmental opportunities specific to each crime" (Boggs, 1965: 899). Such constructions yield valuable information whether crime targets in certain spatial areas are be more exploited than similar targets in other spatial areas, particularly when crime counts are similar and populations at risk differ (Pittman and Handy, 1962; Boggs, 1965). However, calculating these opportunity-based crime occurrence rates meant a deviation from the conventional calculation of crime rates that used the residential population in the spatial unit under analysis as the denominator. As Boggs (1965) states: "[s]ince the number of events, or the numerator, varies with the type of crime, the denominator should likewise vary so that the whole number of exposures to the risk of that specific event is incorporated as the base" (Boggs, 1965: 900). Therefore, if one always uses the residential population in the calculation of crime rates when better measures are available, valuable information is not being incorporated into the analysis. In the 1960s when Boggs put forward her idea, it was clear that using these alternative denominators may result in substantial work and would incur high costs that would have a consequence: most of the information needed to develop an opportunity-based measure was not being collected in common data sources such as the census, such that the developments of opportunity-based crime rates have been few and far between.

But does it really matter which calculation one uses, or is this issue more of an academic curiosity? Some authors argue that there is little to gain from using alternative denominators, because these denominators tend to have high correlations—such as the number of residential units and the residential population (Cohen *et al.*, 1985). They claim that any gains in insight are small relative to the cost and acquisition of the data, and conventional measures are preferred. It is also generally believed that for purposes of forecasting or looking at trends over time it makes no difference which denominator is used (Cohen *et al.*, 1985), although Andresen *et al.* (2003) show that this is not the case for Canadian homicide.

The justification for these claims has been the robust nature of official measures in the calculation of crime rates; the official crime rates are as good as any other gathered measures because they exhibit high correlations in comparative studies—some research has shown that traditional or conventional denominators work slightly better (Cohen *et al.*, 1985). The proponents of alternative denominators in crime rate calculations do not deny this finding. In fact, for certain crimes, the proponents find that the use of traditional or alternative calculations has little impact on the study results because the correlations for these crimes (such as criminal homicide, aggravated assault, and residential burglary) are very high: in some cases, $r = 0.997$ (Boggs, 1965; Cohen *et al.*, 1985). However, for many other crimes it is clear that traditional and alternative calculations are not substitutable, given that their correlations are close to zero, or even negative (Boggs, 1965)— further research has also suggested that for some specific crimes and prevention purposes it may be better to change to a more appropriate denominator (Harries, 1981, 1991). Needless to say, there is no scientific consensus on this matter of the appropriate crime rate calculation—see Reiss (1986), Johnson and Lazarus (1989), Silverman *et al.* (1996), and Sacco and Kennedy (2002) for other critical accounts of crime rate calculation. This causes us to revisit Boggs' opportunity-based crime measures. In doing so, this allows us to examine alternative data that measures the populations at risk to supplement current/traditional measures.

Data and methodology

Measuring the population at risk

In order to best measure the population at risk, the science of knowing where people are is critical (Dobson, 2004). Consequently, so is the need for a reliable and accurate database. The LandScan Global Population Database (developed by Oak Ridge National Laboratory in Tennessee) has been adopted by many US and international government agencies as well as the United Nations. It has become the "de facto world standard for these government bodies for estimating populations at risk from terrorism, technological accidents, regional conflicts, and natural disasters" (Dobson, 2003: 162). The use of this data in areas outside potentially large-scale disasters is vast, including research within criminology.

The LandScan Global Population Database provides a 24-hour ambient population estimate, at the resolution of 30 arc seconds by 30 arc seconds (latitude and longitude), approximately one square kilometer—a "quantum leap" in the precision of population estimates from the previous world standard, P-95 and Rural Cell Population from the US Census Bureau (Dobson, 2003: 163). This estimate measures how many people are expected to be in a given square kilometer at any time of the day and all days of the year, because the measure incorporates diurnal and seasonal population changes. Though this current database does not separate daytime and nighttime populations (it is a 24-hour average), the developers of these data are currently working on a daytime population measure.

Because of our daily activities, people travel to and from their residences, workplaces, and recreational sites. The LandScan Global Population Database incorporates these movements by assigning every square kilometer cell on the planet a value that is based on each cell's relative attractiveness to people pursuing these activities. Using the value in each of these cells, the national or sub-national population, based on census counts, is redistributed (Dobson *et al.*, 2003). The LandScan Global Population Database is then an estimate of the population at the one kilometer by one kilometer scale that "integrates diurnal movements and collective travel habits into a single measure" and its "purpose is to distribute populations based on their likely ambient locations integrated over a 24-hour period for typical days, weeks, and seasons" (Dobson *et al.*, 2000: 849–50).

The census population counts are redistributed to the cells using a probability coefficient based on road proximity, slope, land cover, and nighttime lights. Transportation networks (roads, rail, water, and air) are all excellent indicators of populations, particularly the road network density, which is positively related to population density; slope enters the calculations because human settlements are typically located on relatively flat terrain; land cover (desert, water, wetlands, ice, urban, etc.), due to suitability for human settlement, is an important factor (Dobson *et al.*, 2000); and "[n]ighttime lights are the best available global indicator of where people live, work, and play, and the amount of light emitted is roughly proportional to the number of people" (Dobson, 2004: 577). The overall model is the same for all regions of the world, but the individual variables need to (and do) represent different places differently—the presence of nighttime lights in energy-rich nations has different implications than for energy-poor nations. Census counts are used for population control totals, usually at the provincial level (one administration division below national).

In addition, verification and validation studies are conducted routinely for all regions of the world, and intensely for some regions within the United States by Oak Ridge National Laboratory (Dobson *et al.*, 2000). As such, ground truthing of the data is done to assess the validity of the ambient population estimates. Though there are comparisons of these data with alternatives, we are unaware of any independent verification of these actual data. This lack of independent verification does not in any way invalidate the use of these data, but until such independent verification has taken place, implementation should be done with caution.

Regardless, there are two difficulties in performing verification studies for these data. First, the algorithm used to generate the LandScan Global Population Database is proprietary, despite the fact that the data are freely available for non-commercial use. Consequently, assumptions of the algorithm as well as other factors such as parameter values used in the calculations cannot be verified or compared to empirical estimates. Second, and more important, there are not any alternative estimates of the ambient population at the relevant resolution and geographic coverage that the LandScan data can be compared to, but this should be changing soon. Mobile phone data, a good estimate of ambient populations, are beginning to emerge (albeit with corresponding privacy issues) that can be used for a comparison—see SENSEable City at http://senseable.mit.edu/. The trouble with such alternative estimates is their limited geographic coverage.

The differences between the ambient and census residential populations are, at times, extreme. In the downtown region of Houston, Texas, with a residential population of approximately 7,000, its ambient population estimate is approximately 180,000—off by a factor of 26 (Gold, 2003). Needless to say, the uses of these data for crime rate calculations are numerous. Such radical differences are not present in Vancouver, Canada, the city under study, but the utility of employing the ambient population estimates is apparent below.

It should also be noted that because the ambient population estimates are a 24-hour average for any day of the week and any day of the year, the impact of factors such as weekends and holidays cannot be accounted for in an analysis. Commercial zones of a city tend to be more crowded during the weekend and certain holidays (Christmas, for example). As such, depending on the day of the week or the time of the year, the ambient population estimate is biased upward or downward. Of course all data have their limitations, but this limitation should be kept in mind, particularly if crime data are restricted to particular days of the week or time of the year.

Census data

Census boundary units and their corresponding residential population measures are from the Statistics Canada's Census of 1996 data, packaged by DMTI Spatial Inc., for the City of Vancouver, Canada. The descriptive statistics for the residential population are provided in Table 2.1. In order to avoid data smoothing from large census boundary units, enumeration areas are used in this analysis. In Statistics Canada's Census of 1996, the smallest spatial unit is the enumeration area, followed by the census tract; in Vancouver there are 860 enumeration areas and 87 census tracts—a census tract analysis is not presented here, but such an analysis was done and the results were found to be qualitatively similar. The LandScan data covering Vancouver consists of approximately 200 pixels, therefore the use of census tracts would unnecessarily increase the coarseness of the LandScan data.

Crime data

The ultimate target in violent crime is the person. As such, the appropriate starting point when considering the ambient population and criminal activity is violent crime. In this context, violent crime includes assault, fighting, hold-ups, homicide, robbery, sexual assault, and stabbing. However, to facilitate a comparison, the results for automotive theft are also presented in the tables below. Though the

Table 2.1 Residential and ambient populations, descriptive statistics for enumeration areas

	Mean	Standard deviation	Minimum	Maximum	Aggregate
Residential population	598	402	0	1,832	514,008
Ambient population	636	872	0	8,257	547,109

target of an automotive theft is not a person, because of the car culture in North America the presence of people is a good predictor of the presence of automobiles. The most appropriate population at risk for automotive theft is a direct indicator of the number of automobiles (parking stalls and linear feet of parking, for example), but the provision of automobile theft is done to show that the results are not specific to a particular crime calculation—the results for automotive theft are qualitatively similar to those for violent crime.

The data measuring violent crime within Vancouver is the Vancouver Police Department (VPD) Calls for Service Database 1996. The calls for service are calls requesting police service that have been made directly to the VPD, from within the VPD, or through the 911 Emergency Service and allocated to the VPD. The advantage of these data is their raw form. These are not the official crime statistics from Statistics Canada that are dependent on a criminal charge, but record actual police activity across the city. Consequently, these data provide a richer assessment of violent crime than official statistics. The original data set includes 11,991 violent crimes, but after geocoding the point locations of these crimes the final data set includes 11,853 violent crimes—a 98.8 percent geocoding success rate.

Methodology

The methodology employed in this chapter is simple and straightforward, with the most demanding task being the transformation of the LandScan population data into a form to ease a comparison of ambient and residential populations. Analytically, descriptive statistics, simple correlation, and ordinary least squares regression are employed to show the differences in using these two different population measures.

Results and discussion

There are two major results in this chapter: first, there is the relationship between the residential and ambient populations; and second, there is the relationship between the crime rates using the residential and ambient populations as the denominators in the crime rates. Each is discussed in turn, followed by implications of these results.

Residential versus ambient populations

The residential and ambient populations for the City of Vancouver are shown in Figures 2.1 and 2.2, respectively. The residential population in Vancouver, though quite evenly distributed (it should be noted that this is the goal of the census), is relatively concentrated in the southern half of the city, with the northern coastal area comprising of downtown and the majority of the commercial and industrial areas. The ambient population in Vancouver, however, displays quite a different pattern. Generally speaking, the ambient population is much more clustered in

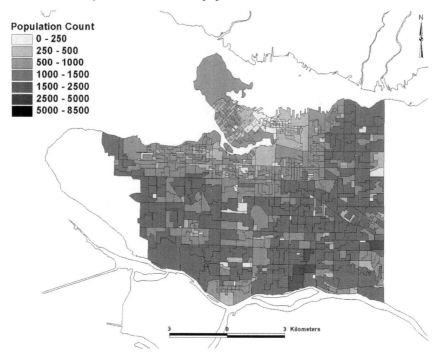

Figure 2.1 Residential population of Vancouver.
Source: Statistics Canada (1996).

particular areas. The general concentration is in the downtown and northern coastal (industrial) areas, as would be expected during daytime hours.

One descriptive statistic worth noting is the aggregated populations in Vancouver, reported in Table 2.1. The residential population is approximately 514,000, with the ambient population being approximately 547,000. We did expect the ambient population of Vancouver to exceed its residential population through an employment draw from the suburbs. However, the purpose of using the ambient population is not to estimate the *aggregated* population of the city, but the *distribution* of that population—the aggregated ambient population may also be of interest if the research is assessing the population at risk for the metropolitan area. The averages for the residential and ambient populations are similar in value, but the variances and ranges of these two populations differ substantially. The ambient population has more than twice the variation of the residential population, itself enough to indicate substantial differences between the two populations. Moreover, the range of the ambient population is almost five times that of the residential population, indicating a significantly different population distribution.

Inferentially, the two populations are related. The correlation, $r = 0.54$ (p-value < 0.001), is positive, but not nearly high enough in magnitude to claim that using

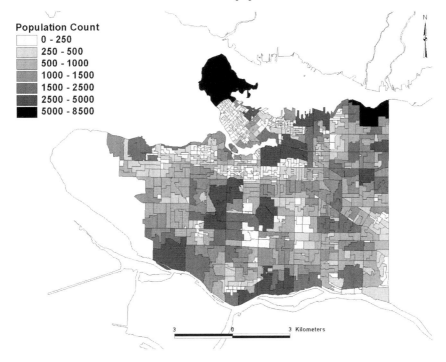

Population Count
- 0 - 250
- 250 - 500
- 500 - 1000
- 1000 - 1500
- 1500 - 2500
- 2500 - 5000
- 5000 - 8500

Figure 2.2 Ambient population of Vancouver.
Source: Oak Ridge National Laboratory (2003) and Statistics Canada (1996).

one population measure versus the other would not affect the results of an analysis. Using the residential population in order to predict the ambient population, the case for substitutability becomes even weaker—see Table 2.2. The Adjusted-R^2 is only 0.287, showing that less than 30 percent of the variation in the ambient population is explained by the residential population. Though the regression coefficient is close to unity, suggesting the two populations move together, with such a low Adjusted-R^2 there is too much noise in the regression output to have any meaningful prediction. At this point in the analysis, it is clear that obtaining the ambient population is worth the effort to supplement conventional calculations.

Table 2.2 Regression results: predicting the ambient population

	Coefficient	*Standard error*	*t-statistic*	*p-value*
Residential population	1.16	0.053	21.87	< 0.001
Constant	−56.88	29.90	−1.90	0.058

Adjusted-R^2 = 0.287

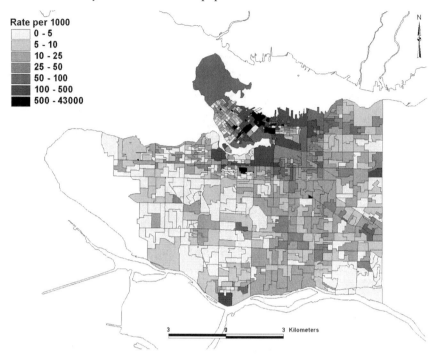

Rate per 1000
- 0 - 5
- 5 - 10
- 10 - 25
- 25 - 50
- 50 - 100
- 100 - 500
- 500 - 43000

Figure 2.3 Residential-based violent crime rate.
Source: Statistics Canada and Vancouver Police Department.

Residential- versus ambient-based crime rates

The residential- and ambient-based violent crime rates for the City of Vancouver are shown in Figures 2.3 and 2.4, respectively. The distribution of the residential- and ambient-based violent crime rates using the legend categories in Figures 2.3 and 2.4 are shown in Table 2.3 to show why the legend categories are presented this way. Legend categories are easily manipulated to produce almost any particular result—see Monmonier (1996). Therefore, the legend categories are chosen to be the same values for each of the violent crime rates to better facilitate a comparison; in addition, the legend categories are chosen such that the relative percentage of each of the residential- and ambient-based violent crime rates is similar. This presentation, then, shows the changes in the distribution of the violent crime rate rather than being a consequence of the legend category selection—the descriptive statistics for the residential- and ambient-based violent crime rates are shown in Table 2.4.

Although the patterns in each of the maps do appear to be somewhat similar, they are actually quite unrelated. The correlation coefficient for the two violent crime rates, though positive and significant, is very low in magnitude, $r = 0.09$ (p-value = 0.008), suggesting that the two violent crime rates have little statistical

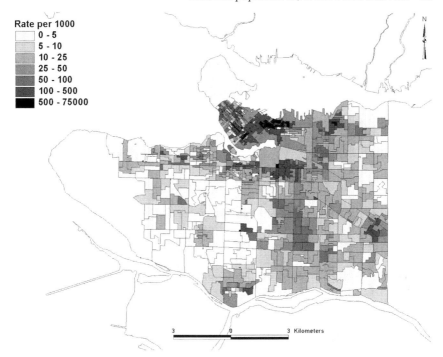

Rate per 1000
- 0 - 5
- 5 - 10
- 10 - 25
- 25 - 50
- 50 - 100
- 100 - 500
- 500 - 75000

Figure 2.4 Ambient-based violent crime rate.

Source: Oak Ridge National Laboratory (2003), Statistics Canada, and Vancouver Police Department.

relationship with each other. As shown in Table 2.5, the residential-based violent crime rate is a poor predictor of the ambient-based violent crime rate. With an Adjusted-R^2 = 0.007, the variation in the residential-based violent crime rate has very little relation to the variation in the ambient-based violent crime rate. Though the estimated parameter is significant at the 6 percent level, strong enough for

Table 2.3 Percentage distribution of violent crime rates

Violent crime rate	Residential-based		Ambient-based	
	%	Cumulative %	%	Cumulative %
0–5	35.81	35.81	29.19	29.19
5–10	17.09	52.90	13.84	43.03
10–25	23.60	76.5	23.14	66.17
25–50	9.77	86.27	11.86	78.03
50–100	5.00	91.27	7.44	88.47
100–500	5.24	96.51	10.12	95.59
500–75,000	3.49	100	4.41	100

Table 2.4 Residential- and ambient-based crime rates, descriptive statistics

		Mean	Standard deviation	Minimum	Maximum
Violent crime	Residential-based rate	161.33	1,609.25	0	43,000
	Ambient-based rate	254.07	2,701.91	0	73,000
Automotive theft	Residential-based rate	558.27	4,688.87	0	76,000
	Ambient-based rate	330.76	1,415.49	0	22,182

retention in a statistical model, its magnitude, $\beta = 0.15$, is far too low to have reliable estimates of the ambient population—the regression results for automotive theft are even weaker. As with the raw population comparison above, an appropriate magnitude to justify the substitutability of the two populations should be close to unity with a high Adjusted-R^2.

The comparison of residential- and ambient-based violent crime rates further illustrates the utility of employing the ambient population in criminological research. The comparison of the raw population numbers does show that the populations are somewhat related, but once violent crime rates are calculated using the different denominators the relationship all but disappears. This virtual absence of any relationship between residential- and ambient-based violent crime rates has strong implications for both the reporting of crime in the academy and public policy circles. In short, residential-based (violent) crime rates may provide misleading information, so ambient-based (violent) crime rates should be calculated to supplement the residential-based rates to guard against possible false inference.

The natural question to ask is why these populations differ so much to make two crime rate calculations essentially unrelated. A measure of daytime population attractiveness, the ratio of the ambient to residential population, is shown in Figure 2.5. It is clear that there are clusters of areas that lose a large proportion of their residential population and areas that significantly gain in ambient populations. Measured using the map classifications, the daytime population attractiveness variable exhibits moderate spatial clustering, Moran's $I = 0.267$, indicating that populations do move from one set of places to another throughout the day.

Table 2.5 Regression results: predicting the ambient-based rates from residential-based rates

	Violent crime	Automotive theft
Coefficient	0.152	0.048
Standard error	0.079	0.01
t-statistic	1.92	4.79
p-value	0.055	< 0.001
Adjusted-R^2	0.007	0.025

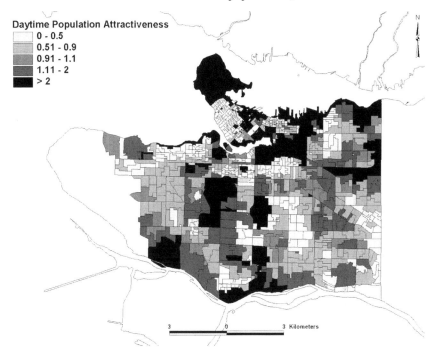

Figure 2.5 Ambient–residential population ratio.
Source: Oak Ridge National Laboratory (2003) and Statistics Canada.

One possible explanation for this particular diurnal movement is land use. Using an overlay technique, daytime population attractiveness and non-residentially zoned areas are shown to have a significant and positive correlation coefficient, $r = 0.246$. The non-residential land uses (commercial, government and institutional, parks and recreation, and resource and industrial) are apparent all across the City, but do exhibit clustering in particular areas. It is in these areas of clustering where daytime population attractiveness is highest.

This should come as no surprise. As stated above, people move away from their residences to work, shop, and take part in recreational activities. With the vast majority of people going to work during the day, the commercial, government and institutional, and resource and industrial land uses are going to be the largest attractors. This is going to be where the victims of violent crime are going to be when they are away from the relatively protected environment of the home. Schmid (1960a, 1960b) states that high levels of crime may occur simply because of the high levels of people in particular places such as central business districts. Though all these areas are not considered the central business district of Vancouver, they all have characteristics of a central business district (employment, shopping, etc.) that draw people to them throughout the day.

An evaluation of ambient population estimates for use in crime analysis

Though instructive thus far, we should not blindly accept the use of a new denominator. The ambient population data is most definitely justified from a theoretical perspective, but how these data work in practice is another matter. The LandScan ambient population data have been used in a number of contexts covering natural disasters (Løvholt *et al.*, 2012), pollution (Ghosh *et al.*, 2010), public health (Xue *et al.*, 2010; Bailey *et al.*, 2011), conservation (Platts *et al.*, 2011), poverty (Elvidge *et al.*, 2009) and population pressure on the environment (Rain *et al.*, 2007). The variety in these applications of the LandScan data clearly shows its utility.

The first known study to evaluate the LandScan ambient population data compares the LandScan data to their own method of estimating urban and rural population in northern Iraq (Mubareka *et al.*, 2008). These authors found that the LandScan data are superior to their own method for urban settlements, but not rural settlements. Compared to seven other global maps of ambient populations, Potere *et al.* (2009) found that the LandScan data also perform well in urban areas. On the other hand, Siljander *et al.* (2011) were able to create a geospatial model that outperforms the LandScan data in Kenya, and Tatem *et al.* (2011) showed that the LandScan data had the greatest uncertainty in low-income regions of the world.

The only study known in a specifically North American context is Patterson *et al.*'s (2009) analysis of quality control efforts used on the LandScan data in the context of schools and their students. These authors found that quality control efforts (that consumed a lot of labor time) did not significantly improve the baseline estimates. Therefore, the LandScan ambient population data may be used with confidence.

Overall, the LandScan ambient population data does reasonably well in these evaluations. Of course, these data have strengths and weaknesses. But given the effort that would be necessary to improve upon the LandScan data, such effort may not significantly alter the results of the analysis, especially if the analysis were in an urban and relatively high-income location. Moreover, the data necessary to make improvements over the LandScan data may not be available to all researchers, whereas the LandScan data are available. Despite these reasonably positive evaluations of the LandScan ambient population, none provides insight to its appropriateness in the spatial crime analysis literature—comparing the ambient population to factors we know attract populations and the corresponding crime.

In the analysis that follows, an evaluation of the ambient population data for its use in crime analysis is undertaken using land use data that captures population attractors. If the ambient population data measures what its providers say it does, there should be a positive relationship between these population attractors and increases in neighborhood populations.

Measurement of the ambient population

The ambient population data are used in a specific format to evaluate their usefulness in (crime) analysis. Because the ambient population represents the 24-hour average population on any given day, there should be places where the population increases or decreases relative to the resident population. For evaluation purposes, the ratio of the ambient to the resident population is used as the dependent variable in the analysis. This ratio represents the average population over the course of a 24-hour day in a given area relative to the number of people that live in that same area: areas that have a ratio greater than 1 have increases in their populations throughout the day, and vice versa. The LandScan 2006 Global Population Database is used in order to correspond with the available 2006 land use data.

Land use data

Land use data are provided by the British Columbia Assessment Authority (BCAA). The BCAA data contain the address for each legal unit of property in British Columbia, with those records for Vancouver selected for this analysis; a geocoding success rate of 99.3 percent for this subset of the BCAA data. This database includes the land use classification for each address, as well as a number of other variables not useful in the current context. There are 149 different land use classifications for the 165,814 legal units in Vancouver, but we focus on residential, commercial, industrial, institutional, recreational, vacant, and other classifications as population attractors—the residential land use classifications are expected to lose populations during the day, not attract them. Specifically, we calculate the percentage of legal unit land uses that are residential (single family dwellings, multi-family dwellings), commercial (grocery stores, restaurants, shopping malls, parking lots, etc.), industrial (factories, mills, lumber yards, etc.), institutional (schools, government buildings, hospitals, etc.), recreational (bowling alleys, campgrounds, parks, recreation centers, etc.), vacant (vacant lots in all land use classifications), and other (parking lots, billboard signs, railways, and cemeteries, for example); in addition to these individual measurements of land use, a mixed land use variable is also calculated: $1-\sum_i p^2$, where p is the percentage of each land use type. With the exception of "residential," positive relationships between these land use classifications and the ambient-resident population ratio are expected.

Empirical methods

The empirical methodology employed here is in two stages: descriptive and inferential analyses. The descriptive analysis reports on the ambient-resident population ratio across the City of Vancouver as well as the distribution of the land use variables. In order to inferentially assess the relationship between the ambient-resident population ratio and the above-listed land use classifications, a spatial regression procedure is employed—the spatial error model. The spatial error model filters out the spatial component within the data for both the dependent and independent variables in order to make proper statistical inference. This specification tends to reject spatial autocorrelation more easily in the residuals for valid statistical inference (versus the spatial lag model) because the spatial effect is filtered from both sides of the equation. As such, the spatial error model is used here rather than the spatial lag model. The general functional form of the spatial error model is as follows:

$$y = X\beta + \rho W\varepsilon + u \tag{2.1}$$

where y is the ambient-resident ratio, $X\beta$ is the matrix of independent (land use) variables and the corresponding estimated parameters, W is the spatial weights matrix that measures the spatial association between the different spatial units, ρ measures the strength of that spatial association, ε is shorthand for $y - X\beta$, and u is the independent and identically distributed error.

Queen's contiguity is used to define the spatial weights. However, the "order" of the queen's contiguity varies depending on the presence of spatial autocorrelation. For example, if two census units (a and b) share a boundary, the order of contiguity is 1. With the introduction of a third census unit, c, that borders census unit b, then a and c are considered contiguous of order 2 because there are two boundaries separating census units a and c. All estimation is performed using GeoDa 0.9.5i (http://geodacenter.asu.edu/), a spatial statistical freeware package developed by Luc Anselin.

Descriptive results

As shown above, Figure 2.5, the ambient–resident ratio does vary significantly across space and the spatial pattern for the 2006 data is very similar. For the census tracts, the average spatial unit does not change its population during the day (average value = 1.0); dissemination areas exhibit a moderate increase during the day (average value = 1.06). Inspecting the mapped results, available from the author, there are some curiosities. For both census tracts and dissemination areas the greatest population increases are in areas expected to have population increases during the day: shopping areas and major transportation thoroughfares. However, there is no increase in the population within Vancouver's central business district, the northern peninsula. In fact, according to the mapped results, population actually decreases during the day in the central business district. It is possible that there is an aggregation issue with this result, but it is present at both spatial scales. Moreover, when all spatial units within the central business district are aggregated together the data still show a decrease in population. This is obviously problematic with these data, but the increases and decreases in most areas in Vancouver are in line with expectations given local knowledge. The large increase in population at the northern-most portion of the peninsula is not part of the central business district but a city park. The substantial increase in its population during the day is likely due to the presence of major roads and ocean shipping in the area that generates a lot of light during the night.

Turning to the land use classifications, the results for residential land use are more in line with expectations by those with local knowledge of Vancouver— maps for all land use calculations are not included for brevity, but are available from the author. For both census tracts and dissemination areas, residential land use dominates Vancouver: 91.75 percent and 92.21 percent averages, respectively. In addition, though there are some changes when the spatial scale changes, the general patterns are remarkably similar with most residential land uses being outside of the central business district as would be expected.

The remaining land use classifications (commercial, industrial, institutional, recreational, vacant, and other) represent a small fraction of addresses in Vancouver with their concentrations in expected areas, particularly for commercial and industrial: commercial land uses are generally found in the central business district and along the major thoroughfares in the city, whereas industrial land uses are located in two primary areas along Burrard Inlet to the north and the Fraser River to the south. Institutional and recreational land uses are relatively evenly distributed across the city as expected given that the most common forms of these land uses are schools and neighbourhood parks, respectively. Aside from a couple of small clusters, vacant land uses appear to be randomly scattered around Vancouver, with other land uses generally being clustered close to the central business district. Overall, there are no unexpected results for the land use classification percentages in each spatial unit of analysis.

Lastly, mixed land use has significant variation across space. Mixed land use is greatest within and close to the central business district, along major thoroughfares, and along the southern border of Vancouver. Because areas with mixed land use attract a variety of different types of people, it is expected that the strongest relationship with the ambient-resident ratio will be with this variable. A preliminary examination reveals that the ambient-resident ratio and mixed land use do have similar spatial patterns. Of course, this relationship must be established empirically.

The bivariate correlations between the independent variables show the expected relationships: residential land use is negatively related to all other land uses, especially commercial, other, and mixed; commercial land use is positively related to industrial and mixed land use, but negatively related to recreational land use.

It should be noted that the primary limitation of these data, and the corresponding maps, is that the percentages are based on addresses, not land use *area*. As such, the large shopping malls in Vancouver with hundreds of stores have the same weight in the calculations as a small coffee shop. Though the maps representing the various land uses are as expected, non-residential land uses are systematically under-represented. Therefore, because of this under-representation and the lack of significant variation (particularly for industrial, institutional, and recreational land uses) within non-residential land uses, the inferential results reported below likely underestimate the impact of non-residential land uses on the ambient–resident ratio.

Inferential results

The spatial regression results are reported in Tables 2.6–2.9; full models are presented in Tables 2.6 and 2.8, with regressions for each land use classification independently shown in Tables 2.7 and 2.9—other land use is not included in the

Table 2.6 Spatial regression results, full model, census tracts

Land use	Census tracts	
	Coefficient	p-value
Residential, %	−0.005	0.19
Commercial, %	−0.018	0.27
Industrial, %	0.033	0.29
Institutional, %	0.177	0.31
Recreational, %	0.381	0.33
Vacant, %	0.032	0.72
Mixed	−0.003	0.79
R^2	0.37	
Queen's contiguity order	1	
Sample size	106	

full models such that the set of independent variables is not perfectly collinear. The census tract results are a moderately better fit to the data than the dissemination area results—the goodness-of-fit variable reported, pseudo-R^2, is the correlation between predicted and actual values; as such it does not have the same statistical interpretation as the traditional R^2 in ordinary least squares—the spatial error model is solved using maximum likelihood. In both cases—census tracts and dissemination areas—spatial autocorrelation is filtered out of the error terms with first-order Queen's contiguity.

For the census tract full model analysis, presented in Table 2.6, none of the land use classifications are statistically significant. However, all land use classifications have their expected signs on the estimated parameters except for commercial and mixed. Though there are only a small number of census tract correlations that are of a magnitude to cause concern for multicollinearity, this may be the reason for the statistically insignificant results shown in Table 2.6. Table 2.7 shows the results for estimating the coefficients in a simple regression format to investigate this possibility. As shown in Table 2.7, all of the land use classifications remain statistically insignificant. As such, at the census tract level, the ambient–resident ratio does not relate to land use calculations as expected.

Table 2.7 Spatial regression results, individual models, census tracts

	Coefficient	p-value	R^2
Residential, %	−0.002	0.47	0.28
Commercial, %	−0.016	0.04	0.30
Industrial, %	0.046	0.01	0.32
Institutional, %	0.26	0.12	0.28
Recreational, %	0.44	0.26	0.28
Vacant, %	0.092	0.28	0.28
Other, %	−0.105	0.32	0.28
Mixed	−0.002	0.70	0.27

Table 2.8 Spatial regression results, full model, dissemination areas

Land use	Dissemination areas	
	Coefficient	p-value
Residential, %	−0.002	0.37
Commercial, %	−0.009	0.16
Industrial, %	0.053	< 0.01
Institutional, %	−0.004	0.89
Recreational, %	0.035	0.56
Vacant, %	−0.002	0.95
Mixed	0.014	0.02
R^2	0.24	
Queen's contiguity order	1	
Sample size	990	

The dissemination area full model results, though having a pseudo-R^2 value of low magnitude, do fare better with the statistical significance of the independent variables. Industrial land use and mixed land use now have their expected positive and statistically significant estimated parameters. In an effort to investigate the issue of multicollinearity within the dissemination results, a simple regression format was used as well, despite the correlations being much lower in magnitude for the dissemination areas than the census tracts. In this case, the results changed substantially: six of the eight variables are now statistically significant at the 10 percent level, with vacant and other remaining statistically insignificant. Moreover, now all land use classifications have their expected signs, negative for residential and positive for all other classifications.

These differences in results for different spatial units of analysis is a common phenomenon in the geography literature, the modifiable areal unit problem (Openshaw, 1984a; Fotheringham and Wong, 1991). The census tract results are not a "problem," per se, just statistically insignificant. These results would be a problem if the results from the different spatial units of analysis had qualitatively different results that are not the case here. The increased number of variables that

Table 2.9 Spatial regression results, individual models, dissemination areas

	Coefficient	p-value	R^2
Residential, %	−0.004	0.03	0.21
Commercial, %	0.009	0.02	0.21
Industrial, %	0.074	< 0.01	0.24
Institutional, %	0.039	0.08	0.20
Recreational, %	0.095	0.07	0.20
Vacant, %	0.031	0.36	0.20
Other, %	0.037	0.28	0.20
Mixed	0.015	< 0.01	0.22

are statistically significant in the full and restricted regression models may be a result of different sample sizes. The census tract results are based in 106 observations whereas the dissemination results are based on 990 observations. This increase in the number of observations most definitely leads to increased variations and, potentially, more statistically significant results. However, as discussed in later chapters, census tract results (some using even fewer census tracts from older censuses) do not have any problems retaining statistically significant variables in a spatial crime analysis context.

Discussion

Most often the population at risk (owing to such reasons of ease of access and cost) is the residential population measured in government censuses. Therefore, any general assessment of risk based on the residential population in a geographical area that cannot assume non-varying populations throughout the day is potentially unrelated to the actual risk. Furthermore, any public or private crime prevention policy using residential-based crime rates as a measure of success or failure may misinform the public, policy-makers, and practitioners, potentially misallocating public or private expenditures to combat crime. The results presented here strongly indicate that the residential population is not the appropriate population at risk, given its difference from the ambient population estimates, using an example of violent crime—an exception would be if crime data were recorded temporally, so risk could be assessed at different times of the day, such as when the population is, largely, expected to be in residence. Other applications of this alternative population at risk may not have such stark differences with conventional crime rates. However, it should be abundantly clear for a need to supplement the conventional crime rates particularly with these new data that are free for non-commercial use.

Moreover, if the characteristics of the ambient population are different from that of the residential population—which is likely to be true given that most residents leave their home census boundary unit during the day—the independent variable, if obtained from a census used to test the criminological theory, may in fact be completely unrelated to the characteristics of the ambient population, being the true population at risk in many crimes. As such, any criminological theories and crime prevention evaluations that are dependent on an ambient population for proper testing need to be re-evaluated, not dismissed.

The points of assessing risk from residential population counts and differing characteristics between residential and ambient populations are easily seen with reference to the percentage of trips residents make outside of their home municipality—these trips are dominantly, though not exclusively, work related. For the City of Vancouver, under study in this chapter, the percentage of trips made outside of the residents' home municipality is relative low, 27 percent, but still large enough to raise questions regarding the counts and measured characteristics of the population. The remaining percentages of all trips, approximately 50–100 percent, show the implications of diurnal movements in a large metropolitan center (Statistics Canada's 1996 Census Journey to Work Survey).

In most cases within the Greater Vancouver Regional District (GVRD), the vast majority of residents leave their home municipality during the day and, by necessity, also leave their home census tract or enumeration area. With such large movements of the residential population out of municipalities, and smaller census units, there is no way to know how many people are actually present in any given spatial unit without some reference to the attractiveness of that spatial unit during given times of the day. Herein lies the utility of the ambient population estimates, described above.

With regard to the characteristics of the populations, greater difficulties are present. In most cases, surveying the ambient population for its characteristics is prohibitive—small area case studies would be able to undertake such a survey. However, neighborhoods do often reflect the characteristics of the residential population. Areas with high levels of income and low levels of unemployment tend to have high land values. These high land values correspond with high leasing costs for commercial areas (an attractor of non-residential populations) and more expensive retail opportunities (Birkin *et al.*, 2002). Therefore, due to the attractors in an area, the ambient population *may* not be too dissimilar than the residential population.

In the context of the evaluation of the ambient population, the empirical results reported above do not support a strong relationship between the ambient population and land use classification. A relationship is clearly present, and most often in an expected way. However, based on the knowledge in the field of environmental criminology, particular land uses attract populations and the corresponding crime (Kinney *et al.*, 2008). Consequently, this is problematic because land uses such as commercial, industrial, and mixed should be associated with increases in ambient populations. This expected result is present for the dissemination area results but only in the simple regression framework. One of two implications may be drawn from these results, and both matter in the current analysis.

First, the land use data, though complete, do not provide a complete picture of the use of land in the present context. As discussed above, the primary limitation of the current land use data is that each address is weighted equally in the calculations because the *area* comprised by each address is not known—the shopping mall example shows the importance of knowing the area represented by each address. Consequently, most commercial addresses (particularly shopping centers) are under-represented in the data. This may be the source of the insignificant spatial regression results, particular for the census tracts. Unfortunately, nothing can be done at this stage regarding this data limitation because parcel data are not available. However, this limitation may not be too serious in this context because of the large area covered by commercial areas and, consequently, fewer addresses in each census unit. As such, commercial land use in these areas is identifiable because the total number of addresses in these census units is smaller when calculating the percentages of each land use.

The second implication is that the ambient population data provided by Oak Ridge National Laboratory are of little value because land use classifications represent population attractors. Though a possibility, this statement is premature.

Before any such claims can be made, the limitations of the land use data discussed above must be dealt with. In addition, the crime analysis work discussed in later chapters will show the ambient population to be rather useful and have expected patterns in the City of Vancouver, generally speaking—there are a few anomalies within Vancouver, but only in particular areas on the fringes of the city. The strongest statement that could be made at this point, even if the land use data issues are resolved, is that researchers should be cautious when employing the ambient population because studies have shown that it is not always representative of expected population patterns—a similar result emerged in a similar study on the City of Surrey in the Metro Vancouver area (Andresen *et al.*, 2012). Because of the limited nature of the ambient population data, this latter statement is followed with a slight modification: researchers should be cautious when employing the ambient population because studies have *indicated* that it *may* not always be representative of expected population patterns.

Despite these limitations, there is an obvious question to pose at this point: what are the implications for the spatial crime analysis literature? As stated above, the use of alternative denominators in the crime analysis literature is supported both theoretically and empirically. The question is whether or not the LandScan ambient population data is a good choice for that alternative. Though we state that researchers must remain cautious, our results still indicate a statistically significant relationship that generally follows expectations. Because of this result, the ambient population probably represents an improvement over using the residential population in the census. If this is the case, error may still be present in spatial crime analyses, but that error is less than in an analysis that uses the residential population. Regardless of these limitations of the ambient population data, ambient population estimates do provide a first step in improving measures of risk, the testing of theory, and the evaluation of criminal justice policy and security initiatives.

Conclusions and directions for future research

Using freely available digital data, this chapter shows the utility of using global ambient population estimates in criminological research. Though the data are not in a ready-made format for incorporation into census data analysis, only a moderate amount of data manipulation is necessary. The results are striking. With virtually no statistical relationship between residential- and ambient-based violent crime rates, any assessment of risk, whether it be descriptive or inferential, based upon residential populations is highly suspect in light of these findings.

These findings indicate that the calculation of crime rates used to measure risk must necessarily incorporate ambient population estimates if risk is associated with the number of persons in a given geographical area and/or crime data are not temporal. This is particularly true for violent crimes because (by definition) violent crimes require the presence of people. In such a situation the ambient population provides a better population at risk because the number of people who reside/sleep in an area (residential population) may not be a good measure of how many people we can expect to be in that area during any time of the day. The above example of the downtown area of Houston, Texas provides an example of such a situation. Of course, there may be those cases where the ambient population is viewed to be the only appropriate denominator in the calculation of a crime rate, but at the very least an ambient-based rate can be used to supplement rather than supplant the conventional calculation.

These new data present an alternative to the conventional calculation of crime rates to infer risk. Inferred risk messages made in commission or omission should be based on the most recent and relevant information available. This may then give a more precise depiction of victimization and educate not only the public, but also academics and practitioners, to a more accurate reflection of their group and personal safety/security. In addition, as the ambient population data science advances into the realm of temporal changes within the day, risk assessment may be calculated not only based on where you are, but when you are there.

As with most analyses, this one leads to more questions than it answers. Consequently, future work in this area needs to consider a number of issues. First, similar analyses in other contexts should be undertaken. Second, if at all possible, parcel data with land use classifications for further evaluation should be employed in such analyses. Though it is argued that the current land use point data still capture concentrations of particular land uses, because the number of addresses is less when the area covered by a particular land use increases, confirmation of this argument is in order. Lastly, similar to some of the other evaluation literature (Potere *et al.*, 2009), other ambient population data sources should be investigated. Though none of these data sources may be ideal, some may better represent population movements and changes that are relevant to the spatial crime analysis literature. We now turn to the application of the ambient population in spatial crime analysis.

3 Role of the ambient population in crime analysis

Introduction

Environmental criminology begins its analysis of the criminal event by asking where and when a crime has occurred (Brantingham and Brantingham, 1991). Through this explicitly spatial–temporal approach to studying crime (broadly encompassing geometric, routine activity, rational choice, opportunity, and pattern theories), significant insight is garnered: human activity patterns and, hence, crime patterns follow both spatial and temporal regularities. The development of geographic information science (GIScience) and the availability of spatially referenced crime data allow the spatial dimension of these theories to flourish. Most often, this occurs through aggregation of criminal event data to census boundary units and analyses in relation to census variables. These types of analyses, however, may be problematic. In order to calculate crime rates for census boundary units, the residential population is most often used. As discussed in the Chapter 2, a potential problem arises because people leave their census boundary units during the day, which is a spatial and temporal regularity. Consequently, crime rate calculations based on the residential population may not provide accurate representations of risk.

The current chapter uses an alternative measure of the population at risk, namely the ambient population (a 24-hour average estimate of the population present in a spatial unit made available through Oak Ridge National Laboratory), in a variety of spatial crime analysis contexts to show its utility. This chapter shows the utility of the ambient population in crime analysis through the use of global indicators of spatial association, local indicators of spatial association, and spatial statistics at two different scales of aggregation and two different years.

If the results from the ambient-based calculations are not qualitatively different from the crime counts and/or crime rate calculations using the more common residential-based populations, little utility is gained from the extra effort to obtain ambient population data. However, if the results are qualitatively different, past evaluations of criminological theory and policy may be called into question. It is shown that alternatively calculated crime rates are not always related to conventionally calculated crime rates. This is important, because the ambient population, as discussed in the previous chapter, is argued to be a better representation of the population at risk for some crime classifications. This shows the importance of keeping up to date with the developments of GIScience technologies and data availability when undertaking a spatial analysis of crime.

Social disorganization and routine activity theory

The spatial, or environmental/ecological, approaches to the theory of crime date back to the early nineteenth century—see Guerry (1833) and Quetelet (1831, 1842). More modern work using a spatial perspective on crime has its roots in the work of Shaw (1929) and Shaw and McKay (1942) as well as research that began in the late 1960s and early 1970s, culminating with the publication of Jeffery (1971) and Newman (1971). The point of departure for the research in this genre is that human behavior is situated in place; therefore, the place in which crime occurs needs to be (at the very least) one of the dimensions of crime investigated—essentially, crime has a geography. Within the geography of crime and criminological research, there are two dominant spatial theories of crime relating back to this early work that inform variable selection in the analyses below: social disorganization theory and routine activity theory.

Not surprisingly, given the spatial nature of these two theories of crime, efforts have been made to integrate them into empirical analyses of crime. Simcha-Fagan and Schwartz (1986), Sampson and Wooldredge (1987), Gottfredson *et al.* (1991), and Smith *et al.*, (2000) have all shown that variables representing both social disorganization and routine activity theories prove to be good predictors of various victimization rates. Therefore, this hybrid approach is undertaken here.

In order to capture social disorganization, variables representing ethnic heterogeneity, social/economic deprivation, family disruption, and population turnover are employed (see Linsky and Straus, 1986; Sampson and Groves, 1989; Stark, 1996; Tseloni *et al.*, 2002; Cahill and Mulligan, 2003). Routine activity theory is about the increased *potential* of criminal victimization as a result of *any* person's activities. To capture this potential, the researcher can measure routine activity variables for neighborhoods across space because the same variables that Cohen and Felson (1979) cite as not being constant over time are also not constant over space within the same time period. Different neighborhoods have different age, ethnicity, and marital status characteristics (the most powerful predictors of victimization found in empirical applications of routine activity theory) and, therefore, different neighborhoods have different routine activities, on average. The variables that affect routine activities, and thus targets and guardianship, revolve around populations; employment status, including the number of hours away from home; income levels; and dwelling values (Cohen and Felson, 1979; Clarke and Felson, 1993; Fisher and Wilkes, 2003; Tseloni *et al.*, 2004).

Data and methodology

All data described below are for 1996 and 2001 in the City of Vancouver, British Columbia, Canada. The Vancouver Census Metropolitan Area (CMA) is the third largest metropolitan area in Canada, based on population (approximately 2 million people), and the largest metropolitan area in western Canada. In 2001, Vancouver had a population of 546,000. In recent years, Vancouver experienced substantial growth in its resident population: 431,000 in 1986, 472,000 in 1991, and 514,000 in 1996. This high rate of growth is often attributed to the 1986 World Exposition on Transportation and Communication that garnered Vancouver tremendous world attention. This attention is expected to continue because of the 2010 Winter Olympics. With an area of approximately 115 square kilometres, the City of Vancouver has 110 census tracts (CTs) and 990 dissemination areas (DAs), defined by Statistics Canada—87 and 860, respectively, in the 1996 census.

Though Vancouver's crime rate trend was decreasing 1991–2005, its crime rate remains substantially higher than the national average. In fact, the Vancouver CMA had the highest crime rates among the three largest metropolitan areas in Canada at 11,367 criminal code offences per 100,000 persons in 2001, more than doubling the rate found in Toronto (5,381 per 100,000 persons) and almost doubling that in Montreal (6,979 per 100, 000 persons). The same relative standing held for the 2001 violent crime rate in the Vancouver CMA (1,058 per 100,000 persons) in comparison to the Toronto CMA (882 per 100,000 persons) and the Montreal CMA (886 per 100,000 persons), but to a lesser degree. These differences in crime rates between these three cities have been decreasing in recent years (Kong, 1997; Savoie, 2002; Wallace, 2003).

In order to avoid the ecological fallacy in the socio-demographic and socio-economic variables, as well as their corresponding crime measurements, smaller spatial units are superior to larger spatial units due to less averaging of the data. In Statistics Canada's Census of 1996, the smallest spatial unit is the enumeration area, followed by the census tract. However, in order to obtain certain socio-demographic and socio-economic variables for the statistical modeling below, there must be a minimum of 250 residents in the census unit for reasons of confidentiality. Of the 860 enumeration areas in Vancouver, 211, or 24.5 percent, have less than 250 residents each and, therefore, do not have the corresponding socio-demographic and socio-economic variables. If these enumeration areas are located randomly across space there is no difficulty with performing the analysis, but these enumeration areas are clustered in the Downtown Eastside of Vancouver. This is a region of high crime, by most measures, in Vancouver and would necessarily have to be excluded in any analysis owing to the lack of socio-demographic and socio-economic variables. To ease this difficulty, crime is measured at the census tract scale for the 1996 analyses, all of which have the necessary socio-demographic and socio-economic information. For 2001, dissemination areas (the new terminology for enumeration areas) do not have the same limitation. As such, the analyses involving the 2001 data use both census tracts and dissemination areas.

Crime data

The discipline of criminology classifies crime into three groups: property, violent, and nuisance/other crimes (Ellis and Walsh, 2000). The utility of the ambient population in crime analysis is best shown using violent crime. Though, in essence, the target in any crime is a person (property and nuisance crimes affect people), violent crimes specifically target people. And given that the ambient population measures the presence of people within a given area, the natural point of departure for considering the ambient population and criminal activity is violent crime. Violent crimes include: assault, fighting, hold-ups, homicide, robbery, sexual assault, and stabbing. However, in the spatial regression context for 1996, break and enter and automotive thefts are also analyzed.

The violent crime data used below come from the Vancouver Police Department's Calls for Service Database (VPD-CFS Database) generated by its Computer Aided Dispatch system. The VPD-CFS Database is the set of requests for police service made directly to the VPD or through the 911 Emergency Service and allocated to the VPD. The VPD-CFS Database contains information on both the location and the complaint code/description for each call. There are two codes for each call: the initial complaint code, and a complaint code filed by the officer on the scene. The code provided by the officer is always taken to be correct. Though the VPD-CFS Database is actually a proxy for actual crime data—because not all calls for service represent actual crimes—the primary advantage of the VPD-CFS Database is this raw form whose data are not dependent on a criminal charge. It should be noted, however, that few calls for service are subsequently unfounded by the VPD. Due to the vast quantity of data available, approximately 30,000 calls for service each month, only certain crimes are investigated. The advantage of these data is their raw form. These are not the official crime statistics from Statistics Canada that are dependent on a criminal charge, but record actual police activity across the city. Consequently, these data provide a richer assessment of criminal activity in Vancouver.

Geocoding of the point locations of any phenomena provides the potential for error. Because of the limitations of computer algorithms, geocoding algorithms have issues regarding their accuracy (see Ratcliffe, 2001). Even when these limitations are not of particular concern, geocoding algorithms are not always able to locate specific point locations: addresses may be recorded incorrectly in the field, only a 100-block is given, or the street network may be out of date. In an effort to quantify the reliability of geocoded spatial point data, Ratcliffe (2004) ran simulations to determine the minimum acceptable hit rate (perfect match). Above this minimum acceptable hit rate, the researcher should have little concern for bias: this hit, or success, rate is deemed to be 85 percent.

The geocoding procedure used for the 1996 data produced 93, 96, and 94 percent success rates for automotive theft, break and enter, and violent crime, respectively. After consultation with the proprietors of the data, it was determined that on occasion an address is improperly recorded in the field and, therefore, cannot be found by the geocoding procedure—either a non-existent street address is provided or only the street block number. With such a high success rate of perfect matches and the nature of the improper address records appears to be random, the analysis is performed without concern for bias (Ratcliffe, 2004). The final data set includes 11,848 violent crimes, 22,896 break and enters, and 36,419 automotive thefts.

For the 2001 data set, a 93 percent hit rate was achieved in the geocoding procedure used in the present analysis—11,629 violent crimes were geocoded from an
original 12,504 violent crimes. Of course, there is always potential for error aris-
ing from converting point data into area data: the modifiable areal unit problem
(Openshaw, 1984a). In an attempt to mediate this error, analyses are undertaken
at two levels of areal aggregation for a sensitivity analysis.

Census variables

The independent variables used in the inferential analysis, discussed below, come
from Statistics Canada's 1996 and 2001 Census of Population. Though some of
the data used in this analysis are obtained from the "short form" of the Census
filled out by all households in Canada, much of the detailed socio-economic data
used in this analysis come from the "long form" of the Census, which is completed by a sample of only 20 percent of Canadian households. All of these data
exclude the institutional population: those living in hospitals, nursing homes, pris-
ons, and other institutions.

The purpose of this analysis is to show differences that arise when using a different population at risk in spatial crime analysis, not to test any particular theory.
However, because there are two theories commonly used in the geography of
crime literature discussed above (social disorganization theory and routine activity theory), variable selection is made with these theories in mind. These variables
are organized as follows: population characteristics, socio-economic status, and
dwelling characteristics.

The population characteristic variables are the presence of young populations
(males, 15–24 and 15–29 years old), never married persons, lone-parent families,
recent immigrants (1986–1996 and 1991–2001), visible minorities, ethnic heterogeneity,[1] population density, population size, and people who have recently
moved. The socio-economic variables include the population receiving government transfer payments,[2] the population aged 20 years and older without a sec-
ondary school diploma, the population aged 20 and older who have obtained a
post-secondary education,[3] persons designated as low income,[4] the unemployment rate for those 15 and older participating in the labor force, average
household income in thousands of dollars, and the standard deviation of that
income. The dwelling characteristic variables include dwellings constructed
before 1961,[5] dwellings in need of major repairs, number of dwellings, households spending more than 30 percent of total household income on shelter,[6]
owner-occupied dwellings, rental units, and average dwelling value. The interested reader is referred to the following previous studies for more information
regarding these variables and their theoretical connections: Shaw and McKay
(1942), Harries (1974), Cohen and Felson (1979), Cohen and Cantor (1980),
Cohen et al. (1981), Hirschi and Gottfredson (1983), Harries (1995), Ackerman
(1998), Kelling and Coles (1998), Morenoff et al. (2001), Sampson (1997),
Sampson et al. (1997), Tseloni et al. (2002), Cahill and Mulligan (2003), and
Andresen (2006a, 2007).

All of the variables used in the 2001 data analysis, with the exception of ethnic heterogeneity, are transformed into natural logarithms—ethnic heterogeneity is an index generated from other variables so it is not transformed. This transformation is undertaken to ease interpretation of results and the comparison of results at different scales. The resulting estimated parameters in the statistical analysis below are then interpreted as elasticities (see Kennedy, 2003). Elasticities measure the degree of sensitivity between the dependent and independent variables: a 1 percent increase in an independent variable leads to a β-percent increase (or decrease if the estimated parameter is negative) in the dependent variable, also transformed into a natural logarithm. The variables in the 1996 data analysis are measured in rates, percentages, and counts. This multitude of methods and measurements allows for the utility of the ambient population data to be shown in an array of different contexts.

The descriptive statistics and correlations for these variables for Vancouver, 1996 and 2001 are available to the interested reader. None of the correlations show any surprising relationships, with the highest of these correlations involving the income and education variables. Average family income has a strong positive relationship with the average dwelling value, university education, and the standard deviation of average family income—these are all standard relationships. Strong negative relationships are present between university education, the unemployment rate, and ethnic heterogeneity. Again, these relationships are standard given that a university education increases employability and recent immigrants may be less likely to have a university education—notable exceptions to this relationship between ethnic heterogeneity and university education exist, but are present in particular places within Vancouver and tend to be associated with the most recent of immigrant populations. With regard to the spatial statistical modeling below, some of the correlations cause concern for collinearity. None of the correlation coefficients are greater than 0.80, a common threshold for concern, but a number of the correlation coefficients are high.

Measures of crime

Employing and mapping different measurements of crime improves crime analysis by allowing a comparison to be made. In this chapter, three measures of crime are used: crime counts, crime rates based on residential populations, and crime rates based on ambient populations—crime rates based on the number of dwelling units are also calculated, but only for the crime of break and enter.

Crime counts are a measure of the volume of criminal activity. Though crime counts may be of interest for those investigating where crime "takes place," crime counts are a restrictive measure of criminal activity because they are in absolute terms—crime counts are absolute, so they do not give any indication of why crime is high in some areas while low in other areas. As discussed in Chapter 2, crime rates are commonly used to assess the risk of crime by controlling for the population at risk.

Empirical methodology

The purpose of this analysis is to show the impact of a different population at risk in crime rate calculations on the spatial analysis of crime. As such, a number of empirical approaches are taken here to show any similarities and differences in different contexts. These different contexts are a descriptive global analysis, a descriptive local analysis, and a spatial regression analysis.

The descriptive global analysis is in two forms: first, the simple correlations between the different calculated crime rates are reported and discussed; and second, the global Moran's *I* statistics are reported and discussed. This global analysis is followed by the descriptive local analysis using the local Moran's *I* of Anselin (1995). Because global measures of spatial association may mask local spatial relationships (see Anselin, 1995; Getis and Ord, 1992, 1996; Ord and Getis, 1995), the use of local indicators of spatial association (LISA) may show that the nature of the clustering for each of the calculated crime rates is qualitatively different. For example, at the global level two different crime rates may exhibit the same (or similar) degree of clustering according to Moran's *I*, but each crime rate may have that clustering occurring in entirely different regions within the study space. In addition, local indicators of spatial association show where and what type of spatial concentrations are occurring—Anselin *et al.* (2006) discuss four categories of local clusters that are mapped and discussed below. Both the global and local Moran's *I* need to have their spatial neighbors defined. This is done using Queen's contiguity.[7] This means that any census unit sharing any boundary, even touching at a corner, with the census unit of concern is considered to be contiguous.

Originally using an ordinary least squares regression model, the null hypothesis of spatial autocorrelation in the error terms is not rejected. Due to the presence of spatial autocorrelation, this is also evident in the spatial patterns of the figures above, the standard assumption in least squares regression of independent errors is violated (Murray *et al.*, 2001). In the presence of positive spatial autocorrelation, present in most socio-economic data, spatial units contiguous (or even close) to one another have similar values for both dependent and independent variables in a statistical analysis. Therefore, if a positive regression error is calculated for one spatial unit, its neighbors are very likely to also have a positive regression error. This phenomenon allows the researcher to predict regression errors spatially, violating the assumption of independence. Though the parameter estimates of the regression model are still unbiased, the variance, and therefore standard deviation, of the errors is not known and standard hypothesis tests are not appropriate—a spatial error model controls for this difficulty. The spatial error model filters out the spatial effect within both the dependent and independent variables. This specification usually makes it easier to reject spatial autocorrelation in the residuals for valid statistical inference (versus the spatial lag model) because the spatial effect is filtered from both sides of the equation. Hence, the spatial error model is used here instead of the spatial lag model. The general functional form of the spatial error model is as follows:

$$y = X\beta + \rho W\varepsilon + u \tag{3.1}$$

where y is the crime rate, $X\beta$ is the matrix of independent variables and its estimated parameters, W is the spatial weights matrix that captures the spatial association between the different census units, ρ measures the strength of spatial association, ε is shorthand for $y - X\beta$, and u is the independent and identically distributed error.

Queen's contiguity is also used to define the spatial weights matrices used in the spatial regression analysis. However, the "order" of the queen's contiguity varies depending on the presence of spatial autocorrelation. For example, if two census units (a and b) share a boundary, the order of contiguity is 1. With the introduction of a third census unit, c, that borders census unit b, then a and c are considered contiguous of order 2 because there are two boundaries separating census units a and c. For the global and local Moran's I, Queen's contiguity is always set to order 1. The final model selection is based on a general-to-specific method: the initial inclusion of all independent variables, removing statistically insignificant variables one at a time. In addition, joint significance tests are performed to prevent the removal of an important, but highly collinear, variable. For each crime rate model, the analysis begins with all independent variables, estimated parameters are tested for statistical significance (p-value $= 0.10$),[8] insignificant variables are removed, and the final models for each crime rate only show the remaining statistically significant independent variables. All estimation is performed using GeoDa 0.9.5i (http://geodacenter.asu.edu/), a spatial statistical freeware package developed by Luc Anselin.

Results

Before the results from the different analyses are presented, it is instructive to consider the different maps representing the resident and ambient populations— see Figures 2.1 and 2.2, respectively. As discussed above, the resident population has a relatively uniform distribution across the city. This is because census boundaries are designed to ensure that samples, and corresponding populations, are as similar as possible. Such a design improves the validity of measurements for comparisons across space. The ambient population shows far more clustering; this is the case in Figure 2.2 as well as similar maps for census tracts and the ambient population data in subsequent years. This is particularly evident, and expected, in the downtown area of Vancouver (the northern peninsula and surrounding areas) and the center of the city that contains the largest shopping areas outside of the downtown area. This is expected because these are the areas of the city with the greatest population draws during the day.

At the municipal level, the actual resident and ambient population counts are not that different, namely 546,000 and 598,000, respectively. This 10 percent increase in Vancouver's population is representative of its drawing of working populations during the day. At the census tract and dissemination area levels, however, the differences are far greater. For census tracts, the average population does not differ much between resident (5,700) and ambient (6,000) populations. The range in population counts is, however, is rather different: 2,600–10,000 for the resident population and 350–85,000 for the ambient population. This is similar for dissemination areas: resident and ambient averages are similar, 565 and 600, respectively, but the ranges are vastly different: 225–2,500 for the resident population and 1–15,000 for the ambient population. Quite clearly, there are significant spatial shifts in Vancouver's population throughout the day when considering these census boundary units.

Turning to the resident- and ambient-based violent crime rates, shown in Figures 3.1–3.4, they do not exhibit such systematic changes in their maps. There are, however, noticeable spatial shifts in the distribution of crime. One notable change is that the crime rates in the center of the city and the downtown area fall in the ambient-based maps because of the higher ambient population.

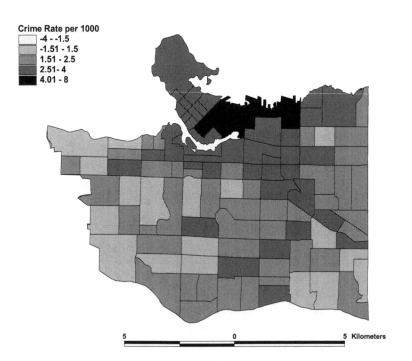

Figure 3.1 Resident-based violent crime rate, natural logarithm, census tracts.
Source: Oak Ridge National Laboratory (2003) and Statistics Canada.

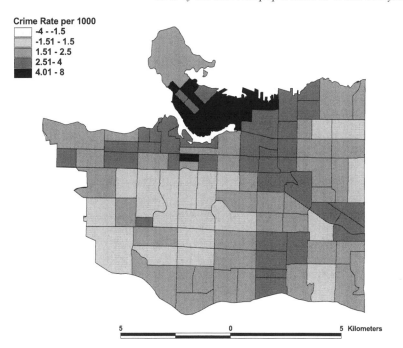

Crime Rate per 1000
- -4 - -1.5
- -1.51 - 1.5
- 1.51 - 2.5
- 2.51 - 4
- 4.01 - 8

Figure 3.2 Ambient-based violent crime rate, natural logarithm, census tracts.
Source: Oak Ridge National Laboratory (2003) and Statistics Canada.

Global analysis

The first results to note from the global analysis are the bivariate correlations between the resident- and ambient-based violent crime rates for the census tracts and dissemination areas, $r = 0.823$ and 0.801, respectively. With such high degrees of correlation, one would expect that there would not be much difference between the results using the resident- or ambient-based violent crime rates. However, as shown below, significant differences are present. It should be noted, using Statistics Canada's 1996 census boundaries and data, that the correlations for census tracts and enumeration areas are $r = 0.737$ and 0.095, respectively. The correlations between the resident- and ambient-based violent crime rates at the census tract level are not too dissimilar, but the correlations between the resident- and ambient-based violent crime rates for the enumeration/dissemination areas are radically different. Though both correlations are statistically significant at the 1 percent level, the magnitude for 2001 indicates that the gains from using an alternative crime rate may be small (as would be argued by Cohen *et al.*, 1985). The magnitude for 1996 indicates that using an alternative crime rate may change the results significantly. And because Vancouver's urban landscape changed very little in those 5 years (the spatial distribution of the population would not have changed very much), this change in the magnitude of the correlation between the resident- and ambient-based violent crime rates is the result of subtle changes in

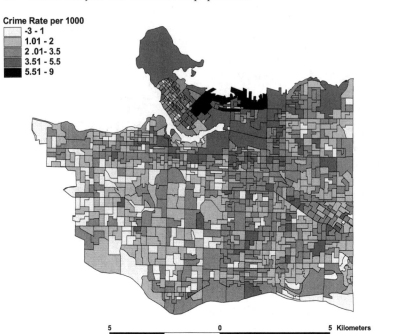

Figure 3.3 Resident-based violent crime rate, natural logarithm, dissemination areas.
Source: Oak Ridge National Laboratory (2003) and Statistics Canada.

the census unit boundaries. The purpose of this discussion is not to invoke the modifiable areal unit problem (see Openshaw, 1984a), but to show that the correlation between the resident- and ambient-based violent crime rates is not necessarily high.

Turning to the global spatial autocorrelation results, positive spatial autocorrelation is present for all of the variables. The Moran's *I* values are statistically significant for all variables except for the resident population of the census tracts. Evident from these Moran's *I* statistics, as discussed above, is that the ambient variables have a stronger degree of clustering than the resident variables, particularly for the dissemination areas. It should be noted, however, that the test statistics are low in magnitude. This result should not come as a surprise because commercial land uses in any city (work and shopping), which attract populations during the day, tend to be far more spatially concentrated than the residential land uses. Of course, the resident population is "concentrated" in places such as suburbs, but commercial land use in a city (square footage, for example) is neither randomly nor uniformly distributed across the urban landscape. And given that the dissemination areas exhibit the greatest differences between the resident- and ambient-based violent crime rates, it is expected that the dissemination areas will also exhibit the greatest differences in the analyses that follow.

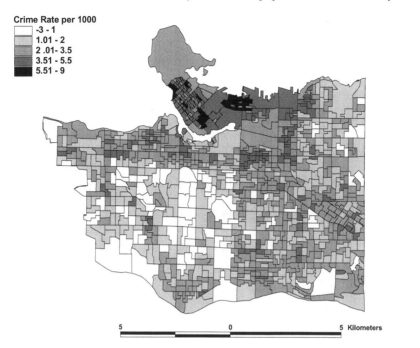

Crime Rate per 1000
-3 - 1
1.01 - 2
2 .01- 3.5
3.51 - 5.5
5.51 - 9

Figure 3.4 Ambient-based violent crime rate, natural logarithm, dissemination areas.
Source: Oak Ridge National Laboratory (2003) and Statistics Canada.

Local analysis

The LISA output is mapped and shown for the census tracts (Figures 3.5 and 3.6) and dissemination areas (Figures 3.7 and 3.8). The areas labeled as "High–High" and "Low–Low" are census units that have high crime rates which are surrounded by other census units with high crime rates and census units which have low crime rates that are surrounded by other census units within low crime rates, respectively. The areas labeled as "High–Low" are census units with high crime rates surrounded by other census units with low crime rates, and vice versa for "Low–High."

In all the figures there are three areas where clustering occurs: the downtown and surrounding areas, the western border of the city, and the eastern border of the city. For the census tracts in Figures 3.5 and 3.6, there is not much change that results from using the resident-based violent crime rate versus the ambient-based violent crime rate. The cluster in the downtown and surrounding areas shifts more into the peninsula, the cluster on the western border moves east, and the eastern cluster is essentially unchanged. The only notable change is the eastward movement of the Low–Low cluster at the western border of the city. The significance of this movement is only because crime is expected to increase as one moves east in Vancouver. Though global statistics may mask local spatial relationships, the

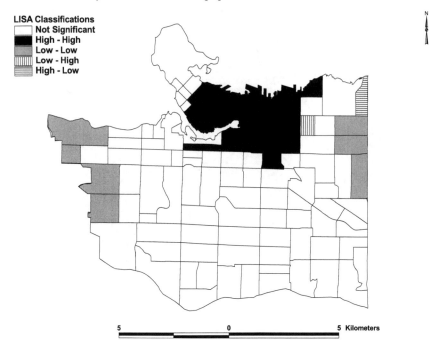

Figure 3.5 Resident-based local indicators of spatial association (LISA) map, natural logarithm, census tracts.

Source: Oak Ridge National Laboratory (2003) and Statistics Canada.

similarity of the global Moran's *I* statistics for the census tracts is mirrored here with the local analysis.

The LISA maps for the dissemination areas, Figures 3.7 and 3.8, show the same general shifting, but the magnitude of the shift is far greater, similar to the global Moran's *I* results. The cluster in the downtown and surrounding areas for the resident-based LISA map shifts almost entirely into the peninsula of downtown and then trails east out of the peninsula. The resident-based LISA map does not exhibit any surprises in that High–High clusters extend as far south as they do, but the ambient-based LISA is more representative of the high crime area of Vancouver. The cluster on the western border of the city shifts eastward (similar to the census tract LISA map), but this cluster's shift is further east and grows significantly in size. Though there is some overlap of the Low–Low areas in the western portion of the city, far more areas of Vancouver are considered to be Low–Low using the ambient-based violent crime rate. This should not be a surprise because of the population draw in the central areas of Vancouver. Rather than being areas that are intrinsically high in crime, they are areas of many opportunities for crime because of the population

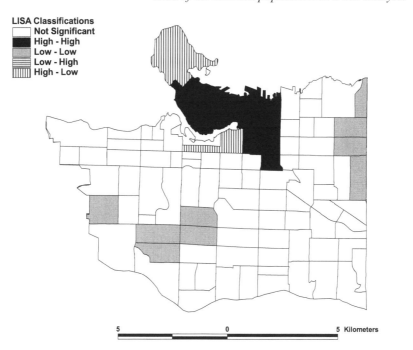

Figure 3.6 Ambient-based local indicators of spatial association (LISA) map, natural logarithm, census tracts.

Source: Oak Ridge National Laboratory (2003) and Statistics Canada.

attraction, particularly during the day. Needless to say, the alternatively calculated violent crime rate has had a significant effect in the analysis of dissemination areas.

Spatial regression analysis, 1996, multiple crime measures

The descriptive statistics and correlations for the 1996 crime measures are presented in Tables 3.1 and 3.2. The different rates, residential versus ambient population-based, for the three types of criminal activity exhibit some significant differences. Automotive theft has similar ranges for both the residential- and ambient-based rates, but the ambient-based average is approximately 133 percent of the residential-based average. The differences regarding break and enter are more extreme; the ranges of the different rates are not too dissimilar, but their averages, as with automotive theft, differ substantially. The residential-based rate is less than half of the dwellings-based rate, with the ambient-based rate in between—all mean rates are statistically different from one another. The violent crime rates exhibit similar differences.

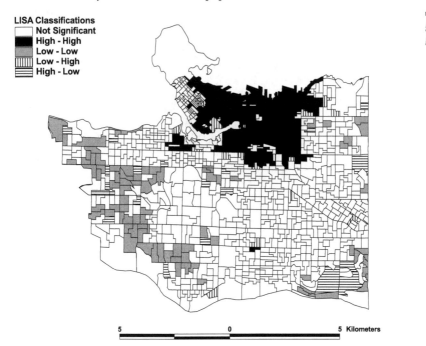

Figure 3.7 Resident-based local indicators of spatial association (LISA) map, natural logarithm, dissemination areas.

Source: Oak Ridge National Laboratory (2003) and Statistics Canada.

Automotive theft

All three measures of automotive theft are highly correlated, $r > 0.65$, across space (spatial randomness is rejected for all three measures) and across measures. All three measures exhibit a concentration of automotive theft in the downtown area (the north-central coastal region of the city), dispersing to the commercial shopping areas, and residential areas. However, with a moderately high correlation value, $r = 0.657$, the residential- and ambient-based crime rates are far from perfect substitutes in any empirical evaluation of theory or policy, possibly leading to qualitatively different results.

Turning to the spatial regression results for automotive theft, the two traditional crime measures—the crime count and residential-based rate—do not show any inconsistent result (see Table 3.3). Both models have a similar R^2, with the residential-based rate model slightly more parsimonious than the crime count model. Considering both the magnitude of the estimated coefficients and the ranges of the independent variables, the unemployment rate has the greatest impact on the dependent variables. When one variable is in both models, the estimated coefficient signs are the same, but there is some variation in variable

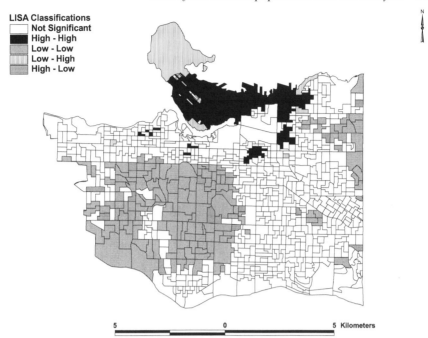

Figure 3.8 Ambient-based local indicators of spatial association (LISA) map, natural logarithm, dissemination areas.

Source: Oak Ridge National Laboratory (2003) and Statistics Canada.

retention between the two models. In particular, residential population, residential population density, and the number of dwellings are present in the crime count model, but absent from the residential-based rate model. This result is not particularly intriguing because the residential-based rate is normalized using the residential population, which is correlated with the number of dwellings. The ambient population, however, is insignificant for both crime counts and residential-based rates, but the ambient-based population density is significant and positive for the residential-based rate. This positive relationship is interpreted as capturing suitable targets for criminal activity; the greater the number of people there are in a given area, the greater the number of automobiles available to steal or steal from—this finding supports the routine activity approach. Noticeably absent from the crime count and residential-based rate models, though present in the ambient-based rate model, is average family income—this proxy for poverty is typically the strongest predictor of crime in the social disorganization framework.

The ambient-based crime rate results are substantially different from both the crime count and residential-based models. The R^2 is 15–20 percent higher than the previous two models, with a respectable value of 0.723. The unemployment rate

Table 3.1 Descriptive statistics for dependent variables, 1996[a]

	Mean	Standard deviation	Minimum	Maximum
Auto theft count, Y_1	418.61	92.76	56.00	7937.00
Break and enter count, Y_2	263.17	24.45	43.00	1902.00
Violent crime count, Y_3	136.18	30.59	6.00	2461.00
Auto theft residential rate, Y_4	75.92	15.65	8.88	978.19
Break and enter residential rate, Y_5	44.59	3.64	6.70	229.18
Break and enter dwelling rate, Y_6	103.64	5.70	19.27	309.87
Violent crime residential rate, Y_7	23.04	4.51	1.38	296.54
Auto theft ambient rate, Y_8	109.04	17.05	6.58	1086.52
Break and enter ambient crime ambient rate rate, Y_9	65.88	5.76	7.76	278.75
Violent, Y_{10}	33.67	5.74	1.14	336.89

Note: [a]All rates are per 1,000 persons.

Source: DMTI Spatial Inc., Oak Ridge National Laboratory, and Vancouver Police Department, calculations by the author.

is insignificant, but average family income is present, though positive. These two variables have a moderately high correlation, $r = -0.594$, so multicollinearity may be the reason why only one of these two variables is present in any model. Overall, the remaining variables are a combination of the variables in the previous two models and the majority of the estimated coefficients are qualitatively similar. Only residential population density and ambient population density have the opposite sign of the previous results.

Table 3.2 Correlations for dependent variables, 1996

Y_1	1									
Y_2	0.877	1								
Y_3	0.965	0.901	1							
Y_4	0.800	0.630	0.727	1						
Y_5	0.759	0.812	0.767	0.857	1					
Y_6	0.558	0.711	0.564	0.650	0.863	1				
Y_7	0.852	0.777	0.904	0.846	0.889	0.655	1			
Y_8	0.745	0.557	0.710	0.657	0.536	0.241	0.667	1		
Y_9	0.459	0.457	0.466	0.351	0.425	0.215	0.433	0.829	1	
Y_{10}	0.712	0.594	0.770	0.565	0.546	0.281	0.737	0.895	0.758	1
	Y_1	Y_2	Y_3	Y_4	Y_5	Y_6	Y_7	Y_8	Y_9	Y_{10}

Key: Y_1: Automotive theft count; Y_2: Break and enter count; Y_3: Violent crime count; Y_4: Automotive theft residential-based rate per 1,000; Y_5: Break and enter residential-based rate per 1,000; Y_6: Break and enter dwelling-based rate per 1,000; Y_7: Violent crime residential-based rate per 1,000; Y_8: Automotive theft ambient-based rate per 1,000; Y_9: Break and enter ambient-based rate per 1,000; Y_{10}: Violent crime ambient-based rate per 1,000.

All Pearson correlations are significant at the 1% level with the exception of Y_6–Y_8 and Y_6–Y_9, which are significant at the 5% level. Non-parametric analysis produces qualitatively similar results.

Source: DMTI Spatial Inc. and Oak Ridge National Laboratory; calculations by the author.

Table 3.3 Spatial regression results, automotive theft, 1996

	Crime count	Residential rate	Ambient rate
Ethnic heterogeneity			
Unemployment rate	99.24(< 0.001)	17.51(< 0.001)	
University degree, %		5.78(< 0.001)	18.24(< 0.001)
Population change, %	8.12(0.017)	3.43(< 0.001)	2.61(< 0.001)
Single-parents, %	−42.78(0.003)		−4.64(0.038)
SD average income, 000s			
Average income, 000s			1.15(0.019)
Rentals, %			
Population, 000s	−133.47(0.003)		−25.94(< 0.001)
Population density, 000s	−45.78(0.003)		16.14(< 0.001)
Number of dwellings, 00s	52.08(< 0.001)		5.89(< 0.001)
Average dwelling value, 000s			
Young population, %			
Ambient population, 000s			
Ambient population density, 000s		16.84(0.009)	−15.81(0.003)
Spatial dependence, *lr*	0.57(0.45)	0.02(0.89)	2.09(0.15)
Weights matrix, Queen's order	4	1	1
R^2	0.577	0.538	0.723
SD = standard deviation.			

Note: *p*-values are reported in parentheses.

The most striking difference is the opposite sign for ambient population density because this variable is present for both of the calculated rates—the opposite sign for residential population density is in regard to the crime count that may be a result of only one variable being normalized. Curiously, increases in the ambient population density decreases the ambient-based crime rate. Therefore, even when the ambient population is controlled for in the ambient-based crime rate, ambient population density still decreases the automotive theft rate. Independent of the residential-based crime rate results, this finding may be interpreted through routine activity theory as the result of guardianship. Of course, the presence of a high population density does not directly imply guardianship because, as shown in the residential-based rate results, it may also imply an increase in the number of targets and increase crime. The main difficulty with interpreting this result is the absence of the ambient population in both models. The *a priori* expectation is that the population increases targets and crime, but the population density increases guardianship and decreases crime—the low correlation of these two variables for both residential and ambient measures indicates that population and population density are capturing different phenomena. Although the residential population and residential population density may not give an accurate account of targets or guardianship because they are nighttime measures, their estimated coefficients are also the opposite of expectations.

Overall, the ambient-based automotive theft rate does not radically alter the estimated results. The ambient-based rate does retain double the number of variables retained in the residential-based results, likely the reason for almost 20 percent more variation of the ambient rate being explained by the independent variables. In addition, the ambient population is a better estimate of the number of people in an area than the residential population given that most people leave their "home" census tract during the day. Knowing how many people are in an area is a better indicator of the number of vehicles in that area being vulnerable to theft.

Break and enter

The crime count, residential-based rate, and dwelling-based rates for break and enter are all highly correlated with each other, all $r > 0.70$, indicating that these three different measures are relatively substitutable—this is particularly true for the residential-based and dwelling-based crime rates, $r = 0.863$. The ambient rate, in contrast, does have positive correlations with the other measures of break and enter, but is clearly measuring a different phenomenon. All correlation coefficients are less than 0.50, with the correlation between the ambient-based rate and the dwelling-based rate being the lowest, $r = 0.215$. Such low correlation values have significant effects on the deployment of police resources. If ambient-based rates considered relevant for crime prevention efforts by police, these efforts may be concentrated in the wrong neighborhoods. All measures of break and enter also strongly reject spatial randomness.

The spatial regression results for break and enter, see Table 3.4, are somewhat different than automotive theft. The crime count, residential-based rate, and dwelling-based rate all show consistent results with respect to the estimated coefficient signs when a variable is present in more than one final model, but the residential-based rate has the greatest variable retention and the R^2 has increased by more than 10 percent for the crime count and residential-based rate.

The social disorganization variables in these first three crime measures have mixed results. The unemployment rate and population change variables, when significant, have their expected positive coefficient signs, but the percentage of university graduates and the level of family income also have positive coefficient signs, contrary to expectations—the results are similar to that of automotive theft. Though the purpose of this paper is not to test social disorganization theory, yet again, but to compare the statistical results of ambient population crime rates with more traditional measures of crime, social disorganization theory does not bode well in these analyses.

The fact that higher proportions of university graduate and family income levels have a positive impact on crime is completely consistent with routine activity theory. Education and income are highly correlated, $r = 0.71$, and are expected to increase criminal activities due to the increased possibility of the presence of desirable goods such as jewellery and consumer electronics—more potential targets. Also, population change and unemployment, though not typically used in a routine activity framework, are consistent with the expectations of routine activity theory as well. Neighborhood population turnover increases anonymity,

Table 3.4 Spatial regression results, break and enter, 1996

	Crime count	Residential rate	Dwelling count rate	Ambient rate
Ethnic heterogeneity				
Unemployment rate	31.29(< 0.001)	6.04(< 0.001)	7.35(< 0.001)	5.21(< 0.001)
University degree, %		0.962(0.004)		
Population change, %		0.275(0.025)		
Single-parents, %				
SD average income, 000s				
Average income, 000s	1.41(0.035)			
Rentals, %				
Population, 000s		−5.07(0.024)		−6.85(0.007)
Population density, 000s	−14.23(< 0.001)	−2.07(0.001)	−4.33(< 0.001)	5.62(< 0.001)
Number of dwellings, 00s	12.42(< 0.001)	0.961(0.023)		1.37(0.003)
Average dwelling value, 000s				
Young population, %	8.16(0.039)	1.49(0.032)	3.71(< 0.001)	3.77(< 0.001)
Ambient population, 000s				
Ambient population density, 000s		4.61(0.001)	7.95(< 0.001)	−12.74 (< 0.001)
Spatial dependence, *lr*	0.19(0.66)	1.62(0.20)	0.29(0.59)	2.24(0.13)
Weights matrix Queen's order	2	2	1	3
R^2	0.678	0.662	0.584	0.749

SD = standard deviation.

Note: *p*-values are reported in parentheses.

decreasing guardianship, and increased unemployment increases the number of people available to offend or be victims of crime. With the strength of the unemployment rate across all results and the sporadic appearance of average family income, unemployment is a far better predictor of criminal activity than poverty, the latter being social disorganization theory's claim to be the best predictor, proxied here with income.

Therefore, whether or not people are working appears to be more important than how much income those people have if they work. A person being in a workplace environment necessarily decreases the chances of becoming a victim of crime and victimizing someone else. Of course, one's presence at work does not eliminate the potential for criminal activity, but by having other tasks to attend to the probability of criminal activity decreases. This is a story of potential, which ties back to the routine activity approach.

As with automotive thefts, the ambient-based rate for break and enter has the highest R^2, 0.749. Curiously, the lowest R^2 is for the dwelling-based rate results, 0.584. The number of dwellings is usually considered the best normalizing variable for break and enter because it objectively measures the number of targets. And if one assumes that the best way to test theory is with the most appropriate measures, the best results should come from that appropriate measure, if the theory is correct. Incidentally, the only social disorganization theory variable present in the dwelling-based results is the unemployment rate.

Once again, population and population density exhibit inconsistent results between the ambient-based rate and the other crime measures. The crime count, residential-based rate, and the dwelling-based rate all have their expected negative relationships with residential population density; residential population, however, has a negative relationship with the residential-based and ambient-based crime rates; and residential population density has an unexpected positive relationship with the ambient-based rate. The only consistency across all crime measures is the positive impact of the number of dwellings on the measures of break and enter. The ambient population is insignificant for all crime measures. The ambient population density has an unexpected positive relationship with the residential-based and dwelling-based rates and an expected negative relationship with the ambient-based rate.

The inconsistent results are probably a result of improper expectations. The residential and ambient populations are significantly and positively related, $r = 0.411$, but residential and ambient population densities exhibit a relatively low positive relationship, $r = 0.102$. If targets and guardianship are to be captured with population and population density, then the ambient population measures are the most appropriate because they are a better indicator of the number and density of people present at any time of the day, rather than at night. Curiously, the more traditional measures of crime do not correspond to expectations, whereas the ambient-based measure does, with the opposite being true for residential population and residential population density. The question then becomes: what are residential population and residential population density measuring, if not targets and guardianship?

Areas in Vancouver, Canada that typically have high residential populations, and in particular high residential population densities, are apartment and condominium developments. These developments are typically found in the safer communities of the city, and through secure parking and entrances provide better protection for automobiles, people, and property. This may explain the negative coefficients for residential population and residential population density with the more common measures of crime. With regard to the residential-based crime rate and its positive relationship with the ambient population density, this appears to be a result of the way the crime rate is normalized—similarly for the dwelling-based crime rate.

Using the ratio of the residential to the ambient population as a measure of daytime population attraction—as the ratio increases, fewer people are present in the day than the night—an explanation manifests itself. The areas in Vancouver, Canada that have high residential population densities also have low measures of daytime population attraction, $r = -0.566$. As a result, any rate calculated with the residential population is artificially low because the normalization variable is in the denominator of the crime rate. Including the ambient population density in the statistical model compensates for that artificially low crime rate with its positive coefficient—this compensation effect is clearly not necessary for the ambient-based rate. Therefore, the differences between the estimated coefficient signs and prior expectations are most likely a result of measurement error in the dependent variable.

Violent crime

As with the two previous crime classifications, violent crime is highly correlated across both space and across measures—spatial randomness is strongly rejected for all crime measures and the lowest correlation coefficient is 0.737. As such, violent crime is the most suitable, in the present context, for substitutability between crime measures.

The spatial regression results in Table 3.5 exhibit the same consistency between the crime count and the residential-based crime rate. This consistency is even more apparent with the final models all being quite similar. Opposed to the results

Table 3.5 Spatial regression results, violent crime, 1996

	Crime count	Residential rate	Ambient rate
Ethnic heterogeneity		−1.17(< 0.001)	−1.18(0.004)
Unemployment rate	41.36(< 0.001)	7.73(< 0.001)	6.39(< 0.001)
University degree, %			
Population change, %	2.89(0.001)	0.587(< 0.001)	0.901(< 0.001)
Single-parents, %		−1.13(0.036)	
SD average income, 000s			3.37(0.001)
Average income, 000s	2.06(0.016)	0.276(0.019)	
Rentals, %	−4.09(0.022)		
Population, 000s	−63.12(0.001)	−5.57(0.009)	
Population density, 000s	−9.81(0.029)	−1.32(0.018)	3.80(< 0.001)
Number of dwellings, 00s	23.39(< 0.001)	1.33(0.001)	0.891(0.018)
Average dwelling value, 000s			
Young population, %			
Ambient population, 000s			
Ambient population density, 000s			−6.84(0.001)
Spatial dependence, *lr*	2.42(0.12)	0.90(0.34)	1.82(0.18)
Weights matrix, Queen's order	4	2	4
R^2	0.713	0.777	0.674
SD = standard deviation.			

Note: *p*-values are reported in parentheses.

of automotive theft and beak and enter, the ambient-based crime rate has the lowest R^2, 0.674, with the residential-based rate having the highest, 0.777. All of the three final models retain few of the routine activity variables, but the social disorganization theory variables do not correspond well to expectations.

As with the previous results, average family income has a positive relationship with crime, but the violent crime models also include ethnic heterogeneity, the percentage of single-parent households, and the percentage of rental residences. All variables have unexpected negative relationships with their respective crime measures. Ethnic heterogeneity in Vancouver, Canada comes dominantly in the form of recent immigrants. In particular, a large proportion of recent immigration has come from Hong Kong and Taiwan, and the majority of these immigrants have high economic status (Ley, 1999; Ley and Smith, 2000). Therefore, the negative relationship between ethnic heterogeneity and crime rates may not only be due to the underreporting of crime often stemming from English as a second language and a lack of knowledge of (Canadian) law (Ley, 2004), but also that these immigrants have been settling in the wealthy (i.e. low crime) regions of the city.

The percentage of single-parent households having a negative relationship with crime rates may not correspond well with social disorganization theory, but does relate to research on intimate partner assault in Canada. DesKeserdy and Ellis (1995) found that once a woman is removed from the residence of her violent partner, but not necessarily the relationship, intimate male violence against that woman decreases. Again, this fits well with routine activity theory—there is a lack of guardianship in the violent male's residence. Of course, not all single-parent households are the result of intimate partner assault, but this example shows that the statistical relationship is only inconsistent with one particular theory, not the existing research.

Finally, we turn to the result for the percentage of rental residences. Given that the majority of rental residences occur in apartment settings in Vancouver, this negative relationship likely corresponds to the explanation above regarding residential population density; the added security of parking and pedestrian entrances adds guardianship to automobiles, property, and, with respect to violent crime, people.

Residential population has the same results as the previous crime classifications: negative relationships with the crime count and residential-based crime rate, and a positive relationship with the ambient-based crime rate—the ambient population density is only significant for the ambient-based rate. The number of dwellings positively impacts violent crime for all these crime measures. Although the number of dwellings is not typically considered in violent crime, this result is likely the manifestation of most violent crime occurring close to the home.

Overall, the results for violent crime are more consistent across crime measures than the previous two crime classifications. The implications for social disorganization theory, however, appear to be worse.

Spatial regression analysis, 2001, multiple scales of analysis

The spatial regression results for 2001, shown in Tables 3.7 and 3.8, are similar to the previous results in that the census tracts are less sensitive to which violent

Table 3.6 Spatial error model results, census tracts

	Resident-based violent crime rate	Ambient-based violent crime rate
Resident population density	−1.99***	−0.97***
Ambient population	−1.57***	−1.55***
Ambient population density	1.86***	0.84***
Population turnover	0.76***	0.63**
Ethnic heterogeneity	0.01	0.01**
Government assistance	0.05***	0.06***
Unemployment	0.65***	0.75***
Average family income		0.75*
Low income	−0.74**	−0.56**
Housing affordability	2.04***	1.66***
Average dwelling value	−0.39	−0.71***
Rentals	−0.66***	−0.75***
Major repair	−0.22	−0.27**
Apartments		0.29**
Pseudo-R^2	0.78	0.88
Moran's I, residuals	−0.011, p-value = 0.42	−0.014, p-value = 0.30
Queen's contiguity order	1	1

Notes: All estimated coefficients are elasticities, except ethnic heterogeneity; ***$p < 0.01$, **$p < 0.05$, *$p < 0.10$.

crime rate is being used in the analysis. This does not mean, however, that there are no changes in the results. As shown in Table 3.6, the goodness-of-fit, measured using a Pseudo-R^2, is notably stronger in the ambient-based output that retains one less variable than the resident-based output, 0.86 versus 0.77. Though a higher Pseudo–R^2 does not necessarily mean a better model,[9] the ambient-based violent crime rate is better able to fit the data than the resident-based violent crime rate. Curiously, with such a difference in the Pseudo-R^2, the signs and magnitudes of the variables retained in both models are almost identical—they are identical in three cases. Consequently, the results for the census tracts do not indicate a strong need for the used of an alternatively calculated violent crime rate, unless one is more satisfied with a higher Pseudo-R^2 value. This is not the case for the dissemination areas.

The results for the dissemination area spatial regression model, shown in Table 3.7, presents a much stronger case for use of an alternatively calculated violent crime rate. Similar to the census tract results, when a variable is present in both outputs its sign is always the same and its magnitude is similar. The primary difference is variable retention and, again, the Pseudo-R^2. The Pseudo-R^2 is much stronger in the ambient-based results (0.60 versus 0.38). Though a Pseudo-R^2 value of 0.38 is acceptable for a spatial cross-section analysis, it is low enough to be noticed, whereas a Pseudo-R^2 value of 0.60 is not.

The most notable result from the dissemination area spatial regression output is the consistency with theoretical expectations. As shown in Table 3.6, there are

Table 3.7. Spatial error model results, dissemination areas

	Resident-based violent crime rate	Ambient-based violent crime rate
Resident population	−0.83***	
Resident population density	−0.58***	−0.35***
Ambient population		−0.77***
Ambient population density	0.24**	
Never married	1.03***	1.01***
Post-secondary	−0.46***	−0.47***
Average family income	−0.37***	−0.37***
Low income	−0.14**	−0.15**
Housing affordability	0.21**	0.21**
Average dwelling value	−0.38***	−0.38***
Apartments	0.13**	0.13***
Pseudo-R^2	0.38	0.60
Moran's I, residuals	−0.001, p-value = 0.21	−0.001, p-value = 0.22
Queen's contiguity order	1	1

Notes: All estimated coefficients are elasticities, except ethnic heterogeneity and Ehet* immigrants; ***$p < 0.01$, **$p < 0.05$, *$p < 0.10$.

a number of inconsistencies with theory present in the census tract results: areas with higher income have more crime, areas with low income and more rentals have less crime, and areas with more homes under major repair have less crime. However, these inconsistencies in the results have been resolved for dissemination areas in Table 3.7, aside from low income. These changing results point to the importance of choosing the appropriate units of analysis in the study of crime. As argued in the "crime at places" literature, smaller units of analysis are critical for understanding the spatial distribution of crime because many "dangerous neighborhoods" only have a few "places" that are truly problematic—there are many safe places in dangerous neighborhoods (Sherman *et al.*, 1989; Taylor, 1997; Weisburd *et al.*, 2004).

Conclusion

The geography of crime literature asks the following question: where and why do crimes occur? As initially stated by Boggs (1965) over 40 years ago, a great deal of attention is given to the spatial referencing of the criminal events, but far less attention is given to the population at risk. Though at that time and for many years afterward, constraints regarding time and money impeded the development of widely available populations at risk appropriate for different crimes, a data set is now available to serve this purpose for some, but not all, crime classifications—the ambient population produced by Oak Ridge National Laboratory. This chapter investigates the utility of this new data set in the context of multiple crime types in two years, at two different scales of aggregation, and multiple methods of analysis.

In the context of the analysis of the 1996 data, crime counts and residential-based crime rates exhibit relatively strong positive correlations for all three crime classifications. The ambient-based crime rates show relatively strong positive correlations among themselves, but less so with the residential-based crime rates—this is particularly true for the crime of break and enter. Therefore, there is no strong case for residential-based and ambient-based crime rates being good substitutes for any of the crime classifications.

Empirically, there are definite differences between the use of the ambient-based crime rate and the other measures of crime. With the exception of violent crime, the ambient population model has superior goodness of fit, potentially due to a better assessment of criminal activity. With respect to the variables representing routine activity theory, there are consistent differences between the ambient-based crime rate results and the other crime measures. These differences are believed to be a result of measurement error in the case of residential-based crime rates and a lack of normalization in the case of crime counts. In addition, this measurement error is apparent for both dependent and independent variables.

Although not an intended result for this chapter, social disorganization theory does not fare well in the statistical models. The social disorganization variables that have unexpected signs for their estimated coefficients can be explained using routine activity theory, as can the remaining social disorganization variables that maintain their expectations on the estimated coefficients. Overall, routine activity theory does quite well in explaining criminal activity in Vancouver, Canada.

These results do not provide any major contradictions of past research on the spatial dimension of crime, but do call into question the appropriateness of residential-based crime rates, in general. If unexpected empirical results for the residential-based crime rates can be explained through measurement error, the confirmation or rejection of theories is probably premature. In addition, the evaluation of public policy using residential-based crime rates may be misinformed. As such, the use of an ambient-based crime rate, if deemed appropriate, should always be employed to avoid measurement error. Past research has indicated that the costs of obtaining better denominators for crime rates may be great, given that the changes in the results may not be significant (Harries, 1981, 1991). However, the financial costs of obtaining these data for non-commercial use is zero and the time commitment is negligible, particularly if research is done jointly with a geographer familiar with geographic information systems.

In the analysis of the 2001 data, it is shown above that the use of the ambient population in crime rate calculations has an impact on the results relative to the conventionally calculated violent crime rate using the resident population. This impact, however, is greater for the analysis involving the dissemination areas, though still present for the census tracts. In all analyses (global, local, and spatial regression) the general result is the same, but the specifics change: positive spatial autocorrelation is always present, but the magnitude is different; each local analysis produced three clusters of census units, but those clusters shifted in both space and size; and the spatial regression results are similar when variables are present in the different models, but the goodness-of-fit and variable retention varied depending on whether the analysis was resident- or ambient-based. The most surprising factor in the context of these results is that the resident- and ambient-based violent crime rates had high bivariate correlations, all $r > 0.80$.

However, because of the similarity in all of these spatial regression results, one may question whether it is worthwhile to incorporate the ambient population into an inferential analysis. Indeed, Harries (1981, 1991) found that although the use of alternative denominators in crime rate calculations did improve measurements, the improvements were most often not worth the costs in both time and money to obtain the alternative denominators. Regardless, there are at least two reasons why the ambient population needs to be considered in spite of these similar spatial regression results.

First, as just stated, other analyses did show qualitatively different results when using the ambient population in crime rate calculations. This is particularly true for the local analysis at the dissemination area level. As such, the utility of the ambient population may be more important in particular contexts. Second, the costs in both time and money for incorporating the ambient population data into an analysis are negligible. The data are free for non-commercial use and are easily incorporated into an analysis with a moderate level of training in GIS software. As such, past concerns regarding resources are now overcome.

These data, however, are not without limitations. The ambient population may not always be the appropriate population at risk. Is the presence of people the appropriate population at risk for homicide, assault, rape, and robbery? Perhaps not, but it is still better than the alternative of the census resident population. And this is the key point: even if the ambient population is not best, it is likely to be better than the resident population when analyzing violent crime. This reduces measurement error. A further limitation is that the ambient population cannot account for varying differences in risk at different times of the day. This limitation, however, is somewhat mediated with LandScan USA that includes a daytime population estimate. Unfortunately, as the name suggests, these data are not available globally.

The primary implication of these results is that the choice of the population at risk alters empirical results. It is unlikely that any particular theory will be discarded through the use of an alternative population at risk, but the theoretical and policy variables of interest may be altered (insignificant variables become significant, and vice versa), possibly altering theoretical interpretations and changing the focus of criminal justice policy. This analysis has then shown the importance of being aware of the latest technologies and available data sets. This is particularly true with the spatial analysis of crime and the developments within GIScience technologies.

4 Diurnal movements and the ambient population

An application to municipal level, crime rate calculations

Introduction

One of the most fundamental components within criminology and criminal justice is the assessment of risk: the risk of criminal victimization, the risk of recidivism, and the risk of repeat victimization, to name only a few. With regard to the general risk of criminal victimization, the crime rate is the most common measure employed. This rate is used to compare the risk of criminal victimization between neighborhoods, municipalities, provinces/states, and nations. But how useful is this measure for making these comparisons? The previous chapters have shown this in the context of neighborhoods, but other scales of analysis are also instructive.

In the 1960s, Sarah Boggs investigated the impact of alternative denominators on various crime rates: the number of automobiles present for automotive theft, the pairs of persons present for violent crime, commercial land use for business-related theft, the number of females for forcible rape, and the number of occupied housing units for burglary. In some cases, changing the denominator had little impact on the crime rate (residential day burglary, forcible rape, criminal homicide, and aggravated assault), but in other cases the impact was significant such that the alternative denominator completely changed the interpretation (automotive theft, grand larceny, non-residential day and night burglary). This finding led Boggs (1965) to state: we must "construct crime occurrence rates on the basis of environmental opportunities specific to each crime" … and … "the number of events, or the numerator, varies with the type of crime, [so] the denominator should likewise vary so that the whole number of exposures to the risk of that specific event is incorporated as the base" (Boggs, 1965: 899–900). Indeed, as stated by Harries (1981), the crime rate has only the *potential* to be a meaningful statistic, referring to the appropriate denominator—see Cohen *et al.* (1985) for a different view on alternative denominators.

Despite the importance of this issue, very little research has been undertaken in recent years. This small literature, however, has been instructive. O'Brien (1989) tests the Easterlin hypothesis using age-specific crime rates, concluding that larger population cohorts have greater propensities toward property crime because there are relatively fewer legitimate economic opportunities. Investigating the trend in Canadian homicide, Andresen *et al.* (2003) compare the conventional homicide rate with an alternative rate that used the number of young (15–30 years) males as the denominator. The two trends are radically different. The conventional homicide rate increases up to the mid-1970s, falling thereafter, whereas the alternative homicide rate increases right up to the early 1990s, then starts to fall. In the neighborhood level spatial crime analysis literature, Andresen (2006a) shows that the standard ecological theories of crime (social disorganization theory and routine activity theory) fare better with an alternative denominator, and Andresen and Jenion (2008) show that there is very little relationship between spatially referenced crime rates that use conventional and alternative denominators for a number of different crime classifications—these two studies employed the same data discussed below. Consequently, recent research (especially on crime in Canada) shows that the alternative denominator issue is still important.

This short chapter incorporates the ambient population data into municipal-level crime rate calculations. The applications of these ambient population data in the previous chapters were all at the neighborhood level. However, as shown below, the same processes that change ambient population counts at the neighborhood level are also present at the municipal level. As such, understanding the nature of population movements and the corresponding impact on the population at risk of criminal victimization is important.

Diurnal movements and the ambient population

The discipline of ecology is generally defined as the study of how organisms survive in an ever-changing environment; in the context of human ecology, it is most often how humans survive in an ever-changing *urban* environment—of course, human ecology applies to rural environments as well. This survival consists of at least two measurable components: space and time. The space component, though complex in its details, is straightforward at an abstract level: we humans must move through our environment (go to different places) in order to survive, undertaking activities such as work, shopping, and recreation. The time, or temporal, component is also straightforward at an abstract level: we tend to undertake most of our activities at particular times. As such, we are very predictable organisms, particularly our group behavior. Amos H. Hawley (1944, 1950) outlines a method of understanding this temporal component involving the concepts of rhythm, tempo, and timing—this work is also the basis for routine activity theory (Cohen and Felson, 1979).

Rhythm is a representation of the periodicity of our activities: every day at 8 a.m. a person leaves home to go to work. Tempo is the measurement of that activity per unit time: a person goes to work once every 24 hours. And lastly, timing refers to how the activities of one person coincide with the activities of another person (Hawley, 1944, 1950). Because of these activities, populations move throughout their urban environment altering the volume of people in different areas: most often, people leave residential neighborhoods and go to commercial areas. As mentioned above, most of the research that investigates this phenomenon is performed at the neighborhood level, but impacts municipal-level populations as well.

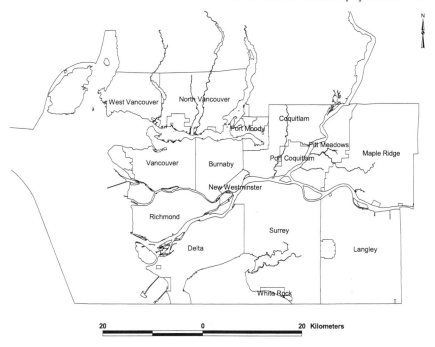

Figure 4.1 Municipalities of the Greater Vancouver Regional District.
Source: Statistics Canada.

As shown in Chapter 2, the majority of commuting trips in the Greater Vancouver Regional District (GVRD) are outside the commuter's home munici- pality—Figure 4.1 provides a reference for the various municipalities in the GVRD. In fact, in some cases the vast majority of commuter trips are outside the commuter's home municipality: New Westminster (80 percent), Port Coquitlam (83 percent), White Rock (84 percent), Pitt Meadows (89 percent), and Port Moody (92 percent). Of course, these municipalities are small and also gain popu- lations throughout the day, so these numbers cannot simply be used to adjust resident populations. Herein lies the utility of the ambient population estimates employed below.

Resident- and ambient-based population counts and crime rates

The resident and ambient populations for GVRD municipalities are presented in Table 4.1—resident populations are based on Statistics Canada's 2001 Census of Population and the ambient population is for the same year, based on data avail- ability. Overall, the GVRD gains population throughout the day: an ambient– resident ratio of 1.05. This gain in the GVRD population comes from outlying municipalities that are dominantly residential. Comparing municipalities, it should be clear that there is a large range in population changes. Vancouver and

Surrey (the two largest municipalities in the GVRD) have virtually no change in their populations. Many people may leave these municipalities during the day, but because of their amenities they also attract large populations during the day. Other municipalities such as West Vancouver, Port Moody, and White Rock have significant drops in their populations representing the more stereotypical bedroom communities. At the other end of the spectrum Burnaby, Pitt Meadows, and Richmond gain significant populations because their commercial areas (employment and/or shopping) attract more people throughout the day than leave.

Consider the example of Richmond. With 47 percent of commuter trips leaving the municipality, this leads to a population loss of approximately 40,000 persons—this assumes 50 percent of the population undertakes commuter trips—and a remaining 125,000 resident population. Combining this information with the ambient population estimate of 245,000 persons, each day 120,000 people enter Richmond. Such a statement would come as no surprise to a person who commutes over one of the five bridges or through the tunnel into this municipality with any regularity and uses its large number of commercial establishments. These population movements impact municipal-level crime rates.

Using the 2001 crime data from the Ministry of Public Safety and Solicitor General, Police Service—in order to be compatible with the ambient population data described above—the resident- and ambient-based municipal-level crime rates (total criminal offenses, less traffic) are shown in Table 4.1 In addition, the rankings of the 15 municipalities are shown in order to provide a measure of change.

There are two ways of comparing the different crime rates shown in Table 4.1, one within each municipality and the other between municipalities. Making comparisons within each municipality shows how significant an impact the municipal-level population at risk of criminal victimization can make in crime rate calculations. Some municipalities that have little change in their populations at risk of criminal victimization have very little change in their respective crime rates—Vancouver and Surrey, for example. In other municipalities, there is a large impact from changing the population at risk of criminal victimization: Pitt Meadows (96 to 49 per 1,000 residents); Port Coquitlam (103 to 125); Richmond (85 to 57); and West Vancouver (66 to 114).

The first measure of the different crime rates between municipalities is the correlation between resident- and ambient-based crime rates. Both parametric (Pearson) and non-parametric (Spearman) correlation coefficients are presented, each having similar results. Having correlation coefficients valued at approximately 0.75, one may believe the two crime rates are quite similar despite the changes within each municipality. Such inference, however, would be misleading, because there are some notable changes for individual municipalities.

The second measure of the different crime rates between municipalities is to compare the rankings within the GVRD, a total of 15 municipalities. The municipalities that have the highest resident-based crime rates also have the highest ambient-based crime rates: New Westminster, Maple Ridge, Surrey, and Vancouver occupy the top four ranks for both crime rate calculations. However, there is far less consistency in the bottom ranks. For example, Pitt Meadows drops

Table 4.1 Resident and ambient populations, resident and ambient population crime rates per 1,000 in year 2001

Municipality	Resident population	Ambient population	Ratio	Resident rate	Ambient rate	Resident rank	Ambient rank
Burnaby	193,954	242,551	1.25	123	98	6	9
Coquitlam	112,905	119,818	1.06	102	96	8	10
Delta	97,429	86,669	0.89	78	87	13	12
Langley	110,645	117,958	1.07	124	116	5	6
Maple Ridge	63,174	60,795	0.96	137	143	3	2
New Westminster	54,656	50,770	0.93	163	176	1	1
North Vancouver	128,749	114,963	0.89	80	89	12	11
Pitt Meadows	14,894	29,241	1.96	96	49	9	15
Port Coquitlam	51,262	42,211	0.82	103	125	7	5
Port Moody	25,842	19,616	0.76	63	82	15	13
Richmond	164,345	244,749	1.49	85	57	10	14
Surrey	348,087	350,457	1.01	140	139	2	3
Vancouver	554,792	554,519	1.00	135	135	4	4
West Vancouver	42,800	24,649	0.58	66	114	14	7
White Rock	18,250	14,380	0.79	85	107	11	8
					Correlation	*p*-value	
				Pearson	0.732	0.002	
				Spearman	0.757	0.001	
Total	**1,981,784**	**2,073,346**	**1.05**				

Sources: Ministry of Public Safety and Solicitor General, Statistics Canada; and Oak Ridge National Laboratory (2003).

from a ranking of 9th highest crime rate to 15th highest crime rate, Richmond drops from 10th to 14th, and West Vancouver rises from 14th to 7th. This latter change is particularly significant from a socio-economic perspective because West Vancouver is the wealthiest municipality (income per capita) in the GVRD; in most ecological studies of crime, the wealthiest area has the lowest crime rate, not the median crime rate. There are also a number of smaller changes, making some municipalities at relatively lower risk of criminal victimization and others higher risk.

Conclusion

The crime rate has a long history of being shown to be problematic at the neighborhood level. The problem emerges because of the improper measure of the population at risk of criminal victimization actually present in a neighborhood. During the day, residential areas have fewer people present than represented in census data, and commercial areas have more. As shown in this chapter, a similar effect is found at the municipal level using a relatively new measure of the ambient population.

The conclusion is clear: using census counts for the population at risk of criminal victimization is problematic at the meso-level of the neighborhood (based on previous research) and the macro-level of the municipality. One question remains: does it really matter? This is a particularly important question, after all, because the correlation coefficients for the two crime rates are quite high. The answer to this question, however, is yes, on three fronts.

First, many municipalities may not be as safe or as dangerous as people think they are. The actual risk of victimization, when based on the population at risk, is not based on how many people *reside* in the municipality, but on how many people are *actually* there. When comparing two or more census metropolitan areas, however, the ambient population may be of little use because these areas tend to be "closed systems" for population movements. This is shown to be the case for the GVRD, a 5 percent change. But still, there may be municipalities that have unjustifiable reputations when one considers the ambient-based crime rate. For example, based on the resident population, Burnaby is ranked sixth in the GVRD, but ranked ninth when based on the ambient population. The reason for this change is because Burnaby is home to the largest shopping mall in British Columbia, namely Metrotown. Because of this, many people outside of Burnaby go to this municipality to shop, leading to significant increases in its population; similarly for Pitt Meadows because it contains a large number of shopping facilities used by the residents of Maple Ridge.

Second, though the number of police officers needed is calculated based on a number of variables such as the volume of crime, road kilometers, and the census population, many police districts may benefit from taking the ambient population into account. Because there are times during the day when all residents may be home, or at least in their home municipality, the resident (census) population should be considered the minimum population in a police district when calculating the number of officers needed. However, municipalities that attract a large volume of people (because of employment and entertainment opportunities) from other municipalities during the day may not have adequate police representation.

Third, researchers and practitioners who undertake ecological studies of crime may benefit from considering ambient population-based crime rates in their analyses, regardless of scale. Andresen and Jenion (2010) have shown that ambient-based crime rates can be significantly different from resident-based rates at the neighborhood level, and the present analysis shows the utility of similar calculations at the municipal level.

Part II

Measurement and analysis of crime specialization

As Part I should have made clear, the calculation of crime rates has the potential for misrepresentation because of variations in the population at risk, the denominator, let alone from issues with the numerator discussed in Chapter 1. But crime does not need to be measured using a population at risk. Rather than measuring risk—however one wishes to define risk—specialization can be measured instead.

A specifically geographical measure provides this alternative, which is not plagued with the lack of a control variable (crime counts) or the choice of an appropriate population at risk (crime rates)—the location quotient. Traditionally used in economic geography to measure employment or industrial specialization since the 1940s (Miller *et al.*, 1991; Isard *et al.*, 1998), Brantingham and Brantingham (1993a, 1995, 1998) introduced the location quotient into criminological research as a descriptive tool.

Well known to many geographers, the location quotient measures the percentage of some activity in a spatial unit relative to the percentage of that same activity in the entire study region. This measurement of the under- or over-representation of an activity has obvious implications for crime analysis at both theoretical and empirical levels. For example, Vancouver, in a Canadian context, may have a low break and enter rate, such that police agencies do not think that break and enters are a problem for Vancouver. However, the low break and enter rate for Vancouver may be an aggregation phenomenon. Certain regions within Vancouver may have a problem with break and enters, but on average Vancouver has a low break and enter rate. Alternatively, certain regions within the city may have a low break and enter rate but have a disproportionate share of that crime. Both of these phenomena are captured well with the location quotient.

In Part II, three chapters investigate the utility of this measure of specialization. Chapter 5 starts out by showing how to calculate the location quotient with a crime-specific interpretation. It then goes on to show how the location quotient is different from the crime rate for a number of crime types. These differences are mapped and are drastic in some cases.

Chapter 6 presents a descriptive analysis using the location quotient in two contexts: one provincial and one municipal. In the provincial descriptive analysis, a long-standing pattern is investigated using crime rates and location quotients. It is shown that crime rates exhibit an increasing east-to-west pattern, well established in the academic literature, but that same pattern does not manifest itself with the location quotients. For example, violent crime is greater in western Canada than eastern Canada, but given that you are going to be a victim of crime, you are not more likely to be a victim of violent crime in the west than the east. In other words, we in the west are not more violent in a relative sense. In the municipal descriptive analysis, it is shown that municipalities that have high levels of crime do not necessarily specialize in that crime, and vice versa.

Lastly, Chapter 7 investigates the location quotient in an inferential context. Chapter 7 is a similar investigation as done in one of the sections of Chapter 3. As such, it provides a good comparison to see the different interpretations when considering crime specialization instead of crime risk.

Overall, crime specialization, measured using the location quotient, proves to be instructive in crime analysis. The interpretations of the location quotient are obviously different, but from an inferential perspective the same relationships tend to stand. Moreover, when considering crime specialization and the location quotient, one is forced to ask different questions, which allows for a deeper insight into the spatial patterns of crime.

5 Measuring crime specialization using the location quotient

Introduction

Recent research in spatial criminology has shown that calls for police service are highly concentrated with 5 percent of street segments (or less) accounting for 50 percent of such calls (Sherman *et al.*, 1989; Weisburd *et al.*, 2004; Andresen and Malleson, 2011). In addition, this recent research (some of which is presented in Chapter 10) has shown that spatial crime patterns, particularly at small and microspatial units of analysis, vary significantly across crime classifications (Andresen, 2009a; Andresen and Malleson, 2011). This has a number of implications for the measurement of crime.

One obvious implication from this research is that the "opportunity surfaces" for different crimes, though they may overlap, are going to be different—the opportunity surface for a crime may be thought of as the distribution of targets for a crime across the landscape. If one considers the theoretical perspectives within environmental criminology, such a statement is trivial: considering routine activity theory (Cohen and Felson, 1979; Felson and Cohen, 1980, 1981), a crime occurs when a motivated offender and a suitable target converge in time and space without the presence of a guardian, and this convergence occurs at a place; the geometric theory of crime (Brantingham and Brantingham, 1981, 1993b) posits that crimes occur at discrete locations (places) within the boundaries of our activity spaces; and rational choice theory (Clarke and Cornish, 1985; Cornish and Clarke, 1986) puts forth that crimes are the result of context-specific choices that consider the immediate environment (places) within which a crime may occur. The places that matter for these convergences, regardless of the theoretical perspective, are going to be different for different crime types: commercial burglary and robbery can only occur in commercial districts, residential burglary can only occur in residential districts, for example. Consequently, whether you wish to consider theory or just the fundamental aspects of our built environment, crime must specialize at places. Locations that have a multitude of opportunities may specialize in a multitude of crime types. As such, it is important to consider that crime specialization does not imply any mutual exclusiveness. Therefore, just as multiple different crime types may be highly concentrated at the same place, the same may be true for crime specialization. Though this is sometimes true, it is shown below that this is far from a monolithic phenomenon.

Because crime specialization and crime concentration may or may not occur at the same places, the consideration of both these phenomena must be considered separately. We have known for at least 180 years that crime concentrates, and the places of that concentration vary by crime classification (Guerry, 1833; Quetelet, 1842). There is no reason to think that crime specialization is any different and that it follows the same pattern as crime concentration. Typically, crime concentration is measured using a crime rate, such that places with high crime rates have greater levels of crime per capita than places with low crime rates. The key to understanding crime specialization, however, is that it may occur in places that have low levels of crime per capita; if a place has very little crime but only one type of crime, then clearly specialization is occurring. As such, the form of measurement that is necessary must consider the crime mix in some form. Location quotients provide an excellent example of this form of crime measurement.

Calculation of the location quotient and its use in spatial criminology

The location quotient is a geographic measure of specialization that has a long history in economic geography. One of the benefits of the location quotient is that it only relies on data for the phenomenon in question: if you are analyzing crime, you only need crime data. This proves useful because, as discussed in the previous chapters, in measuring concentration (crime rates) a number of methodological issues emerge, because the measures require other data (Andresen, 2006a). Of course, the location quotient still suffers from all the problems associated with crime reporting issues and the dark figure of crime, discussed in Chapter 1, a concern in quantitative-based studies of crime dating back to at least the early nineteenth century (Bulwer, 1836). Regardless, the location quotient is calculated as follows:

$$LQ_{in} = \frac{C_{in}/C_{tn}}{\sum_{n=1}^{N} C_{in} / \sum_{n=1}^{N} C_{tn}},$$

(5.1)

where C_{in} is the count of crime i in sub-region n, C_{tn} is the count of all crimes in sub-region n, and N is the total number of sub-regions. In this context, the location quotient is a ratio of the percentage of a particular type of crime in a sub-region relative to the percentage of all crime in the region as a whole; neighborhoods within a city, for example. If the location quotient is equal to one, the sub-region has a proportional share of a particular crime; if the location quotient is greater than one, the sub-region has a disproportionately larger share of a particular crime; and if the location quotient is less than one, the sub-region has a disproportionately smaller share of a particular crime. Specifically, if a sub-region has a location quotient of 1.20, that sub-region has 20 percent more of that crime than expected given the percentage of that crime in the region as a whole—that sub-region then "specializes" in that crime classification. Miller *et al.* (1991) provide the following classifications that are useful for interpreting the location quotient:

highly under-represented areas, $0 \le LQ \le 0.70$; moderately under-represented areas, $0.70 < LQ \le 0.90$; averagely represented areas, $0.90 < LQ \le 1.10$; moderately over-represented areas, $1.10 < LQ \le 1.30$; and highly over-represented areas, $LQ > 1.30$.

Brantingham and Brantingham (1993a, 1995, 1998) introduced the location quotient into criminological research in the early 1990s, but since this initial use almost two decades ago, its adoption as a standard criminological measurement has been slow. With a primary concern for violent crime, Brantingham and Brantingham (1993a, 1995, 1998) used the location quotient to measure the crime mix and specialization within a municipality; they compared the location quotient results to those for crime counts and crime rates. The larger municipalities in their study, not surprisingly, had the highest counts. However, after controlling for population size, the larger municipalities no longer ranked at the top of the list, but tended toward the bottom of the list. Smaller hinterland municipalities topped the list when using crime rates. Yet another ranking emerged with the location quotient: some municipalities with high crime rates also had high location quotients, but there were also a number of municipalities that had low crime rates with high location quotients. Consequently, there were municipalities that had low risk of crime in general (low crime rates), but specialized in violent crimes.

Though this phenomenon—specializing in a particular crime when the risk of crime is rather low—is interesting in itself (and the focus of this chapter), this property may allow one to investigate a curious result that emerges when considering crime rates. In the context of illegal drugs in the United States, Rengert (1996) expected the north central region of the United States to have the greatest proportions of marijuana crimes (of all drug-related crimes) because of a lack of a coastline and its agricultural base. (Heroin and cocaine are expected to be greatest in coastal regions because of a greater need to transport the drugs internationally.) However, Rengert (1996) found that the spatial pattern of marijuana crimes effectively followed the same spatial pattern as heroin and cocaine when using calculations based on the crime rate: the north central region of the United States is ranked last. However, when Rengert (1996) used the location quotient to consider crime specialization, the pattern reversed. Therefore, the other regions of the United States had greater volumes and corresponding rates of marijuana crimes than the north central region, but if one were to commit a drug crime in the north central region it would most likely to be related to marijuana.

Curiously, aside from one study that used the location quotient as a component in a composite index, its use in criminology was absent for 10 years. In more recent research, McCord and Ratcliffe (2007) use the location quotient to measure crime intensity across neighborhoods, and find that drug markets tend to cluster close to pawnshops, drinking establishments, and mass transit stations. Andresen (2007), included in Chapter 7, performs an inferential analysis (spatial regression) using the location quotient as a dependent variable, and finds that if independent variables are interpreted as attractors of a particular crime, it performs well in a predictive manner. Ratcliffe and Rengert (2007) use the location quotient to identify areas that have greater intensities of shootings, relative to the city as a whole.

Andresen (2009b), included in Chapter 6, investigates the phenomenon of crime rates in Canadian provinces increasing as one moves east to west—crime rates in the federal territories are even higher than in the western provinces. Andresen (2009b) uses the location quotient to show that simply because all crime rates are greatest in the west does not mean that western provinces specialize in all crimes. In fact, crime specialization is present in all provinces for at least two crime classifications in each province. This analysis vividly shows that crime concentration (crime rates) does not necessarily imply crime specialization. Most recently, Block *et al.* (2012) use the location quotients in the context of automotive theft in the United States. They find that states and counties that contain or are near heavily-trafficked borders and ports specialize in automotive theft; Block *et al.* (2012) speculate that this is an indication for the presence of a "theft for export" problem in these areas. Moreover, these are not always areas that have high rates of automotive theft.

The location quotient's popularity in spatial crime analysis has increased recently, but its general lack of adoption in widespread criminological research is surprising because it allows for the measurement of crime specialization.

An example of mapping the location quotient

In order to perform the calculations below (crime rates, location quotients, and other measures of specialization), crime data are necessary. All crime data shown are for 2001 in the City of Vancouver, British Columbia, Canada. The areal unit of analysis is the dissemination area (DA) as discussed in previous chapters. Discussions regarding the location quotient are helpful in order to show its utility, but examples comparing the spatial patterns of crime rates and location quotients are most instructive. As such, the location quotients for seven crime types are shown below: assault, robbery, sexual assault, theft, theft from vehicle, theft of vehicle, and burglary.

The mapped location quotients for assault are shown in Figure 5.1b. The map for the crime rate per 1,000 for all crime types, Figure 5.1a, represents a typical crime pattern for Vancouver: very low crime in almost all areas, with the exception of the Downtown Eastside, right at the beginning of the downtown peninsula; the crime rate per 1,000 is of moderately high magnitude in and around the Downtown Eastside, but very quickly dissipates to a low or even non-existent level. As such, the reader is referred to the crime maps in chapters 2 and 3 for a reference to this pattern and only the maps of the location quotients are shown here—maps for a direct comparison to the location results presented here are available from the author.

The location quotient map reveals a very different spatial pattern. There is a high degree of specialization in assault in the Downtown Eastside, as would be expected given the high magnitude of the crime rate. However, this high degree of specialization is not highly concentrated in and around the Downtown Eastside. Other areas of downtown experience specialization in assault, namely commercial areas with alcohol outlets. High values of the location quotient also continue eastward from the Downtown Eastside along the northern coastline of the city. Moreover, the east side of Vancouver has many areas that specialize in assaults,

(a)

Assault rate per 1000

☐ 0 - 15
▨ 15.01 - 50
▨ 50.01 - 125
▨ 125.01 - 300
■ 300.01 - 700

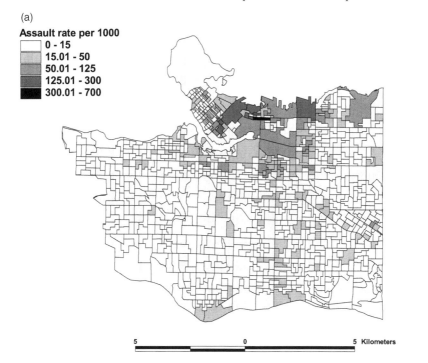

(b)

Assault location quotient

☐ 0 - 0.7
▨ 0.701 - 0.9
▨ 0.901 - 1.1
▨ 1.101 - 1.3
■ > 1.30

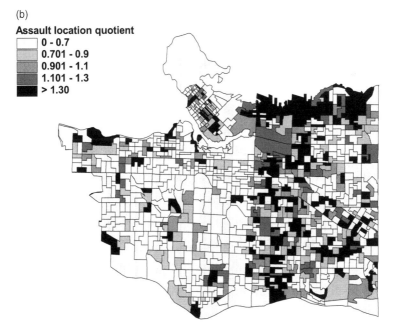

Figure 5.1 Crime rate (a) and location quotients (b), assault, Vancouver, 2001.

(a)

Robbery rate per 1000

- 0 - 1.5
- 1.51 - 7.5
- 7.51 - 20
- 20.01 - 50
- 50.01 - 165

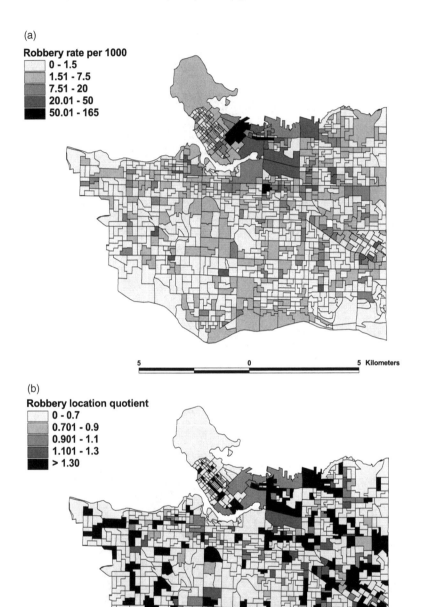

(b)

Robbery location quotient

- 0 - 0.7
- 0.701 - 0.9
- 0.901 - 1.1
- 1.101 - 1.3
- > 1.30

Figure 5.2 Crime rate (a) and location quotients (b), robbery, Vancouver, 2001.

most of which are centered along major arterial roads. Even the wealthier area of the west side of Vancouver has a number of "pockets of violence," often in areas with commercial and recreational land use.

Figure 5.2b shows the location quotients for robbery. The crime rate map for robbery, Figure 5.2a, is quite similar to the crime rate map for assault: a high concentration of crime in the Downtown Eastside that dissipates rapidly as one moves away from that area. The area that has the highest crime rates for robbery is approximately the same size as for assault, with more dissemination areas being in the top legend categories. Unlike assault, a few areas have noticeably high levels of robbery across Vancouver, but these areas are connected to major arterial roads and/or commercial areas; some of these areas are in the wealthy west side of Vancouver.

The location quotient map, again, tells a very different story. In the case of robbery, much of the Downtown Eastside has average representation relative to the city as a whole. Robbery is a crime that has specialization in areas across Vancouver, though more concentrated within the east side of the city. Similar to the mapped results for assault, the specialization of robbery occurs along the major arterial roadways within Vancouver. Of course, this is an obvious result. In order for a robbery to take place, there must be at least two people: one offender and one target. There are going to be more people, so more targets, along major arterial roadways.

Also interesting is the other areas of specialization in robbery within the downtown peninsula. The two "strips" laying in the northwest direction are Davie Street and Robson Street. These two streets, as well as the others close by, are densely populated most of the day, with relatively wealthy residences, high-end retailers, alcohol outlets, and a lot of youth. For reasons discussed in previous chapters, these particular areas of downtown are primed for a crime such as robbery.

Sexual assault in Vancouver is a relatively rare event in police statistics. The sexual assault rate in the Downtown Eastside areas is high but there are relatively few of such incidents, with a scattering over a few other areas around the city. Almost all of the areas are within the east side of Vancouver, but that may simply be a reporting issue.

The location quotient map for sexual assault, Figure 5.3b, represents a radically different phenomenon. The specialization of sexual assault is scattered across all Vancouver with the only potential clustering occurring in the northeastern portion of the city. Similar to robbery, there is a pattern of the areas of specialization to be close to or on major arterial roadways, and there are more of these arterial roadways within the east side of Vancouver, potentially accounting the moderate appearance of clustering in the northeastern portion of the city.

The map for the location quotients of theft, Figure 5.4b, also reveals an interesting pattern. Not only is more of the downtown area now specializing in theft, but the majority of the areas with specialization in theft lie within the west side (wealthier) portion of Vancouver. This is both contradictory to common perceptions and makes sense. Most often we believe crime to be higher in relatively poorer areas of the city, but there will be more attractive targets for theft in those

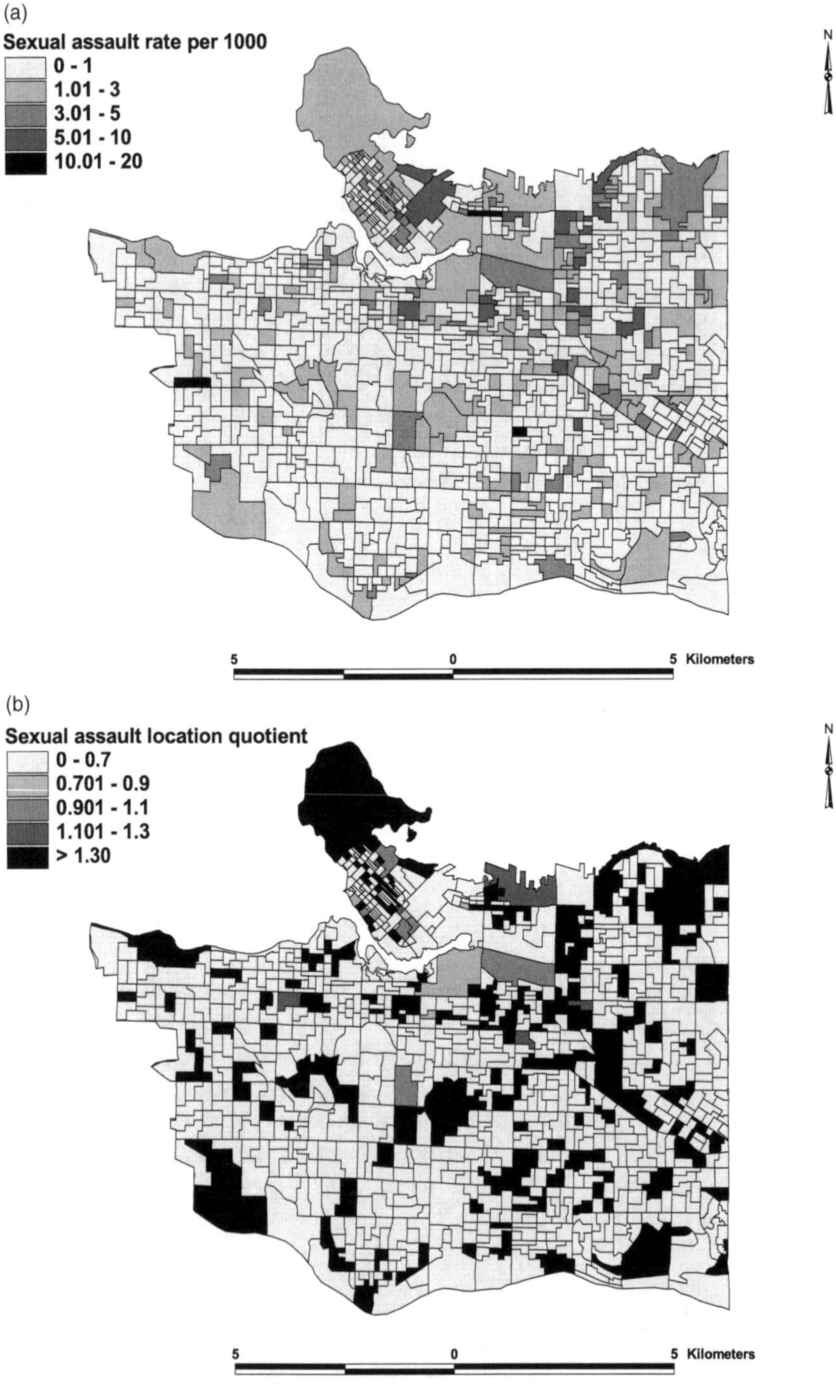

(a)

Sexual assault rate per 1000

- 0 - 1
- 1.01 - 3
- 3.01 - 5
- 5.01 - 10
- 10.01 - 20

N

5   0   5 Kilometers

(b)

Sexual assault location quotient

- 0 - 0.7
- 0.701 - 0.9
- 0.901 - 1.1
- 1.101 - 1.3
- > 1.30

N

5   0   5 Kilometers

Figure 5.3 Crime rate (a) and location quotients (b), sexual assault, Vancouver, 2001.

(a)

Theft rate per 1000

- 0 - 30
- 30.01 - 100
- 100.01 - 200
- 200.01 - 400
- 400.01 - 1200

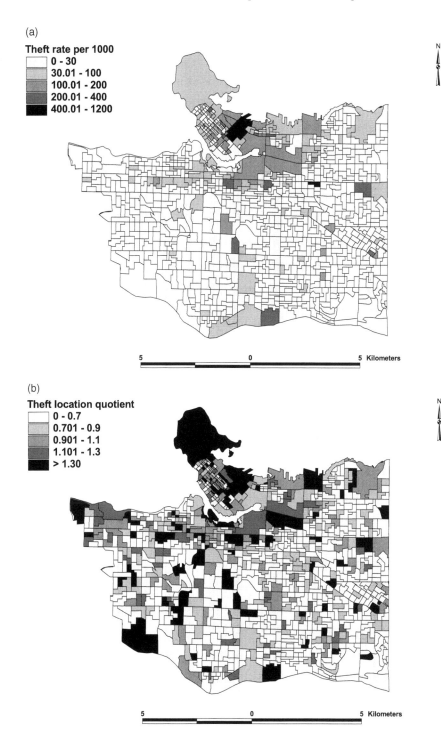

N

5   0   5 **Kilometers**

(b)

Theft location quotient

- 0 - 0.7
- 0.701 - 0.9
- 0.901 - 1.1
- 1.101 - 1.3
- > 1.30

N

5   0   5 **Kilometers**

Figure 5.4 Crime rate (a) and location quotients (b), theft, Vancouver, 2001.

wealthier areas. This demonstrates a clear advantage to using multiple measures of crime, particularly a measure of specialization, which allows for these nuances to be easily identified.

The location quotient map for theft from vehicle is shown in Figure 5.5b. The crime rate map, Figure 5.5a, is most similar to that of assault: the highest crime rates are in the downtown and Downtown Eastside areas, with low crime rates across the rest of Vancouver. Generally speaking, all the crime rate maps are very similar thus far, as discussed above.

The location quotient map identifies the downtown area as almost completely highly specialized in theft from vehicle. This is also easily understood when considering opportunity. The downtown area has many parking areas for cars because of the large number of people who work in downtown. These cars are parked all day with relatively low guardianship aside from the more expensive and exclusive paring facilities. The downtown area also has a large number of commercial areas: shopping malls, boutique shops, clubs and bars, museums, and art galleries. These are also attractions that lend to people parking their vehicles for relatively long periods of time with little or no guardianship. This will be particularly the case for those who try to avoid parking in the expensive parking facilities and leave their vehicle away from the crowds, often in alleys with no guardianship.

Though difficult to interpret without local knowledge of Vancouver, the apparently random scattering of areas for theft from vehicle specialization tend to be along the major arterial roadways, mass transit stations, and other commercial areas where people will leave their cars unguarded for a long periods of time.

The theft of vehicle map for the location quotients is shown in Figure 5.6. Again, in the context of crime rate per 1,000, a similar pattern emerges with a concentration in the downtown area that dissipates as one moves away from this area. The high crime rates in the areas in the center of the city are in the area of the largest shopping center in Vancouver outside of the downtown area. As such, a high rate of theft of vehicle is not surprising here.

The location quotient map, however, has quite a different spatial pattern. A large portion of the downtown area (the central business district) is highly under-represented in theft of vehicle; only the shopping areas have a high degree of specialization in theft of vehicle. Again, this is indicative of crime opportunity. The central business district of the downtown area has parking facilities that are dominantly underground or multi-story, above-ground parking lots with attendants. Consequently, it is much more difficult to steal an entire vehicle in these areas than it is to steal items within the vehicles parked in these areas. The shopping and commercial outlet areas of downtown, however, dominantly have street parking and unattended parking lots. Vehicles are much easier to steal in these areas because there are fewer (most often zero) physical barriers, much unlike the multi-story parking facilities with attendants.

The rest of Vancouver has many areas with a high degree of specialization in theft of vehicle. The only noticeable pattern that emerges is that there are more areas with a high degree of specialization on the east side of the city. This may be

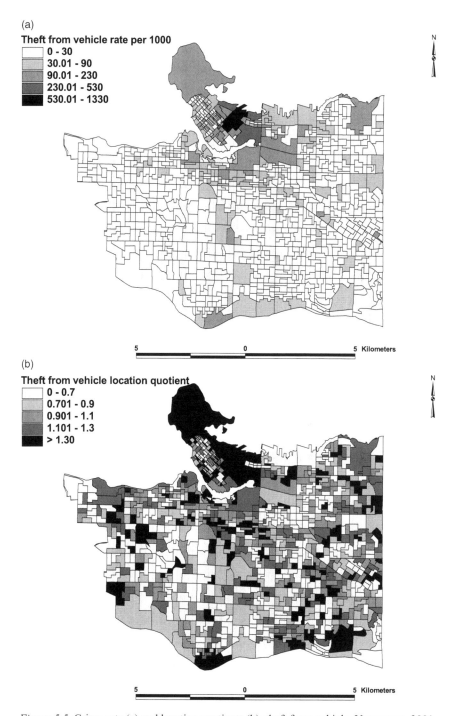

Figure 5.5 Crime rate (a) and location quotients (b), theft from vehicle, Vancouver, 2001.

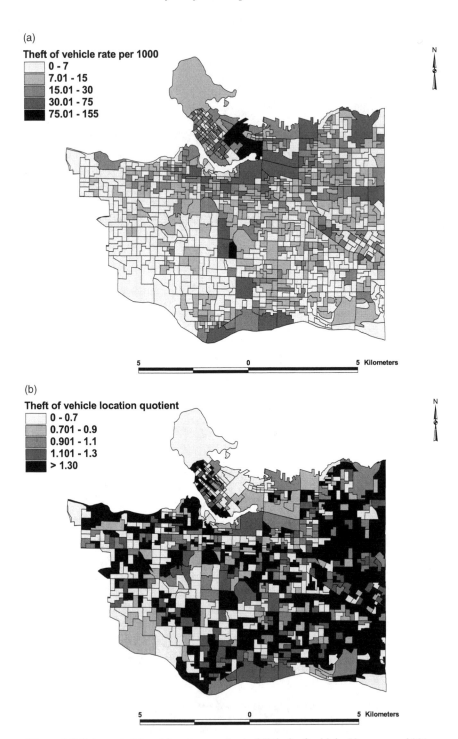

Figure 5.6 Crime rate (a) and location quotients (b), theft of vehicle, Vancouver, 2001.

explained through the security hypothesis: relatively wealthier areas will have newer vehicles with better security features (Tseloni *et al.*, 2010; Farrell *et al.*, 2011), so there has been a shift in theft of vehicle from early to late model vehicles that manifests itself on the east side of the city that is not as wealthy.

The most interesting comparison of general crime rate per 1,000 pattern to the location quotients is in the case of burglary, Figure 5.7. As with the previous crime types, the crime rate map for burglary follows the general pattern for Vancouver, and most Western cities, being highest in the downtown area and dissipating as one moves away from that area. The location quotient map, however, shows a high degree of widespread specialization, precisely in places where we would not expect them, *a priori*.

The first aspect of the location quotient map of burglary to notice is the absence of any burglary specialization in the central business district. This is, of course, an expected result. There are a few areas in the downtown shopping and commercial areas that are specialized in burglary, but these are most often commercial outlets, not residential.

Though there is a high degree of burglary specialization within the east side of Vancouver, almost the entire west side of Vancouver is classified as highly over-represented. This is an unexpected result because the burglary crime rate per 1,000 is so low within much of the west side of Vancouver. In fact, these maps partially shroud how low the burglary rates are within the west side of Vancouver because there are only five legend categories. An inspection of the raw data (or a map with many more legend categories) reveals that burglary in these areas is remarkably low.

But once we consider opportunity, the reason behind this result is clear. The homes in these areas, because they are wealthy, are more likely to have expensive items to steal, particularly jewellery. As such, if you are going to travel to the west side of Vancouver to commit a crime, it will likely be a burglary. If vehicle security had not increased like it did in recent years, theft of vehicle specialization would likely be high in these areas as well.

Final thoughts on location quotient and crime specialization

The crime rate maps for the different crime types all basically show the same spatial pattern that is all too common in spatial criminology: high crime in the downtown areas that (most often) decreases monotonically with distance away from the downtown area. Though there will be subtleties across the different crime types, as are shown above, the basic story is almost always the same.

The location quotient is now clearly not in a similar vein. Rather, the location quotient, though sometimes following a similar pattern as the crime rate, shows substantially different spatial patterns from crime type to crime type. These different patterns, as argued above, are representative of the opportunity surface of crime. Different places are abundant in different types of opportunities, so it is no wonder that these places "specialize" in different crime types.

(a)

Burglary rate per 1000

	0 - 15
	15.01 - 30
	30.01 - 50
	50.01 - 90
	90.01 - 210

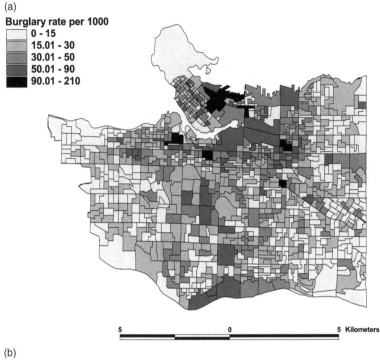

5   0   5   **Kilometers**

(b)

Burglary location quotient

	0 - 0.7
	0.701 - 0.9
	0.901 - 1.1
	1.101 - 1.3
	> 1.30

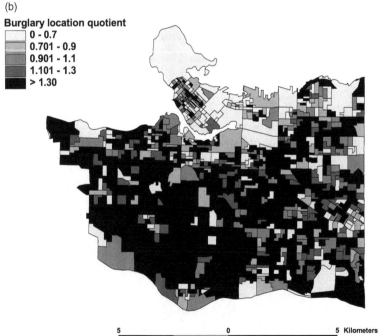

5   0   5   **Kilometers**

Figure 5.7 Crime rate (a) and location quotients (b), burglary, Vancouver, 2001.

This descriptive exercise follows in the stream of the previous chapters that discussed a different way of calculating the crime rate. As with that work, changing the ways in which we measure crime can have significant implications for the interpretations we are able to make. Based on the work presented thus far, and what follows, the message is abundantly clear: if we are to get a comprehensive understanding of crime, we must measure it in a multitude of ways.

6 Crime specialization across the Canadian provinces and Metro Vancouver's municipalities

Introduction

One set of crime statistics that is particularly interesting is the pattern of Canadian provincial crime rates: a generally increasing crime rate moving east to west that has been present for at least 40 years (see Silver, 2007 for a recent example of this reporting). Curiously, there has been relatively little research investigating this phenomenon, with only two studies finding statistically significant relationships. The earliest investigations of this phenomenon (Giffen, 1965, 1976) find moderate support for higher provincial crime rates being related to population growth and the presence of urbanization; Hartnagel (1978) finds little support for the age and sex composition of provincial populations affecting provincial crime rates; Kennedy *et al.* (1991) find that provincial homicide rates are related to income inequality and social disorganization; Hartnagel (1997) finds that provinces with greater inward migration have greater crime rates; and most recently, Daly *et al.* (2001) find that income inequality partially explains differences in lethal levels of violence.

But how much of this pattern is truly present? Certainly the crime rates are higher as one moves west across the Canadian landscape, but are the western provinces really more violent, for example, or is there simply more crime in these provinces with the proportion of violent crime similar to that of the rest of the provinces? This chapter adds to the criminological literature through the use of a geographical measure of crime, the location quotient, which was discussed in Chapter 5. Rather than measuring crime relative to some population at risk, the location quotient measures crime specialization: how much of crime X is in a given province relative to the whole of Canada? Or, how much of crime X is in a given municipality relative to the whole metropolitan region? The location quotient has been used in a number of ecological studies of crime, but not in the context of understanding the east-to-west pattern of crime in Canada or at the municipal level. As shown below, this different measure of crime reveals that the western provinces do not disproportionately specialize in all crime classifications. Rather, different provinces specialize in different crime classifications. Therefore, although one may be more likely to be a victim of crime in the western provinces, as indicated by provincial crime rates, one is not more likely to be a victim of all crimes. In addition, municipalities that have high crime rates do not necessarily have a high degree of crime specialization in that crime, and vice versa.

Data and measurement methodology

All crime counts and crime rates used in the provincial calculations below are obtained from Silver (2007) and Statistics Canada's Socio-Economic Information Management System, consisting of violent crimes, property crimes, and other crimes. Violent crimes include total violent crimes, homicide, assault (levels 1, 2, 3),[1] sexual assault, and robbery. Property crimes include total property crimes, burglary, motor vehicle theft, and other theft. Other crimes include mischief, drugs (total), and total federal statutes. Each of these crime classifications is measured at the national and provincial levels for the year 2006 and based on incidents, not charges, to avoid any provincial biases in criminal justice prosecution. The municipal level data are from the Province of British Columbia (2012). Though these data do represent municipalities across the entire province of British Columbia, the focus here is on the Greater Vancouver Regional District (GVRD)—see Brantingham and Brantingham (1998) for an analysis considering all of British Columbia's municipalities. Data are available for total crime, violent crime, property crime, motor vehicle theft, and drug offences.

The measurement of crime takes two forms: the crime rate and the location quotient. The crime rate is the standard crime measurement of the number of crimes per 100,000 population (province) and the number of crimes per 1,000 (municipalities). As discussed in Part I, the crime rate has a relatively long history of being shown to be problematic in measuring crime (see Boggs, 1965; Harries, 1981, 1991), particularly in neighborhood analyses, but at the municipal, provincial, and national levels there is generally much less concern. However, a difficulty does arise at this scale in the Canadian context with Canadian regions that have populations less than 100,000, such as each of the three territories: Yukon, Northwest, and Nunavut. The Yukon Territories, for example, has a population (2006) of 31,229. Consequently, when making crime rate calculations per 100,000, one crime in the Yukon Territory generates a crime rate of 3.2 per 100,000. A good case in point is homicide in Nunavut. Nunavut, with a population (2006) of 30,782, had two homicides in 2006 and a corresponding homicide rate of 6.5 per 100,000. Though this crime rate is technically correct, it may be misleading to an uninformed public which may make false inferences about this region of Canada. Because of this difficulty in interpretation, the discussion of crime rates below focuses on the provinces and not territories. As such, if one only uses a rate when analyzing crime, this provides limited information, especially for areas with small populations.

As discussed in Chapter 5, the location quotient is a specifically geographical measure that provides an alternative measurement to the crime rate and is not plagued with the difficulties of crime rates (Isard *et al.*, 1998). This measure does not correct for the problem outlined above regarding Canadian regions with relatively low populations, but it does add new information that may help interpreting such crime statistics.

In the context of this chapter, the location quotient is a ratio of the percentage of a particular type of crime in a province/territory relative to the percentage of that same crime in all of Canada. The five-classification scheme of Miller *et al.* (1991)

described in Chapter 5 is utilized here. This provides a measurement of under-, over-, or expected representation of criminal activity. For example, Ontario has a low robbery rate relative to the rest of Canada (below the national average), potentially leading police agencies to believe that robbery is not a problem in Ontario. However, as shown below using the location quotient, Ontario is one of three provinces that exhibit a specialization in robbery—these provinces (Quebec, Ontario, and Manitoba) have a disproportionate share of robbery. Therefore, robbery *is* a problem in Ontario to which police agencies should direct their resources. Though both the robbery and overall crime rates in Ontario are relatively low, given a person is going to be a victim of a crime in Ontario that person is 21 percent more likely to be a victim of a robbery relative to the risk of robbery in Canada as a whole.

Therefore, the usefulness of the location quotient is to supplement the use of crime rate calculations in understanding crime patterns, including the Canadian provincial trend. By having crime specialization, one more dimension of crime may be understood. In particular, the crime mix can be known. Measuring the crime rate tells us the volume of per-capita crime, and measuring the location quotient tells us the specialization or intensity of that volume relative to a larger geographical region, namely Canada and Metro Vancouver in the current context.

Provincial crime rates and location quotients

Provincial crime rates

The various provincial level crime rates, listed above, are shown in Table 6.1. The historical pattern of the western Canadian provinces and Territories having higher crime rates than central and eastern Canada is apparent, particularly for property crime. Not only do crime rates increase, on average, moving westward, but the regions in Canada that are above the Canadian average are all in western Canada except for Nova Scotia in the case of violent crime. Though this pattern is not always so apparent, it is the general pattern for all of the sub-categories of crime available in Silver (2007) except for counterfeiting currency, which is not shown. (Other *Criminal Code* offenses are also not shown here, but this category does follow the same geographical pattern mentioned above.) The primary exception to this pattern is for mischief. Within this crime classification, the Atlantic provinces (Newfoundland and Labrador, Prince Edward Island, Nova Scotia, and New Brunswick) are also above the Canadian average, but here as well the western provinces and Territories most often have crime rates that are far greater. Overall, it should be noted that the strength of the east-to-west trend in Canadian crime varies considerably across crime types and does appear to have lessened in recent years.

Regardless, as mentioned above, this geographical pattern of crime in Canada has remained stable for many years and continues, despite western Canada having the largest drops in many crime categories (Silver, 2007). This phenomenon leads to an obvious question: why is crime so high in the west? Though the current

Table 6.1 Crime rates per 100,000: Canada and provinces, 2006

	YT	NT	NU	BC	AB	SK	MB	ON	QC	NB	NS	PEI	NL	Canada
Homicide	0.0	0.0	6.5	2.5	2.8	4.1	3.3	1.5	1.2	0.9	1.7	0.7	1.4	1.9
Assault[a]	2,655	5,834	5,893	980	888	1,671	1,243	563	540	706	919	624	734	735
Sexual assault[a]	195	373	598	75	64	125	108	56	67	67	86	48	67	68
Robbery	58	36	39	110	93	150	182	87	91	29	85	17	23	94
Violent crime	3,007	6,448	6,764	1,218	1,101	2,039	1,598	756	756	849	1,135	714	851	951
Burglary	1,467	2,332	1,965	1,088	768	1,228	1,074	541	867	599	735	537	737	768
Motor vehicle theft	445	927	620	682	725	633	1,376	303	507	187	263	115	131	487
Other theft	2,840	2,719	1,351	3,425	2,449	2,434	2,200	1,574	1,463	1,484	1,984	2,033	1,266	1,941
Property crime	5,107	6,357	4,256	5,685	4,480	4,776	4,951	2,811	3,114	2,562	3,514	3,000	2,363	3,588
Mischief	5,476	13,251	9,558	1,436	1,764	3,208	2,781	798	616	1,181	1,598	1,577	1,561	1,160
Drugs (total)	468	769	672	617	258	275	183	239	266	248	218	127	128	295
Total federal statutes[b]	22,249	4,4423	33,401	1,2563	10,423	15,320	12,348	6,291	6,629	6,672	8,747	7,522	6,669	8,299

Notes

[a]Levels 1, 2, 3.

[b]This classification is sometimes referred to as Total Incidents.

analysis does not aim to understand why the rates of crime are consistently higher in western versus eastern and central Canada, it does aim to shed light on the perception that all crime is more problematic in the west.

Provincial location quotients

The various provincial level location quotients are shown in Table 6.2. It should be noted that some of the results shown in the figures are artifacts of the classifications of under-, average, and over-representation. For example, Manitoba and New Brunswick are over-represented for violent crimes, whereas Ontario is not shown as over-represented despite appearing to have a very similar location quotient value. However, inspection of Table 6.2 reveals that all these provinces have very similar location quotient values for violent crime. As such, the reader should always refer to both the figures and the tables in order to obtain a complete picture of the provincial differences.

As should be clear from Table 6.2, there is a substantial difference between the patterns of crime rates and location quotients. As mentioned above, with the exception of Nova Scotia, violent crime rates are highest in the western provinces and the Territories. Turning to the location quotient for violent crimes, however, Saskatchewan and Manitoba are the only western provinces that are over-represented in violent crime along with New Brunswick, Nova Scotia, and Newfoundland. Aside from Nunavut, there is no trend of increasing or decreasing violent crime location quotients as one moves across the country. Moreover, even for those provinces that are over-represented, that overrepresentation is moderate.

The location quotient for property crime has the opposite geographical pattern as the location quotient for violent crime: the property crime location quotient has no particular trend moving east to west, aside from a significant drop for the Territories. Moreover, no province or Territory is over-represented with regard to property crime. In fact, most provinces have percentages of property crime that do not deviate significantly from the national average. Therefore, despite the depiction of the provincial property crime rates, if one is to be a victim of crime there is no evidence to show that property crime is significantly more prevalent in any specific province or group of provinces than Canada as a whole.

In Table 6.2, it is quite clear that specialization in different crime types is common for all provinces and, therefore, all three regions of Canada. In fact, separating Canada into its three regions, Table 6.2 shows that over-representation in a crime type occurs in eastern Canada 15 times, central Canada 7 times, and western Canada 15 times—the Territories have over-representation 10 times. Consequently, crime specialization varies across the Canadian landscape and is far from being concentrated in western Canada. With regard to central and eastern Canada, Ontario only has one crime classification that is over-represented (robbery), whereas Quebec and Newfoundland have five crime classifications that are over-represented. These results for Ontario and Newfoundland are not unexpected: given the size of Ontario, it is not uncommon for this province to represent (and in many ways define) the Canadian average; and given the small size of

Table 6.2 Location quotients: provinces, 2006[a]

	YT	NT	NU	BC	AB	SK	MB	ON	QC	NB	NS	PEI	NL
Homicide	0.00	0.00	0.88	0.89	**1.22**	**1.18**	**1.20**	**1.10**	0.82	0.63	0.88	0.43	0.92
Assault[b]	**1.35**	*1.47*	*2.02*	0.88	0.96	**1.23**	**1.14**	1.01	0.92	**1.20**	**1.19**	0.94	**1.24**
Sexual assault[b]	1.08	1.01	*2.22*	0.73	0.75	0.99	1.07	1.08	**1.23**	**1.22**	**1.20**	0.78	**1.23**
Robbery	0.23	0.07	0.10	0.77	0.79	0.86	*1.30*	**1.21**	**1.22**	0.39	0.85	0.20	0.31
Violent crime	**1.18**	*1.25*	*1.79*	0.84	0.92	**1.16**	**1.13**	1.05	1.00	**1.11**	**1.13**	0.83	**1.11**
Burglary	0.71	0.56	0.64	0.94	0.80	0.87	0.94	0.93	*1.41*	0.97	0.91	0.78	**1.19**
Motor vehicle theft	0.34	0.35	0.32	0.92	**1.19**	0.70	*1.90*	0.82	*1.30*	0.48	0.51	0.26	0.33
Other theft	0.55	0.26	0.18	**1.16**	1.01	0.68	0.76	1.07	0.94	0.95	0.97	**1.16**	0.81
Property crime	0.53	0.33	0.30	1.05	1.00	0.72	0.93	1.03	1.09	0.89	0.93	0.93	0.82
Mischief	*1.76*	*2.11*	*2.08*	0.82	**1.21**	*1.50*	*1.61*	0.91	0.67	**1.27**	*1.31*	*1.51*	*1.68*
Drugs (total)	0.59	0.48	0.57	*1.38*	0.70	0.51	0.42	1.07	**1.13**	1.05	0.70	0.48	0.54

Notes

[a] Bold figures indicates moderately over-represented, bold and italic figures indicate very over-represented.

[b] Levels 1, 2, 3.

Newfoundland it is not surprising it has a criminological situation that is unique. The result for Quebec, however, is rather curious because of its size.

Three specific crime classifications are worthy of special note here because they either most clearly challenge conventional thought on provincial crime patterns (motor vehicle theft and sexual assault) or have a potential explanation for the location quotient result (drugs). The first, motor vehicle theft, is over-represented in Quebec, Manitoba, and Alberta. The fact that these provinces are over-represented is not particularly interesting, though Manitoba is highly over-represented; it is the absence of British Columbia that is curious. Historically speaking, British Columbia's motor vehicle theft rate has been 25–40 percent greater than the Canadian average with the largest differences being the most recent (Statistics Canada, 2007a). In addition, one of British Columbia's larger municipalities (Surrey) has even been titled the motor vehicle theft capital of the world. One may attribute British Columbia not being over-represented in 2006 as a result of efforts by the police to reduce the motor vehicle theft rate (see Silver, 2007), but in 2001, the year before Surrey earned its title, British Columbia's motor vehicle theft location quotient was 1.00. As a result, with regard to crime specialization, very little has changed in the past 5 years.

The second crime classification of interest is sexual assault. As shown in Table 6.1, the crime rates for sexual assault follow the general violent crime pattern in Table 6.1, aside from Alberta being below the national average. The location quotient for sexual assault, however, approximately follows the opposite pattern, aside from Prince Edward Island and Nunavut. The location quotients are not particularly large, but there are approximately 20 percent more sexual assaults in the Atlantic provinces and Quebec relative to Canada as a whole. There is no obvious explanation for this pattern here, but clearly sexual assault specialization occurs in the eastern portion of Canada, not in the west.

The third crime classification of special interest is one for which an explanation can be found within the literature, namely drugs. The crime rates for drugs are only above the national average in British Columbia and the Territories—over 60 percent of drug charges are related to marijuana. As discussed in Plecas *et al.* (2005), both British Columbia and the Territories have above-average marijuana growing operations based on founded police reports, with British Columbia leading all of Canada, consistent with these reported crime rates. The location quotient, however, does continue to indicate British Columbia as over-represented in drugs, but also identifies Quebec. Plecas *et al.* (2005) identify Quebec as having a greater than average marijuana-growing operations and Bouchard (2007), using a capture–recapture model, estimates that the Quebec marijuana-growing industry is larger than previously thought. A question still remains: why British Columbia and Quebec?

Easton (2004) provides at least a partial answer in the case of British Columbia: growing marijuana is highly profitable and penalties are low. Easton (2004) conservatively estimates that marijuana-growing operations have a 50 percent profit rate that will likely be similar across the rest of Canada as well—Rengert (1996) estimates that marijuana-growing operations have a profit rate ranging from 100 to 400 percent. Though profitability is going to be a factor in the participation of illegitimate activities, this does not explain the geographic pattern of the location quotients. The regional pattern of criminal justice responses to drugs, however, does provide insight. The penalties for marijuana are lower in British Columbia versus the rest of Canada: crimes cleared by charge in British Columbia are 22 percent, but 61 percent in the rest of Canada (Easton, 2004). In addition, for those convicted of a charge, punishments are low: almost 60 percent spend 1 day or less in prison, almost 90 percent spend 90 days or less in prison, and those who are fined pay approximately $2,000 (Easton, 2004; Plecas *et al.*, 2005). Assuming similar clearance rates and sentencing in Quebec (based on volume, Quebec is the second largest marijuana producing province in Canada), the enforcement and sentencing of one drug may provide a good explanation for the pattern found using the location quotient for all drug charges, particularly because marijuana dominates the drug crime category.

More generally, the crime specialization that is occurring in different provinces for different crime classifications may be understood through crime/criminal adaptation to provincial environments. Though a complete analysis is beyond the scope of this chapter, the most recent work of Felson (2006) provides insight here. Crime adapts to ever-changing environments; crime finds its niche; and crime thrives where it is not threatened by a predatory species—think of the criminal justice system as (one of) crime's predator(s). Such an ecological interpretation reveals itself with the drug example for British Columbia. As noted above, the risk of punishment and actual punishment are lower in British Columbia than other areas of Canada with regard to the marijuana industry. Therefore, the marijuana industry is more likely to thrive in British Columbia than other areas of Canada. At this stage, such explanations are admittedly conjecture, but using the location quotient forces one to pose and attempt to answer questions that crime rates do not.

Municipal level location quotients

In the previous section, the utility of measuring crime specialization was shown using provincial level data. Though the question of why there is a regional pattern to crime in Canada's provinces was not answered, using the location quotient it was shown that, relatively speaking, Canada's western provinces do not unilaterally have more violent crime or property crime than other provinces. Moreover, in the case of property crime, none of the provinces and territories had any over-representation.

The various crime rates and location quotients are shown in Table 6.3. Because of the nature of the location quotient calculations, discussed in Chapter 5, the total crime rate is not calculated in location quotient form; it is shown here for reference. There is clearly quite the variation in crime rates across the GVRD. New Westminster has the highest crime rate in the GVRD, with West Vancouver having the lowest. The general pattern shown in Table 6.3 is consistent with data representing previous years, such as those presented in Chapter 4.

A similar pattern is present for violent crime. New Westminster and Surrey have the highest violent crime rates, with the lowest crime rates in West Vancouver

Table 6.3 Municipal level crime rates and location quotients (LQs), Metro Vancouver, 2006

Municipality	Crime rate	Violent crime rate	Violent crime LQ	Property crime rate	Property crime LQ	Motor vehicle crime rate	Motor vehicle theft LQ	Drug Rate	Drug LQ
Burnaby	10,919	1,485	0.86	7795	1.03	838	1.04	368	0.60
Coquitlam	8,656	1,247	0.91	5851	0.97	660	1.03	559	1.15
Delta	6,947	1,128	1.02	4859	1.01	521	1.01	334	0.86
Langley	11,505	1,433	0.79	8034	1.00	1,022	1.20	651	1.01
Maple Ridge	11,490	1,562	0.86	7355	0.92	1,005	1.18	487	0.76
New Westminster	12,879	2,374	1.16	7,614	0.85	978	1.03	907	1.26
North Vancouver	7,235	1,118	0.97	4,811	0.96	332	0.62	396	0.98
Pitt Meadows	9,517	1,233	0.82	6,277	0.95	663	0.94	233	0.44
Port Coquitlam	10,843	1,450	0.84	7,390	0.98	737	0.92	380	0.62
Port Moody	6,432	790	0.77	4,884	1.09	414	0.87	428	1.19
Richmond	7,276	942	0.82	5,244	1.04	429	0.80	526	1.29
Surrey	11,310	2,045	1.14	7,638	0.97	1,156	1.38	639	1.01
Vancouver	10,751	1,832	1.08	7,771	1.04	615	0.77	654	1.09
West Vancouver	5,835	866	0.94	4,371	1.08	169	0.39	266	0.81
White Rock	7,702	1,168	0.96	4,774	0.89	539	0.95	1047	2.42
Crime Rate – LQ correlation		0.68		−0.26		0.90		0.83	
GVRD	10,006	1,586		6,954		741		561	

GVRD = Greater Vancouver Regional District.

and Port Moody; the violent crime rate in Port Moody is almost one-third the level of the violent crime rate in New Westminster. More interesting, however, is the relationship between the crime rates and their corresponding location quotients, measured using Pearson's correlation coefficient. For violent crime, the correlation coefficient is 0.68. This shows that the two measurements move together for violent crime, but there is much variation between the two crime measurements that is not accounted for if only one is considered; in other words, just because an area under study has a high violent crime rate does not mean that it specializes in that crime as well. This is similar to the provincial level analysis in the previous section of this chapter.

These differences are apparent when comparing the violent crime rate to the violent crime location quotient—see the map of the GVRD in Chapter 4 for municipality reference. Vancouver, New Westminster, Surrey, and Maple Ridge are all in the highest level of violent crime rate category. However, when considering the violent crime location quotient, Vancouver has average representation, New Westminster and Surrey are moderately over-represented, and Maple Ridge is highly under-represented.

The comparison of crime rates to location quotients is most stark when considering property crime. The correlation coefficient is not only of low magnitude, but negative in sign, −e0.26. As such, the places with high magnitudes of property crime do not specialize in property crime, on average. The property crime rate is greatest in Vancouver, Burnaby (this municipality has British Columbia's largest shopping center), and Langley. However, all of these municipalities have average representation when considering the location quotient. Perhaps, most interesting for this comparison is New Westminster, which has one of the highest property crime rates, but is the most underrepresented municipality when considering the property crime location quotient. Only White Rock has a low property crime rate and an under-representation of property crime.

The comparison of crime rates to location quotients for motor vehicle theft and drug offenses is the most similar with correlation coefficients of 0.90 and 0.83, respectively. For motor vehicle theft, in particular, the resulting maps show similar patterns for crime rates and location quotients. Drug offences show some differences between crime rates and location quotients (Vancouver, Surrey, and Langley, specifically), but no drastic changes occur.

This brief discussion using data at the municipal level has shown the utility of using a crime specialization variable such as the location quotient at another scale. Though the ranking of municipalities using the location quotient was similar to crime rate rankings for motor vehicle theft and drug offences, this was not the case for property crime and only moderately the case for violent crime. These differences were shown in the previous chapter in that the spatial pattern of the location quotient was significantly different from the spatial pattern of the crime rate in the case of burglary. A similar result is shown in different context using a census tract analysis in the Chapter 7.

Conclusions and directions for future research

The quantification of social phenomena, including crime, is a reality of contemporary society whether we accept the notions behind the reasons for that quantification or not. The testing of theoretical frameworks is in part performed because of that quantification, policy decisions that allocate scarce societal resources are based on that quantification, and we decide where we would like to live because of our interpretation of that quantification. Consequently, how we quantify social phenomena is critical, such that we are able to cull as much information as possible from the data we collect.

In the context of crime data, this chapter shows the utility of supplementing the crime rate with the location quotient in an analysis of crime, even in a descriptive context. When only considering the crime rate, crime simply appears to be higher in western Canada versus the rest of the country. Indeed it is true that crime rates are higher in western Canada than the rest of Canada. However, given that a person is going to be a victim of crime in Canada, the likelihood it will be a particular crime type varies regionally.

Showing that different provinces and municipalities specialize in different crime classifications, however, is only the beginning because understanding why that specialization occurs is critical if we wish to formulate criminal justice policies to reduce crime. An explanation is hypothesized above regarding the specialization of drugs in British Columbia, but more work needs to be done in order to understand the specialization of drugs as well as the other crime classifications available. Future research not only needs to understand these specializations that exist at the provincial level, but to generate and/or apply new measures of crime to supplement the measures we already have in order to increase our understanding of this social phenomenon that impacts all of our lives.

Future work can also be done in a number of contexts for testing criminological theory. Three such contexts are immediately apparent. First, though Andresen (2007) has used the location quotient to test both social disorganization theory and routine activity theory with good success (see Chapter 7), this is only one application within one municipality; the attempt to replicate results should be undertaken at a number of different geographical scales of analysis and a number of different locations. Second, criminological theory testing may also be undertaken using victimization surveys and crime classifications that can be calculated at the provincial level to investigate whether or not the dark figure of crime is apparent in crime specialization. Third, the location quotient may be used to specifically interrogate opportunity theories of crime. As indicated above, criminal penalties in drug crimes differ across the provinces—similar variation is likely to be present for a number (or all) other crime classifications as well, depending upon perceived problems within a province. Such variation in penalties represents part of the opportunity structure of crime because it captures the cost of criminal participation relative to its benefit. Therefore, location quotients may be used to uncover where these increased opportunities exist, or test the relative importance of different deterrent factors in crime specialization. These types of analyses may then inform theory by confirming or rejecting hypotheses.

This form of criminological theory testing using the location quotient may then lead to a wider application of the location quotient in criminological research. If the criminological research community recognizes the utility of this different form of measurement, a location quotient may be calculated in any area of criminology that calculates rates or by anyone interested in specialization/intensity within the regions of a larger geographical area.

7 Location quotients, ambient populations, and spatial analysis of crime in Vancouver

Introduction

This chapter uses the location quotient to measure criminal activity in Vancouver, Canada in a spatial analytical framework, similar to the 1996 analyses in Chapter 3. Crime data for Vancouver, 1996, are the same as those used in Chapter 3, as is the set of variables and analytic method. The location quotients for automotive theft, break and enter, and violent crime are modeled using the two most common spatial theories of crime: social disorganization theory and routine activity theory.

Descriptive results

The maps for the dependent variables are shown in Figures 7.1–7.3 (descriptive statistics and correlations are available from the author). Though normality is an issue with some of the variables, particularly the crime counts, the different crime measures are mapped using standard deviations. Despite the limitation of using standard deviation classifications, this method of presentation shows best the different crime measures in comparable units and, therefore, the utility of employing the location quotient in crime analysis.

The spatial pattern of the location quotients for automotive theft bears little resemblance to the automotive theft crime rate, with the correlation being slightly negative and essentially zero. The downtown area (the north-central coastal region in the city) as well as the census tract in the center of the city (representing the largest shopping center within the City of Vancouver, outside of the downtown area) both have high crime rates and are over-represented for automotive theft. The rather small proportion of census tracts with a high location quotient are largely represented in these areas, with the remainder of the city having average or under-representation in this criminal activity. With the large number of automobiles present in the downtown area and shopping centers in most cities, this location quotient appears to capture well the attractiveness of particular areas for automotive theft.

The results for break and enter, Figure 7.2, are quite different, with the spatial pattern of the break and enter location quotients being almost the opposite of the automotive theft location quotients—the crime rate and location quotients

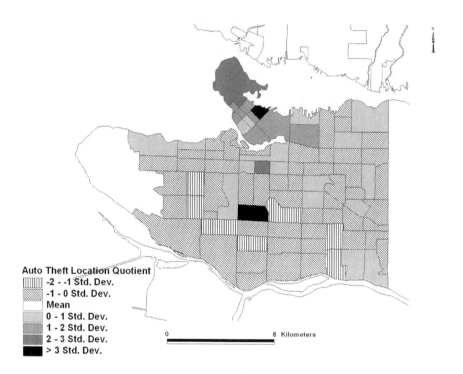

Figure 7.1   Automobile theft, location quotients.

Source: DMTI Spatial Inc. and Vancouver Police Department. Std. Dev. = standard deviation.

for break and enter have a significant negative correlation, $r = -0.53$. The downtown area, Downtown Eastside, and the shopping center at the center of the city are poorly represented for break and enter; the high number of commercial and low number of residential land use components of these areas are simply not attractors to break and enter crime. The west side of Vancouver has a low break and enter crime rate, despite a high crime count due to the number of residential units, a statistic which usually leads the public to believe that the risk of break and enter crimes in that area is low. Although it is true that the crime rate itself is low, if a person in that area is going to be a victim of crime, it is very likely to be a break and enter. It is precisely this relationship that is used to explain why some people who live in areas with low crime *rates* have a high fear of crime. A large proportion, approximately 47 percent, of the census tracts in Vancouver are highly over-represented in the crime of break and enter, with those areas having lower proportions of rental residences and higher incomes.

Violent crime, Figure 7.3, also exhibits a substantially different spatial pattern between the crime rate and the location quotients—they exhibit a low, though significant, positive correlation. The downtown area, Downtown Eastside, and

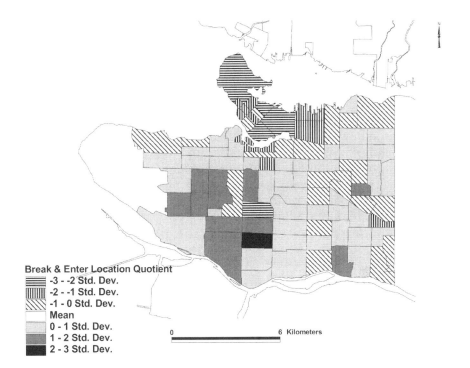

Figure 7.2 Break and enter, location quotients.
Source: DMTI Spatial Inc. and Vancouver Police Department. Std. Dev. = standard deviation.

major corridors have the highest crime rates and crime counts of violent crime in the City of Vancouver. These areas, owing to their commercial land use and transit systems, necessarily have high volumes of people, which is a necessary crime attractor for areas specializing in violent crime. The variation of the location quotients is greater, with more areas of downtown and major corridors exhibiting high values as well as large portions of the east side of Vancouver specializing in violent crime.

The correlations for the dependent variables exhibit either negative or zero correlation. This is qualitatively different from the correlations for the various crime rates and crime counts, which all exhibit strong positive correlations. This result exemplifies the differences between using location quotients versus crime rates and crime counts. Areas with a high crime rate or count in one crime classification usually have a high crime rate or count in another. They are typically hotspots for crime, in general. However, having no relation, or a negative relation, between the different location quotients shows that specialization in criminal activity occurs in particular places, adding significant new information to the geographical analysis of crime.

Inferential results

As discussed in Chapter 3, in all of the final spatial regression models reported in Table 7.1 spatial dependence is controlled for using a Queen's contiguity spatial weights matrix: fourth, third, and second order contiguity for automotive theft, break and enter, and violent crime, respectively. Given that spatial regression is performed using maximum likelihood estimation, there is no R^2 calculated, but a Pseudo-R^2 is provided to assess the models' goodness of fit. Violent crime has the lowest Pseudo-R^2 (0.42), followed by automotive theft (0.45), and break and enter (0.58). Although these Pseudo-R^2 values are relatively low, they are impressive given these data are a spatial cross-section and the parsimonious nature of the three statistical models—these results are on par with the results of Cahill and Mulligan (2003) using crime rates.

The final statistical model for automotive theft retains population change, average income, all four population variables, and average dwelling value. Areas with high degrees of population change have increased levels of automotive theft specialization, consistent with a lack of guardianship, as discussed above. Increases in average income also increase this specialization, potentially capturing the availability of targets: areas with higher average incomes are more likely to have high-valued vehicles to steal. One limitation of this interpretation is that it assumes all vehicles are chosen based on value and desirability, which is not necessarily the case with joyriding or automotive theft to commit another crime. However, no such distinction can be made with the data used in this analysis. Average dwelling value has a negative relationship with automotive theft, likely due to guardianship issues. More expensive neighborhoods with a higher proportion of vehicles in garages with alarms provide fewer targets, and thus attract less criminal activity. The ambient population and ambient population density have positive and negative relationships with automotive theft specialization, respectively. The presence of more people, and their vehicles, provides more targets, but high densities of people are able to provide more guardianship for those vehicles—less opportunity to break into or steal a vehicle undetected.

Places with high residential populations have a negative relationship with automotive theft specialization and places with high residential population densities have a positive relationship with automotive theft specialization. Given that residential populations are not a good indicator of where people actually are throughout the day, it must be the characteristics of these places that attract specific criminal activities to them. High population density is associated with apartment buildings, which tend to have parkades for their residents. Although these parkades typically have security measures to increase guardianship, once that security is breached the availability of targets appears to dominate. The negative relationship with the residential population is more difficult to interpret. It may be the case that places with high residential populations are characterized by high levels of employment, removing automobiles (targets) from those places during the day.

The final statistical model for break and enter retains the percentage of university graduates and average income. Increases in both variables decrease the

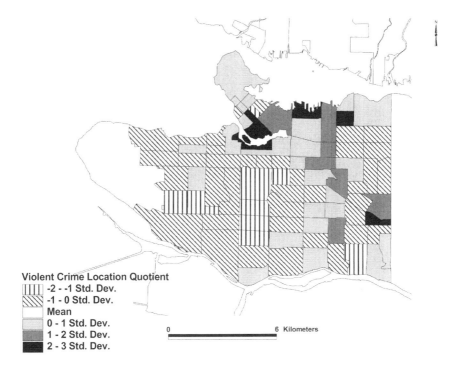

Figure 7.3 Violent crime, location quotients.

Source: DMTI Spatial Inc. and Vancouver Police Department. Std. Dev. = standard deviation.

specialization of those places for break and enter. The unemployment rate and population change also have negative coefficients. In order to increase the level of specialization in break and enter, an area needs to decrease unemployment and increase neighborhood stability. In addition, considering both the estimated coefficients and range of values for the variables remaining in the final model, the unemployment rate has the largest magnitude impact on the location quotient for break and enter. This result for unemployment is easily understood when considering crime attractors: areas with low unemployment have higher proportions of people at work during the day. Vacant homes (targets) most definitely attract break and enter specialization. An inspection of Figure 7.2 reveals that the areas with the greatest positive deviations in location quotient values (the west side of Vancouver and the wealthier neighborhoods of the east side of Vancouver) are areas with high incomes, high levels of education, high employment, and a high degree of home ownership.

Increased population density and ambient population is associated with decreases in break and enter specialization, whereas increases in the number of dwellings, average dwelling value, and ambient population density increases break and enter specialization. The interpretation of these results is straightforward for the number of dwellings and average dwelling value: places with more dwellings have more potential targets for break and enter, and places with higher average dwelling values are more likely to have greater payoffs to a break and enter, and are thus more attractive targets. Increased residential population density and ambient population decreases break and enter specialization. Increases in the residential population, while holding the number of dwellings constant, implies higher density housing, or apartment buildings. With decreased access to an apartment building—multiple security doors and fewer access points per housing unit—break and enter offenders are likely to find easier targets in areas dominated by single family dwellings. An increased ambient population negatively affecting break and enter specialization may be interpreted as increased guardianship. Though this is the opposite of the case of automotive theft, the ambient population does not represent, directly or indirectly, the ultimate target of criminal offenders. Therefore, their presence hinders, rather than facilitates, crime. The ambient population density is more problematic for interpretation. The explanation for this positive relationship is most likely due to the strong negative relationship between the location quotients for automotive theft and break and enter, $r = -0.84$, manifesting itself in opposite signs for all parameters on variables in common for the two final statistical models.

The statistical result for violent crime retains the smallest number of explanatory variables, explaining its relatively low Pseudo-R^2 value. Increases in both the unemployment rate and the percentage of single-parent households increases the level of specialization in violent crime. The percentage of recent immigrants, only present in the final model of violent crime, is negative and of a moderate magnitude. The clustering of ethnic groups in the city potentially constitutes a form of social cohesion. In the City of Vancouver, the vast majority of ethnic heterogeneity comes from relatively recent immigration, hence the use of this measure to capture ethnic heterogeneity in this analysis. Due to both cultural familiarity and social networks, recent immigrants tend to cluster in particular areas, potentially leading to social cohesion in these areas. However, another possibility is the under-reporting of crime in areas with large proportions of recent immigrants. Having English as a second language and/or a lack of knowledge in (Canadian) law influences the probability of criminal activity being reported to the police (Ley, 2004).

The positive relationship between the percentage of single-parent households and the location quotient for violent crime runs contrary to some research in Canada on intimate partner assault. DeKeseredy and Ellis (1995) find that intimate male violence against women decreases when the woman is removed from the household of the male offender. The increased specialization in violent crime in areas with high proportions of single-parent households may simply be due to increased activity outside of the home related to childcare and child-related services. This result may be interpreted as a lack of guardianship because an increased level of activity outside the protective environment of the home increases susceptibility to criminal victimization.

Table 7.1 Spatial regression results[a]

	Automotive theft	Break and enter	Violent crime
Ethnic heterogeneity, % recent immigrants			−0.008
Unemployment rate, %		−0.039	0.034
University degree, %		−0.014	
Population change, %	0.003	−0.006	
Single-parents, %			0.016
Average income, 000s	0.003	−0.005	
Population, 000s	−0.049		
Population density, 000s	0.019	−0.035	
Number of dwellings, 00s		0.012	
Average dwelling value, 000s	−0.001	0.001	
Ambient population, 000s	0.036	−0.050	
Ambient population density, 000s	−0.031	0.045	
Spatial dependence, *LR*	(0.301)	(0.122)	(0.297)
Weights matrix, Queen's order	4	3	2
Pseudo-R^2	0.447	0.577	0.415

Notes: [a]All variables shown are significant at the 5 percent level. *p*-values for spatial dependence are reported in parentheses.

Conclusion

This chapter uses the location quotient to investigate the spatial dimension of criminal activity in Vancouver, Canada. Although the use of this measure of crime is rather underutilized, it provides yet another understanding of why particular crimes occur in particular places by capturing those characteristics that attract criminal activity. The strength of the location quotient in empirical studies is its ease of calculation. If spatially referenced crime data for an urban center are available for calculating spatially varying crime rates, then location quotients can be calculated using that same data.

Overall, the workhorse spatial theories of criminal activity bode well for the location quotient. This research has shown that the use of the location quotient forces the researcher to ask different questions as to why theory does not match observations in the context of a specific criminal event, strengthening our understanding of that criminal event. Therefore, the purpose of the location quotient is to supplement the use of crime counts and crime rates rather than replace them. Future research using the location quotient should not only be done on other urban centers, but across time. As mentioned above, location quotients are able to identify specialization in crime, even in the presence of a small crime count. However, if crime counts are low in a given area, that area may be subject to high variability in crime counts and, hence, location quotients. Therefore, a longitudinal approach is best undertaken to minimize any small number effects.

One potential criticism of the location quotient is that an area may have very little crime with a high proportion of that crime being a specific crime type.

For example, suppose most census units have 100 criminal events evenly spread across different crime types, with one census unit only having 10 criminal events. If that same census unit had 8 of those criminal events as break and enters and only 40 percent of all crimes in the city were break and enters, that census unit would have a location quotient of 2, indicating specialization in break and enters. This may be considered misleading because there is so little crime taking place in this one spatial unit. But this is precisely the strength of the location quotient in spatial crime analysis. The use of crime counts or crime rates in such a spatial unit would very likely not give much attention to this area. Such low crime counts or low crime rates would not be considered very interesting because research questions are set up to explain crime and very little crime happens there. However, for all intents and purposes, if there is only one type of crime occurring in that area, there is probably something special about that area that attracts particular criminals into that space. Crime counts and crime rates ignore this information, but the location quotient exemplifies it. Despite this strength of the location quotient, low counts of a crime in an area may lead to high variability over time, though the counts in the present analysis occur over the span of a year to minimize this problem. Regardless, interpretations should be made with caution.

A second potential criticism of the location quotient involves the estimated coefficients in a statistical analysis of multiple crime categories: if one crime category has a positive estimated coefficient for an independent variable, another crime category will necessarily have a negative estimated coefficient for that same variable. However, there is no guarantee of such a systematic relationship. If one spatial unit has a high location quotient for one crime category, it may have a high location quotient for all other crime categories as well. In other words, any given unit may have a disproportionate share of only one crime category or all crime categories. Only if crime specialization forms in clusters that are in different places for each crime will such a negative relationship between estimated coefficients occur. Therefore, if this negative relationship between estimated coefficients is found, great insight is gathered regarding the spatial distribution of crime.

Part III

Crime stability and crime aggregation

In this last part of the book, the stability of crime patterns and their appropriate aggregations are investigated. Independently of how we calculate crime rates with various populations at risk or using alternative measures such as the location quotient, we make a number of assumptions regarding the stability of crime patterns and how to aggregate crime types. By their very nature, all data that we analyse are historical because they have to be collected before they can be analysed. And even though most crimes are unique, in some sense, we group them together in various classifications. These are concerns for crime measurements in general, but specifically for spatially referenced crime data.

The first aggregation considered in Part III is the aggregation of various types of crime. Most often we hear about "crime," "violent crime," "property crime," etc., but do these classifications mean anything? Or are they simply artifacts of how we used to measure criminal activity? Though research is increasingly using disaggregate crime data as police agencies make such data available for analysis, we are still presented with these aggregated crime types. I do it myself! Even when disaggregate crime data are available we may aggregate crime types for efficacy in analyses: armed robbery and strong-arm robbery, commercial burglary and residential burglary, etc. When we do this, particularly in spatial crime analysis, we (implicitly) assume that the spatial patterns of these disaggregate crimes are the same. Otherwise, if these crime types are aggregated the resulting pattern is muddled with any results potentially being meaningless.

In Chapter 8, this aggregation is investigated from a spatial perspective using two Canadian cities: Ottawa and Vancouver. Generally, it is found that most often the aggregations commonly made are not justified because of the lack of similarity in the resulting spatial patterns. Moreover, the spatial patterns of disaggregate crime types are least similar when considering the spatial unit of analysis most commonly used in the spatial crime analysis literature, namely the census tract. Only when using micro-spatial units of analysis in a particular context do the spatial patterns of different crime types become sufficiently similar to justify aggregations.

Not only do we aggregate crime across various crime types, but across time as well. Most often a full year of data (sometimes a calendar year, other times a fiscal year) is analyzed in conjunction with census data for that same year. But does it make sense to aggregate data that cover such a long time span? Is the spatial pattern of a crime the same in the summer as in the winter? If not, do any analyses suffer from the same problem as described above? In Chapter 9, this aggregation issue is investigated in the context of assault, the most common crime type analyzed in this context. Spatial crime patterns of assault are compared across two different spatial units of analysis, comparing all year to both seasons and individual months. At the census tract level—the most common spatial unit of analysis in the spatial crime analysis literature—none of the spatial patterns are similar enough to justify aggregation. Only at the dissemination area level does a higher degree of similarity emerge, but in the context of month-to-month similarity; the spatial patterns of assault are similar between any two given months, but when aggregated to the year, those similarities disappear. Therefore, aggregating spatially referenced crime data to yearly observations may also generate meaningless results.

In the context of the stability of crime patterns, the implications are critical for theory testing, policy, and practice. Any analysis of historical crime data must assume ecological stability if we are to make inferences which are relevant for the present. Otherwise, we are only considering historical relationships. If there is no ecological stability and we base theory testing, public policy, and practice on these relationships, all of our efforts may be in vain. In Chapter 10 this stability is investigated. It is found that only at the micro-spatial unit of analysis do the analyses indicate ecological stability. As with the previous chapters, the most commonly used census tract does not fare well with this issue.

Lastly, Chapter 11 investigates spatial heterogeneity within larger spatial units of analysis. Most researchers cite the potential for the modifiable areal unit problem in their results but only undertake their analyses at one spatial scale. Sometimes this is because of data limitations, but other times research is cited stating that spatial aggregation in not an issue in spatial crime analysis. This chapter shows that there is a high degree of spatial heterogeneity within census tracts, and their equivalent in England. At times, there is no relationship at all between the patterns of larger spatial units of analysis and the smaller spatial units of analysis within them.

Overall, it is clear that there are many stability and aggregation issues when undertaking a spatial crime analysis. These issues must be known when they are being used, with the potential consequences acknowledged.

8 The (in)appropriateness of aggregating across crime types

Introduction

Much of the research in spatial crime analysis disaggregates property and violent crimes into their detailed crime types, but this is not always possible because of data availability and confidentiality (see, for example, Miethe *et al.*, 1987; Murray *et al.*, 2001; Cahill and Mulligan, 2003; Weisburd *et al.*, 2004; Andresen, 2006a, 2007, 2011). Though largely beyond the control of the researcher—and this practice of aggregation is decreasing as crime data quality improves and confidentiality issues are resolved—are such aggregations appropriate? This question is of critical importance because high quality crime data are not always available to the researcher and this may have implications for the results.

If two qualitatively different spatial point patterns are aggregated, how useful will any analysis of these aggregated data be for theory and/or criminal justice policy? Though many crime types may have some (or many) similarities, there are theoretical reasons for why we would expect one crime to have a different opportunity surface and, hence, spatial pattern from another. Similarly, a policy prescription for assault will likely be different from a policy prescription for robbery. Consequently, an aggregated crime analysis may not provide meaningful information with regard to either theory or policy.

In this chapter a new area-based spatial point pattern test is used to investigate the similarity of disaggregated crime types; we analyze the similarity across these disaggregate crime types and an aggregate measurement of crime in two Canadian cities. Common units of analysis in spatial criminology are the various census administrative units such as census tracts, census block groups, and dissemination areas (Cahill and Mulligan, 2003; Andresen, 2006a, 2007, 2011). A more recent trend in spatial criminology is to use also micro-spatial units of analysis such as the street segment (Sherman *et al.*, 1989; Weisburd *et al.*, 2004; Andresen and Malleson, 2011). As such, in our investigation of the similarity of spatial crime patterns, we use three spatial units of analysis (census tracts, dissemination areas, and street segments) in order to investigate the impact of spatial scale on the similarity of spatial patterns for disaggregate and aggregate crime types. Generally speaking, we find that such aggregations are inappropriate, but there are some exceptions.

Data

Crime data from Vancouver, British Columbia and Ottawa, Ontario are used in the analysis below. Information regarding Vancouver and its crime data are described in previous chapters. However, unlike the analyses in previous chapters, the crime types are disaggregated as much as possible because of the current interest. The crime types of assault, burglary, robbery, sexual assault, theft, theft from vehicle, and theft of vehicle are all analyzed below. Total counts and percentages of both aggregate and disaggregate data used are presented in Table 8.1.

Ottawa, the capital city of Canada, is located along the Ottawa River in south-eastern Ontario. It sits adjacent to the Quebec border and is situated west of Montreal, Quebec and north-east of Toronto, Ontario. The 2006 Census data from Statistics Canada reveals that Ottawa is the fourth most populous city in the country with a population of approximately 812,000, up almost 5 percent from the previous census of 2001 (Statistics Canada, 2007b). The Ottawa census metropolitan areas (CMAs), excluding the Quebec portion of Ottawa-Gatineau, is considered the sixth most populous metropolitan area in Canada with a population of over 926,000 in 2009, up almost 6 percent from 2005 (Gannon, 2006; Dauvergne and Turner, 2010).

The total number of criminal code offences in the Ottawa CMA has steadily decreased from 6,326 per 100,000 persons in 2003 to 5,775 per 100,000 persons in 2006, and 4,558 per 100,000 persons in 2009 (Wallace, 2004; Silver, 2007; Dauvergne and Turner, 2010). In 2006 the Ottawa CMA's crime rate was slightly greater than that of the Toronto CMA (5,020 per 100,000 persons), slightly below that of the Montreal CMA (6,912 per 100,000 persons) and nearly half that of the Vancouver CMA (10,609 per 100,000 persons) (Silver, 2007).

Official police incident data from 2006 were obtained from the Ottawa Police Service website: <http://www.ottawapolice.ca/> whose officers patrol the City of Ottawa. This publicly accessible data contains information pertaining to four crime types: commercial break and enter, residential break and enter, robbery, and theft of vehicle. Within each of these crime types, details of the date, time and location (street names and 100 blocks) were recorded. Total counts and percentages of both aggregate and disaggregate data used are presented in Table 8.1.

For both Vancouver and Ottawa, the crime data are geocoded to the street network and subsequently aggregated to their respective census boundary units using a spatial join function. Our street networks recognize which side of the street a point is geocoded. If that particular street is a boundary for a spatial unit, the point is assigned to the census unit on the appropriate side of the street in the spatial join. Though shorter street segments may have a lower probability of having a criminal event, *ceteris paribus*, the randomization process in the spatial point pattern test minimizes the potential for having less scope for change than longer street segments. Lastly, the interpolation issue of geocoding algorithms, whereby a point's position on a street segment might be inaccurate, is not a concern here because no inference is made at a finer scale than the street segment.

Spatial units of analysis

Three levels of analysis are used below: census tracts, dissemination areas, and street segments. As discussed in Chapter 3, census tracts are relatively small and stable geographic areas that tend to have populations ranging from 2,500 to 8,000 persons—the average is 4,000 persons. Dissemination areas are smaller than census tracts, equivalent in size to a census block group in the US census— approximately 400 to 700 persons, composed of one or more blocks. And street segments, or 100-blocks, consist of the distance between two consecutive intersections and include all addresses located on either side of the street block. With an area of approximately 115 square kilometers, the City of Vancouver has 110 census tracts (CTs) and 990 dissemination areas (DAs), defined by Statistics Canada, and 11,730 street segments. The City of Ottawa covers approximately 2,800 square kilometers, consisting of 184 CTs, 1,275 DAs, and 32,789 street segments.

Spatial point pattern test

In order to investigate the appropriateness of crime type aggregation, a testing methodology that identifies changes in spatial crime patterns at multiple scales is necessary. The spatial point pattern test developed by Andresen (2009a) and corresponding index serves this purpose well because it can be used to independently identify changes or differences in the spatial patterns of crime at different spatial scales. This spatial point pattern test has been applied to investigate pattern changes in international trade (Andresen, 2010b) and for testing the stability in crime patterns (Andresen and Malleson, 2011).

The spatial point pattern test of Andresen (2009a) is area-based,[1] and is concerned with the similarity between two different spatial point patterns at the local level. This particular spatial point pattern test is not concerned with null hypotheses of random, uniform, or clustered distributions, but may be used to compare a particular point pattern with these distributions. An advantage of the test, as we demonstrate here, is that it can be calculated for different area boundaries using the same original point data sets. The spatial point pattern test is freely available in a graphical user interface: < http://code.google.com/p/spatialtest/>. The test is computed as follows:

1. Nominate a base data set (assault, for example) and count, for each area, the number of points that fall within it.
2. From the test data set (burglary, for example), randomly sample 85 percent of the points, with replacement.[2] As with the previous step, count the number of points within each area using the sample. This is effectively a bootstrap created by sampling from the test data set.
3. Repeat (2) a number of times (200 is used here).
4. For each area in the test data set, calculate the percentage of crime that has occurred in the area. Use these percentages to generate a 95 percent non-parametric confidence interval by removing the top and bottom 2.5 percent of all counts (5 from the top and 5 from the bottom in this case). The minimum

and maximum of the remaining percentages represent the confidence interval. It should be noted that the effect of the sampling procedure will be to reduce the number of observations in the test data set but, by using *percentages* rather than the *absolute counts*, comparisons between data sets can be made even if the total number of observations are different.

5. Calculate the percentage of points within each area for the base data set and compare this to the confidence interval generated from the test data set. If the base percentage falls within the confidence interval, then the two data sets exhibit a similar proportion of points in the given area. Otherwise they are significantly different.[3]

The purpose of this spatial point pattern test is to create variability in one data set so that it can be compared statistically to another data set. The 85 percent samples generated each maintain the spatial pattern of the test data set and allows for a "confidence interval" to be created for each spatial unit that may be compared to the base data set. Therefore, statistically significant changes/differences are identified at the local level.

The output of the test consists of two parts. First, there is a global parameter that ranges from 0 (no similarity) to 1 (perfect similarity): the index of similarity, *S*, is calculated as:

$$S = \frac{\sum_{i=1}^{n} s_i}{n} \tag{8.1}$$

where s_i is equal to one if two crimes are similar in spatial unit i and zero otherwise, and n is the total number of spatial units. As such, the *S*-Index represents the proportion of spatial units that have a similar spatial pattern within both data sets. This raises an obvious question: at which point do we consider two spatial point patterns similar? Though there is no established rule of thumb that we are aware of to answer such a question, we turn to the literature discussion correlations. In a discussion of the variance inflation factor (VIF) and multicollinearity in a regression context, O'Brien (2007) states that a VIF ranging from 5 to 10 tends to cause concern. In a bivariate context this approximately leads to a correlation coefficient that ranges from 0.80 to 0.90. As such, we will use the value of 0.80 to indicate that two spatial point patterns are similar.

Second, the test generates mappable output to show where statistically significant change occurs; i.e. which census tracts, dissemination areas, and street segments have undergone a statistically significant change. Though this spatial point pattern test is not a local indicator of spatial association (LISA; see Anselin, 1995) and there is much more to LISA than being able to produce maps of results, it is in the spirit of LISA because the output may be mapped.[4]

Results

Before results of the spatial point pattern test are presented, it is instructive to investigate the spatial concentrations of crime in Ottawa and Vancouver in the same manner as Sherman *et al.* (1989), Weisburd *et al.* (2004), and Andresen and Malleson (2011). As shown in Table 8.1, a small percentage of street segments in Ottawa and Vancouver account for 50 percent of the various crime types. Specifically in the case of Ottawa, less than 2 percent of all street segments account for 50 percent of crimes, even in the case of total crimes in this particular data set. Vancouver's concentration is also high with less than 8 percent of street segments accounting for 50 percent of the various crime types.

Perhaps more interesting, particularly in the context of a comparison between these two locations, is the percentage of street segments that have *any* crime. Though we must keep in mind that the Ottawa data set is restrictive in the number of crime types available, a very low percentage of street segments accounts for all of its crime; more than 90 percent of Ottawa was free from these reported crimes in 2006. The concentrations in Vancouver are lesser than Ottawa, but still noteworthy for certain crime types. Overall, just over 60 percent of street segments accounted for all of the Vancouver reported crime in these types during 2001. In the cases of robbery and sexual assault, only 5 and 3 percent of street segments, respectively, account for all of these crimes in Vancouver. Though this percentage is greater than in Ottawa, it is a similar result in both cities that robbery has (one of) the greatest concentrations of crime.

Within these street segments that have any crime, there are still further concentrations evident in the last column of Table 8.1. In all cases, less than 50 percent of street segments within any crime account for 50 percent of all crime. This indicates that there are concentrations of crime within concentrations of crime, or hotspots within hotspots.

Turning to the results of the spatial point pattern test, the results for Ottawa's CTs and DAs are shown in Tables 8.2a and 8.2b, respectively. As outlined above, the CT (Table 8.2a) is a common unit of analysis in spatial criminology. Immediately apparent from the CT results is that none of the crime types is even close to the threshold value of 0.80 to indicate similarity. Moreover, the lowest magnitude values of the *S*-Index are for comparisons with "total crime." This most definitely indicates that the most aggregate form of crime statistics—though in the case of Ottawa is not exhaustive—bares little resemblance to any of the disaggregate crime types.

The DA results are a little more promising. Many of the comparisons are at or approaching the threshold value of 0.80. However, only the various types of robbery have achieved the threshold value, all having values greater than 0.85. The results from the CT and DA levels of analysis clearly indicate that disaggregate crime types are necessary if the researcher is concerned with their respective spatial patterns.

The street segment results (Table 8.3a) are quite different from the CT and DA results. Rather than indicating a problem with crime type aggregation, the street segment results indicate that the spatial patterns are similar enough not to matter, with no *S*-Index value below 0.87. However, one may argue that this result is an artifact of the high concentration of crime in Ottawa: all crime in 2006 occurred within 9.52 percent of street segments. Therefore, the high *S*-Index value is

Table 8.1 Counts and percentages for crime types (aggregate and disaggregate)

	Count	Percentage	Percentage of street segments accounting of 50% of crime	Percentage of street segments that have any crime	Percentage of street segments with crime that account for 50% of crime
Ottawa, 2006					
Commercial break and enter	1,460	19.5	0.55	2.31	23.78
Residential break and enter	2,517	33.6	1.36	4.86	27.95
Total break and enter (aggregate)	**3,977**	**53.1**	**1.67**	**6.61**	**25.30**
Commercial robbery	145	1.9	0.01*	0.30	27.84
Individual robbery	241	3.2	0.31	0.65	47.66
Other robbery	362	4.8	0.30	0.82	35.93
Total robbery (aggregate)	**748**	**10.0**	**0.38**	**1.46**	**26.10**
Theft of vehicle	**2,765**	**36.9**	**0.99**	**4.50**	**22.02**
Total (without double counting)	**7,490**	**100.0**	**1.70**	**9.52**	**17.87**
Vancouver, 2001					
Assault	7,643	13.4	1.62	18.75	8.64
Burglary	13,025	22.9	7.61	39.43	19.31
Robbery	1,251	2.2	0.84	5.32	15.87
Sexual assault	440	0.8	1.12	2.99	37.32
Theft	11,255	19.8	2.58	26.79	9.64
Theft of vehicle	6,273	11.0	5.97	27.11	22.01
Theft from vehicle	16,991	29.9	2.64	18.75	8.64
Total (without double counting)	**56,878**	**100.0**	**5.02**	**61.42**	**8.18**

*actual value: 0.000823

present because there are so many zero values. In order to address this concern, we performed the analysis at the street segment level only, including the street segments that had at least one reported crime from at least one of the crime types. The results of this sensitivity analysis are shown in Table 8.3b.

Clearly evident from Table 8.3b is that the results are essentially unchanged. Some of the *S*-Index values have gone up and others down, but not by any great magnitude. As such, these results indicate that at the micro-spatial level of analysis, crime aggregation may not pose a problem in an analysis.

The results for Vancouver's CTs and DAs are presented in Tables 8.4a and 8.4b, respectively. In the context of CTs, the overall result for Vancouver is very similar to that of Ottawa: spatial patterns of crime are rather dissimilar. However, unlike

Table 8.2a Indices of similarity, census tracts, Ottawa, 2006

	X1	X2	X3	X4	X5	X6	X7	X8	X9
Commercial break and enter, X1		0.179	0.245	0.293	0.337	0.272	0.332	0.239	0.168
Residential break and enter, X2			0.380	0.190	0.321	0.277	0.250	0.207	0.190
Total break and enter (aggregate), X3				0.185	0.310	0.277	0.245	0.293	0.429
Commercial robbery, X4					0.582	0.533	0.451	0.152	0.027
Individual robbery, X5						0.473	0.457	0.141	0.049
Other robbery, X6							0.630	0.196	0.109
Total robbery (aggregate), X7								0.212	0.147
Theft of vehicle, X8									0.288
Total (without double counting), X9									

Table 8.2b Indices of similarity, dissemination areas, Ottawa, 2006

	X1	X2	X3	X4	X5	X6	X7	X8	X9
Commercial break and enter, X1		0.535	0.560	0.704	0.719	0.712	0.714	0.613	0.440
Residential break and enter, X2			0.477	0.394	0.438	0.444	0.455	0.450	0.411
Total break and enter (aggregate), X3				0.336	0.385	0.392	0.411	0.440	0.497
Commercial robbery, X4					0.920	0.909	0.884	0.677	0.391
Individual robbery, X5						0.864	0.849	0.651	0.392
Other robbery, X6							0.880	0.658	0.403
Total robbery (aggregate), X7								0.632	0.418
Theft of vehicle, X8									0.495
Total (without double counting), X9									

Table 8.3a Indices of similarity, street segments, Ottawa, 2006

	X1	*X2*	*X3*	*X4*	*X5*	*X6*	*X7*	*X8*	*X9*
Commercial break and enter, X1		0.939	0.938	0.959	0.959	0.958	0.954	0.943	0.915
Residential break and enter, X2			0.903	0.911	0.915	0.913	0.911	0.901	0.881
Total break and enter (aggregate), X3				0.882	0.855	0.885	0.886	0.881	0.873
Commercial robbery, X4					0.994	0.991	0.990	0.968	0.926
Individual robbery, X5						0.983	0.981	0.961	0.923
Other robbery, X6							0.979	0.958	0.922
Total robbery (aggregate), X7								0.948	0.916
Theft of vehicle, X8									0.890
Total (without double counting), X9									

Table 8.3b Indices of similarity, nonzero street segments[a], Ottawa, 2006

	X1	*X2*	*X3*	*X4*	*X5*	*X6*	*X7*	*X8*	*X9*
Commercial break and enter, X1		0.946	0.972	0.951	0.950	0.954	0.950	0.948	0.956
Residential break and enter, X2			0.972	0.977	0.979	0.978	0.972	0.968	0.945
Total break and enter (aggregate), X3				0.933	0.933	0.936	0.935	0.937	0.949
Commercial robbery, X4					0.994	0.993	0.995	0.976	0.950
Individual robbery, X5						0.989	0.991	0.967	0.944
Other robbery, X6							0.991	0.963	0.944
Total robbery (aggregate), X7								0.956	0.937
Theft of vehicle, X8									0.950
Total (without double counting), X9									

Note: [a]Used 9.52 percent of street segments (count: 3,122 of 32,789).

Ottawa, the *S*-Index values corresponding to "total crime" do not stand out as either high or low relative to the other *S*-Index values.

A similar result is present for DAs. Generally speaking, there have been some moderate increases in the *S*-Index values, but some *S*-Index values have decreased. The most notable difference between Vancouver and Ottawa for the DA results is that no crime types have highly similar spatial patterns. However, this only occurred in Ottawa within the various disaggregations of robbery.

Finally, the results for Vancouver's street segments are presented in Table 8.5a. Unlike the results for Ottawa, Vancouver's street segments do not indicate that the spatial patterns of the various crime types are similar aside from Robbery—Sexual assault. Curiously these are the crime types in Vancouver that exhibited the highest degrees of concentration in Table 8.1. We also performed the sensitivity analysis on Vancouver street segments (Table 8.5b) with no qualitative changes in the results. The values of the *S*-Index do fall without all the zero values, substantially in some cases, but the general result holds. Therefore, based on the results for Vancouver, none of the spatial units of analysis indicate that crime type aggregation matters for spatial patterns, aside from Robbery—Sexual assault.

Table 8.4a Indices of similarity, census tracts, Vancouver, 2001

	X1	X2	X3	X4	X5	X6	X7	X8
Assault, X1		0.099	0.264	0.382	0.173	0.091	0.245	0.118
Burglary, X2			0.099	0.255	0.109	0.127	0.136	0.172
Robbery, X3				0.373	0.255	0.155	0.245	0.191
Sexual assault, X4					0.291	0.300	0.309	0.318
Theft, X5						0.127	0.264	0.227
Theft of vehicle, X6							0.118	0.236
Theft from vehicle, X7								0.227
Total (without double counting), X8								

Table 8.4b Indices of similarity, dissemination areas, Vancouver, 2001

	X1	X2	X3	X4	X5	X6	X7	X8
Assault, X1		0.194	0.376	0.395	0.286	0.224	0.257	0.231
Burglary, X2			0.209	0.234	0.199	0.267	0.275	0.352
Robbery, X3				0.721	0.251	0.241	0.219	0.206
Sexual assault, X4					0.282	0.274	0.244	0.225
Theft, X5						0.236	0.305	0.311
Theft of vehicle, X6							0.338	0.382
Theft from vehicle, X7								0.379
Total (without double counting), X8								

Table 8.5a indices of similarity, street segments, Vancouver, 2001

	X1	X2	X3	X4	X5	X6	X7	X8
Assault, X1		0.629	0.725	0.719	0.650	0.565	0.539	0.370
Burglary, X2			0.604	0.592	0.619	0.544	0.547	0.460
Robbery, X3				0.895	0.674	0.608	0.530	0.313
Sexual assault, X4					0.662	0.604	0.519	0.289
Theft, X5						0.564	0.556	0.366
Theft of vehicle, X6							0.593	0.480
Theft from vehicle, X7								0.361
Total (without double counting), X8								

Table 8.5b Indices of similarity, non-zero street segments[a], Vancouver, 2001

	X1	X2	X3	X4	X5	X6	X7	X8
Assault, X1		0.473	0.625	0.612	0.501	0.395	0.367	0.159
Burglary, X2			0.389	0.373	0.452	0.363	0.384	0.328
Robbery, X3				0.852	0.530	0.456	0.356	0.091
Sexual assault, X4					0.514	0.452	0.342	0.063
Theft, X5						0.396	0.392	0.174
Theft of vehicle, X6							0.448	0.325
Theft from vehicle, X7								0.207
Total (without double counting), X8								

Note: [a]Used 61.4 percent of street segments (count: 7,204 of 11,730).

Discussion and conclusions

The results of all the analyses indicate that crime in Ottawa and Vancouver is highly spatially concentrated. This result is consistent with the previous research of Sherman *et al.* (1989), Weisburd *et al.* (2004), and Andresen and Malleson (2011). Moreover, analysis of the different crime types in Ottawa indicates that crime is far more concentrated in this city than those studied by other researchers. Considering how relatively few street segments are retained in order to conduct the sensitivity analysis, these data provide additional support for Sherman *et al.*'s (1989) assertion that within a larger area, such as a neighborhood, many sub-areas are relatively free of crime. As a result, if such chronic street segments produce the vast majority of crime, and analyses are conducted at a larger scale, it can give the illusion that the entire area is problematic.

The spatial point pattern test revealed that the aggregation of crime types was only justified for CTs and DAs within the robbery types for Ottawa. It is worthy of note, however, that the *S*-Index values generally increased moving the analysis to the DA. With regard to street segments, the spatial patterns across crime types exhibited a high degree of similarity in Ottawa, but not in Vancouver, aside from Robbery—Sexual assault.

In order to show these results visually, the output from the spatial point pattern test for total crime compared to assault, burglary, and theft as well as burglary compared to theft from vehicle using DAs is shown in Figures 8.1–8.4. These four comparisons for Vancouver are shown because they are common violent and property crimes. The dissemination area results are shown because they show the greatest visual variation that is easy to interpret. Output from any of the other spatial point pattern tests is available from the author to the interested reader. Figure 8.1 shows the results for Total Crime—Assault with a clear pattern of differences. Assault, aside from a small number of deviations, has a much greater concentration than Total Crime in the eastern half of the city—particularly along the northern border. In the northern peninsula that contains the central business district the places there are a few dissemination areas that have greater concentrations of Assault, but these are dominantly areas with drinking establishments and nightlife. Total Crime—Burglary, Figure 8.2, shows a much different pattern of differences that is almost opposite to those in Figure 8.1. Burglary's spatial pattern differs from Total Crime by being greater in Vancouver's western half of the city, though not to the same degree. Intuitively, this makes perfect sense. Most burglaries occur in residential areas where fewer people are walking around. Of course there are residences in areas of mixed land use that also contain drinking establishments, but this is not the norm in Vancouver. And in Figure 8.3, Total Crime—Theft, a different deviation from Total Crime, is apparent; theft has greater spatial concentration in the central business district and other shopping areas in the city.

As stated above, because of the different opportunity surfaces for different crime types, one would expect their spatial patterns to differ. However, this is all too often ignored in the spatial crime analysis literature. Though comparisons to Total Crime may appear to be extreme cases, a comparison of Burglary and Theft from Vehicle in Figure 8.4 (the two most common property crimes in the Vancouver data) shows very similar results to those shown in Figure 8.2. Total Crime may not be a common aggregation of crime types, but the aggregation of two or more property crimes into a property crime classification is not uncommon in the spatial crime analysis literature. Moreover, the differences shown in these maps are far from random, preventing any claim of the differences in the spatial patterns not impacting results.

The implications from these analyses are twofold. The first is in regard to the high degree of the concentration of crime. The second is in regard to the appropriateness of aggregating crime types.

With such high concentrations of crime identified in a growing number of city-level analyses, there is a need to identify approaches to crime prevention that we

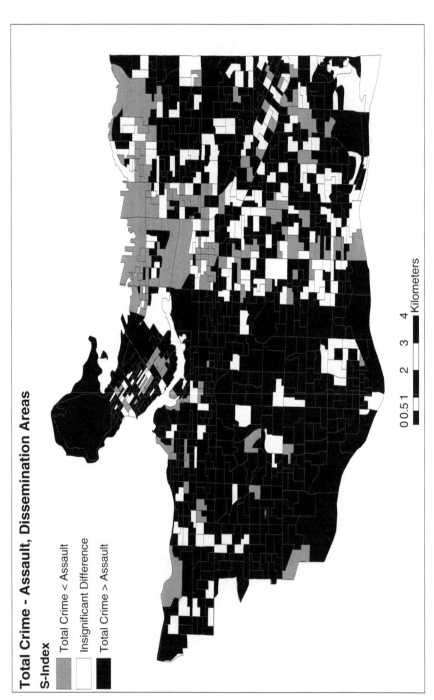

Figure 8.1 Total Crime—Assault, Vancouver, dissemination areas, 2001.

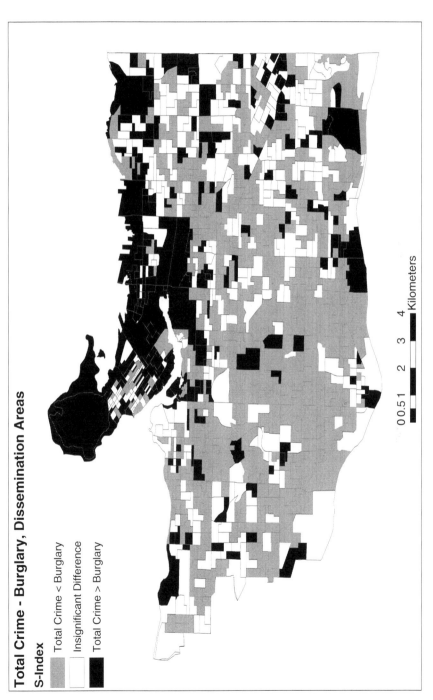

Total Crime - Burglary, Dissemination Areas

S-Index

- Total Crime < Burglary
- Insignificant Difference
- Total Crime > Burglary

0 0.5 1 2 3 4 Kilometers

Figure 8.2 Total Crime—Burglary, Vancouver, dissemination areas, 2001.

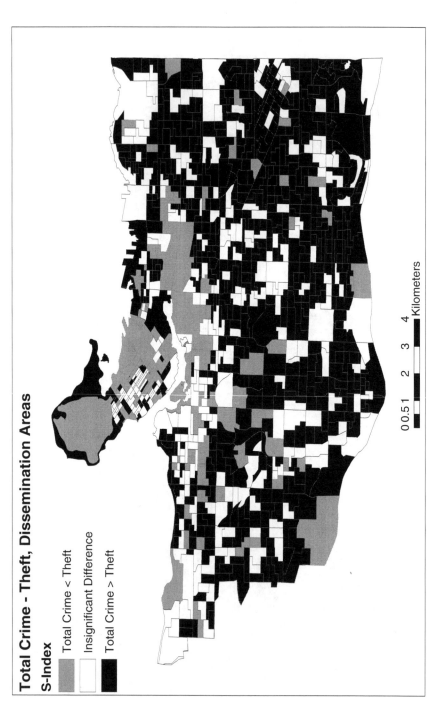

Figure 8.3 Total Crime—Theft, Vancouver, dissemination areas, 2001.

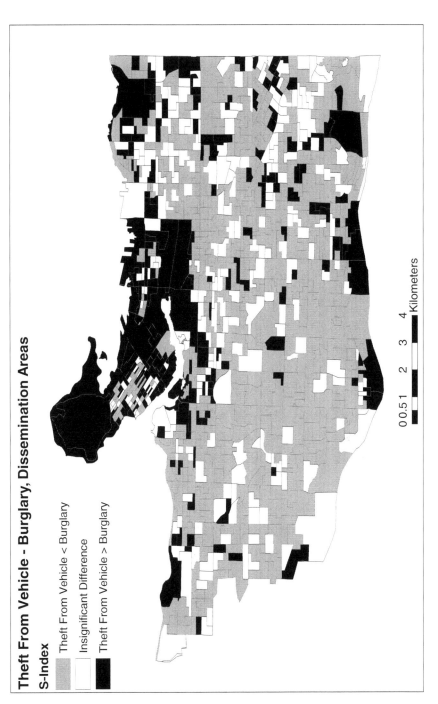

Figure 8.4 Theft from Vehicle—Burglary, Vancouver, dissemination areas, 2001.

may undertake to reduce that crime. Because of the fact that there is such a high degree of concentration of crime for all crime types, approaches such as situational crime prevention (Clarke, 1980, 1997) and crime prevention through environmental design, more generally (Jeffery, 1969, 1971, 1977), may be highly effective to reduce criminal opportunities. Ottawa provides an excellent example: most of the crime types in Ottawa experienced all of their crime within less than 5 percent of street segments and 50 percent of crime within 1.5 percent of street segments— this is also true for robbery and sexual assault in Vancouver. With such high concentrations of crime, crime prevention investigations may be able to identify the aspects of the environment that are conducive to crime and remove them.

This analysis reveals that aggregating across crime types is generally not appropriate if the researcher is concerned the varying spatial patterns of crime. The only exception to this result is the street segment analyses in Ottawa. Though similar analyses in other contexts are necessary to substantiate this claim, it may be the case that if crime is clustered to the same extent as in Ottawa the spatial patterns of crime are remarkably similar. Overall, it should be clear that the aggregation of crime types is not appropriate in most spatial analyses of crime; such aggregations may be appropriate in research that uses micro-spatial units of analysis, such as may be found in the crime-at-places literature.

9 The spatial dimension of crime seasonality

Introduction

As outlined by Cohen and Felson (1979), changes in our routine activities have an impact on crime rates. Cohen and Felson (1979) were concerned with long-run changes in the nature of routine activities to explain the substantial increases in crime rates during the 1950s and 1960s. They hypothesized, and found support, that our increasing amount of time spent outside the relatively protective environment of the home increased risk of victimization because of increased opportunity for crime: empty homes for residential burglary and more people outside who may be victims of violent crime. The increased amount of time people spent outside the relatively protective environment of the home had a number of sources: increased incomes led to more spending on dining out and going to shows; the economic development of small, light-weight, and valuable consumption goods; and the increased role of women in the workplace and post-secondary institutions. These were indeed widespread societal changes impacting not only the United States, but also Western societies more generally.

Changes in routine activities do not have to be as dramatic, representing massive societal change, in order to impact crime rates. A very large body of research has employed routine activity theory to investigate the varying levels of criminal victimization based on lifestyle (Kennedy and Forde, 1990) and across space (Andresen, 2006a). Another aspect of routine activities that impact criminal victimization varies over time, but with regularity. Depending on the time of year, our routine activities change to some degree. Of course, there are the routine activities that change very little: going to work, going to school, etc. However, our leisure activities change throughout the year.

Particularly in temperate climates, much of the fall, winter, and spring are spent indoors. This is the time of year when there is relatively more rainfall and cooler temperatures that make spending time outside relatively uncomfortable. With the onset of drier and warmer weather in late spring through summer, we spend more time outside—schoolchildren are also out of school during two of the summer months. As such, the movement outside of the relatively protective environment of the home described by Cohen and Felson (1979) for systemic societal change, also occurs on a periodic basis.

It should come as no surprise that much recent work on the effect of seasonal oscillations on crime rates uses routine activity theory as a theoretical framework. However, as reviewed below, this literature does not directly consider the spatial dimension of seasonality. Of course, the spatial dimension is implicit in these investigations because fair-weather activities will take us to different locations, but no explicit accounts are known at this time. In this chapter such an investigation is undertaken. There are two primary research questions for this research: first, to establish the degree of spatial change at different times of the year; and, second, in line with the underlying theme of the book, to establish the appropriateness of aggregating monthly crime data (assaults, to be consistent with much of the literature on this topic) to yearly counts. The expectation for the first research question is that a substantial degree of spatial change occurs. In the current study area Vancouver, Canada, many summertime activity nodes (beaches, outdoor shopping, etc.) are at different locations than wintertime activity nodes. The expectation for the second research question is that it is not always appropriate to be aggregating monthly crime counts to yearly crime counts if one wishes to truly understand the spatial dimension of crime.

Previous research on the seasonality of crime and routine activity theory

Though research on the impact of routine activities on crime did not emerge until the 1980s, research on the seasonality of crime dates back to the early nineteenth century in France through the work of Adolphe Quetelet. Quetelet (1842) found that in France crimes against persons (violent crimes) reach a maximum during the summer months (June), whereas crime against property (property crimes) reach a maximum during the winter months (December). Quetelet (1842) argues that the increase in property crimes during the winter months is due to a shortage of basic needs, primarily food. With regard to violent crimes, Quetelet (1842) states two explanations for the increase in the summer: a decrease in reasoning powers because of the heat (mental alienation) and more frequent interactions with individuals outside (personal collisions). The former refers to a temperature/ aggression theory of crime and the latter to routine activity theory—see Hipp *et al.* (2004) for a discussion of the temperature/aggression theory of crime.

Before our review turns to the studies explicitly concerning routine activity theory, the work of Lewis and Alford (1975) is worthy of discussion. In an analysis of monthly assault data from 56 municipalities in the United States, Lewis and Alford (1975) found that assault does not correlate well with latitude. In other words, assaults are not greater in those cites that have warmer temperatures in all seasons. Rather, Lewis and Alford (1975) found that the seasonal nature of assault emerged at approximately the same time each year for all municipalities under analysis, regardless of latitude. Consequently, it is not absolute temperature that impacts the seasonal pattern of assaults, but relative changes in temperature that lead to people (regardless of where they live) to spend more time outside the protective environment of the home.

Turning to studies that explicitly consider routine activity theory as an explanation for the seasonality of crime, Field (1992) analyzed annual, quarterly, and monthly data in England and Wales to investigate the impact of temperature on crime. Field (1992) found that temperature has a positive relationship with violent and property crime types: violent crime, sexual offences, burglary, theft, and criminal damage—a statistically insignificant relationship was found with regard to robbery. Field (1992) attributed these results to routine activity theory because temperature/aggression theory does not predict an increase in property crime. Overall, if the temperature is one degree above normal, crime is expected to increase by 2 percent.

In an investigation of robbery and homicide in Israel, Landau and Fridman (1993) found support for a seasonal relationship for robbery but not homicide. More interesting is their explanations for why they did not find the expected seasonal variations in these crimes in all months. With regard to robbery, Landau and Fridman (1993) were quick to point out that their results do not imply a deterministic relationship between seasons and crime, but that seasons have an impact on human interactions that include criminal activity, consistent with routine activity theory. With regard to homicide that does not display a seasonal effect, Landau and Fridman (1993) suggested why this may be the case when other violent crimes exhibit a seasonal effect. There are two facts critical for their explanation: first, for homicide, almost all cases are reported to the police and subsequently show up in criminal justice statistics; and second, victims are less likely to report victimizations from family members and close acquaintances. Therefore, as hypothesized by Landau and Fridman (1993), our increased routine activities outside the relatively protective environment of the home may simply be leading to an increase in the reporting of violent crimes between strangers and/or not-so-close acquaintances. The difficulty with this explanation is that there is not consistency in the literature on this finding. In an analysis of United States' homicide data, Rotton and Cohn (2003) did not find a seasonality effect, but in an analysis of homicide in Brazil, Ceccato (2005) found that homicides peaked in the warmer seasons of summer and the fall.

Farrell and Pease (1994) investigated domestic disputes, burglaries, and motor vehicle theft in Mereyside, England. Similar to the work of Quetelet (1842), Farrell and Pease (1994) found that a (potentially) violent crime (domestic disputes) displayed its peak in warmer weather; a property crime (burglary) exhibited its peak in the cooler months; and another property crime (motor vehicle theft) displayed no evidence of seasonality—domestic disputes had another lower peak in the Christmas season. This highlights the importance of remembering that relationships between crime and other factors are rarely monolithic; this point is further driven home with Cohn and Rotton's (2000) analysis of burglary (as well as theft and robbery) in Minneapolis which found a peak in the warmer months of the year.

Van Koppen and Jansen (1999) further showed the importance of understanding routine activity theory in the context of temporal variations. Van Koppen and Jansen (1999) analyzed the daily, weekly, and seasonal variations of commercial robbery data in the Netherlands. With regard to seasonal fluctuations, commercial robberies were greater in the winter months. They explained this through the routine activity theory concept of guardianship: there are more dark hours in the day during the winter months. As such, there is no need to search for complicated explanations for understanding a pattern in crime.

Lastly, Semmens *et al.* (2002) found that seasonality is not only present for actual crime, but also the fear of crime, namely burglary, mugging, vehicle crime, and vandalism. Using data from a survey of 576 respondents in Glasgow and Sheffield, Semmens *et al.* (2002) found that the fear of burglary and vehicle crime both peak at the end of the fall when nights are longest, whereas mugging and vandalism did not appear to have any seasonal effect. Once again, this shows that the seasonality effect on crime varies; not only does it vary by crime type and geography, but also the form of measurement.

Data and methods

The data used in this analysis are assaults that occurred in the City of Vancouver in 2001, described earlier in the book, using both census tracts and dissemination areas. The method of analysis, Andresen's (2009a) spatial point pattern test and criterion for similarity (0.80), was also described previously, in Chapter 8. The temporal frequencies of these data, however, deserve specific discussion here.

The seasonal and monthly counts and percentages of assaults in Vancouver are shown in Table 9.1. Clearly evident from these numbers is that assaults peak in the summer and are the lowest in the winter, as predicted by a routine activity theory approach. Moreover, from a monthly perspective, most assaults occur in July, followed by June and August, and the fewest assaults occur in December. This pattern is most evident in the monthly pattern of assault, but is also evident in the daily counts of assaults over the year. Moreover, even though July has the greatest number of assaults for any given month, there is a lot of variation within each month such that the greatest counts in December are more than the fewest counts in July. Once again, this points to the cautious approach necessary when making generalizations.

Results of the spatial point pattern test

The results for the spatial point pattern using census tracts are shown in Tables 9.2 (all year and seasons) and 9.3 (all year and months). Immediately obvious from Table 9.2 is that the Indices of Similarity are all low, most being below 0.50. The Indices of Similarity are the greatest when comparing all year to the various seasons. As expected, there are significant variations across the seasons. The least similarity is between fall and winter and the greatest between all year and spring. The monthly results, Table 9.3, do not fare any better than the seasonal results. The Indices of Similarity are never greater than 0.60 and most often below 0.50. Needless to say, at the census tract level there is very little temporal similarity.

The dissemination area results, Tables 9.4 and 9.5, are more promising. The Indices of Similarity between all year and the various seasons have now increased

Table 9.1 Frequencies of assault, by month and season, Vancouver, 2001

Time frame	Count	Percentage
All year	5,227	100.0
Spring	1,324	25.33
Summer	1,545	29.56
Fall	1,224	23.42
Winter	1,134	21.69
January	388	7.42
February	377	7.21
March	401	7.67
April	413	7.90
May	458	8.76
June	513	9.81
July	536	10.26
August	484	9.26
September	469	8.97
October	421	8.05
November	398	7.61
December	369	7.06

in magnitude, most of which are approaching the value of 0.70. However, the results that have the lowest magnitude are related to all year. Consequently, the most common temporal aggregation is least related to any of the particular seasons. The results for the monthly analyses present some curiosities. The Indices of Similarity for any month to any other month are 0.80 or greater more often than not. Consequently, when considering monthly data, the spatial pattern of any given month is substitutable for another. However, when comparing all year to any given month, the Indices of Similarity decrease considerably, ranging from 0.411 to 0.446. Therefore, the subsequent aggregation of all months in a year distorts the spatial pattern for the most common temporal aggregation of (spatially referenced) crime data, namely the year.

The mapped output from the spatial point pattern test is shown in Figures 9.1–9.4, for the comparisons of all year to the four seasons—other results are available to the interested reader from the author. Figure 9.1, all year—spring, is a comparison of all year to a still relatively cool and wet season in Vancouver. However, there are the beginnings of noticeable shifts in the spatial patterns of

Table 9.2 Indices of Similarity, all year and seasons, census tracts, Vancouver, 2001

	Spring	Summer	Fall	Winter
All Year	0.546	0.491	0.518	0.391
Spring		0.418	0.382	0.382
Summer			0.355	0.355
Fall				0.327

Table 9.3 Indices of Similarity, all year and months, census tracts, Vancouver, 2001

	X2	X3	X4	X5	X6	X7	X8	X9	X10	X11	X12	X13
All Year, X1	0.355	0.464	0.418	0.436	0.455	0.364	0.482	0.418	0.391	0.427	0.409	0.373
January, X2		0.546	0.518	0.455	0.400	0.491	0.482	0.500	0.300	0.446	0.464	0.500
February, X3			0.309	0.427	0.373	0.391	0.364	0.455	0.436	0.473	0.436	0.418
March, X4				0.373	0.427	0.336	0.409	0.391	0.427	0.364	0.400	0.446
April, X5					0.436	0.491	0.500	0.418	0.446	0.573	0.482	0.418
May, X6						0.446	0.382	0.409	0.355	0.355	0.355	0.391
June, X7							0.536	0.436	0.473	0.400	0.455	0.364
July, X8								0.446	0.427	0.355	0.418	0.409
August, X9									0.455	0.391	0.464	0.446
September, X10										0.400	0.382	0.391
October, X11											0.436	0.500
November, X12												0.455
December, X13												

Table 9.4 Indices of Similarity, all year and seasons, dissemination areas, Vancouver, 2001

	Spring	Summer	Fall	Winter
All year	0.566	0.543	0.554	0.507
Spring		0.674	0.656	0.661
Summer			0.662	0.648
Fall				0.673

crime. Most evident in Figure 9.1 is increased proportions of assaults occurring in the northern downtown peninsula which contains Vancouver's largest park. Also noticeable are increases in the west side of Vancouver (particularly northwest) where some of the city's most popular beaches are located. Because of their smaller sizes, the dissemination area results are somewhat different, but the general movement of assaults to recreational areas is still present.

The mapped output of census tracts for all year—summer, Figure 9.2, shows some changes that are expected: shifting spatial patterns of assault to recreational and commercial areas. However, in the case of the dissemination area results there is a very clear shifting of the spatial pattern of assault to recreational and commercial areas, most notably the northern downtown peninsula.

The mapped output of census tracts for all year—fall, Figure 9.3, show the most expected results for a season of reasonably good weather, especially the early time of the fall in Vancouver. There is a very clear shift in the spatial pattern of assaults into the northern downtown peninsula, the northeastern park area, and the northwestern area of Vancouver that contains many popular shopping areas as well as a number of beaches. Curiously, the dissemination area results do not exhibit this shifting spatial pattern.

The mapped output of census tracts and dissemination areas for all year—winter, Figure 9.4, also show an expected result. Though some areas in the northern downtown peninsula still exhibit shifts of the spatial pattern of assault, there is a general moving away from the primary recreational areas and the outdoor shopping locations in Vancouver.

Discussion

This chapter has investigated the spatial dimension of the seasonality of crime considering assaults in the City of Vancouver, 2001. The results show that, as expected, the spatial patterns of assaults differ by season and by month from the aggregation of annual assaults. Moreover, the mapped output of the spatial point pattern test indicates that the changes from season to season are also as expected: there is a shift toward assaults during the warmer times of the year in recreational and outdoor shopping areas.

Table 9.5 Indices of Similarity, all year and months, dissemination areas, Vancouver, 2001

	X2	X3	X4	X5	X6	X7	X8	X9	X10	X11	X12	X13
All year, X1	0.411	0.412	0.445	0.427	0.446	0.423	0.445	0.426	0.437	0.434	0.433	0.415
January, X2		0.849	0.851	0.839	0.824	0.822	0.823	0.822	0.818	0.849	0.839	0.842
February, X3			0.836	0.829	0.812	0.800	0.807	0.817	0.805	0.828	0.819	0.833
March, X4				0.805	0.800	0.790	0.786	0.790	0.815	0.812	0.817	0.819
April, X5					0.825	0.798	0.795	0.822	0.826	0.821	0.828	0.821
May, X6						0.791	0.800	0.821	0.794	0.800	0.805	0.811
June, X7							0.813	0.816	0.809	0.802	0.813	0.804
July, X8								0.794	0.793	0.789	0.804	0.787
August, X9									0.826	0.821	0.829	0.818
September, X10										0.807	0.810	0.801
October, X11											0.812	0.815
November, X12												0.822
December, X13												

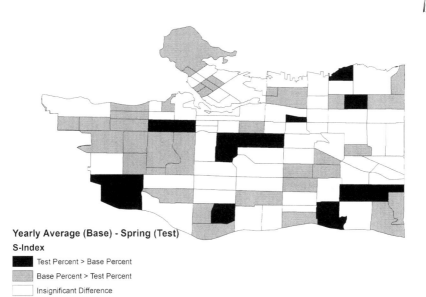

Yearly Average (Base) - Spring (Test)
S-Index

- ■ Test Percent > Base Percent
- ▨ Base Percent > Test Percent
- ☐ Insignificant Difference

Figure 9.1 Spatial point pattern output, yearly average—spring, Vancouver, 2001.

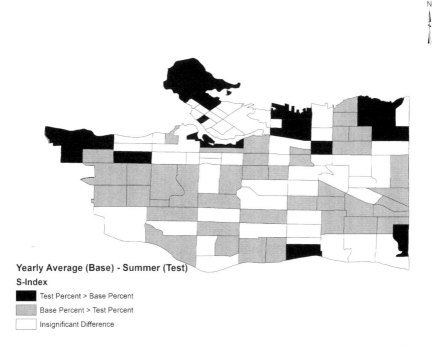

Yearly Average (Base) - Summer (Test)
S-Index

- ■ Test Percent > Base Percent
- ▨ Base Percent > Test Percent
- ☐ Insignificant Difference

Figure 9.2 Spatial point pattern output, yearly average—summer, Vancouver, 2001.

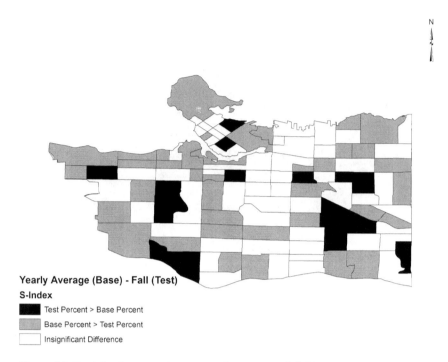

N

Figure 9.3 Spatial point pattern output, yearly average—fall, Vancouver, 2001.

Not only has this research shown that the spatial patterns of assault shift throughout the year, but also that changing the spatial scale of resolution has an impact on the analysis. Invoking the modifiable areal unit problem is hardly new in the spatial crime analysis literature, but as shown in previous chapters, changing the spatial sale of analysis does not always change the results in a meaningful way. However, in the current analysis, the monthly results from the spatial point pattern test were markedly different from the seasonal results. Comparing the spatial patterns of assault within the various months, they were most often quite similar. Only when individual months were compared to the yearly aggregate (all year) did the Indices of Similarity fall below an acceptable level. The results for the spatial point pattern test on the seasons always had Indices of Similarity that were too low in magnitude for the spatial patterns to be considered similar.

The implications of these results may be organized along the lines of theory and policy/practice. If one is testing theory using spatially referenced crime data and corresponding socio-demographic and socio-economic data, which aggregation of crime data is appropriate? Is it meaningful to use the yearly aggregate of data as most often used in the spatial crime analysis literature?

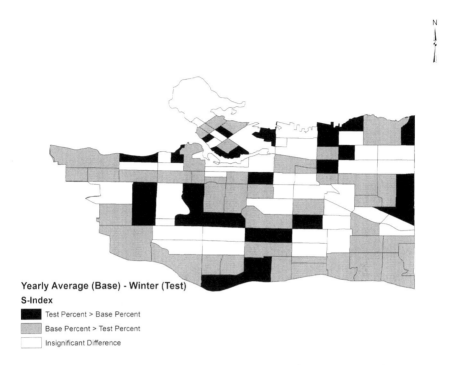

N

Yearly Average (Base) - Winter (Test)
S-Index

█ Test Percent > Base Percent

▓ Base Percent > Test Percent

☐ Insignificant Difference

Figure 9.4 Spatial point pattern output, yearly average—winter, Vancouver, 2001.

No analysis was performed here to answer this question and, perhaps, the changes in the spatial patterns of assault shown here would not alter any inferential analysis, but the results shown in this chapter do raise the question of the appropriateness of such a methodological decision.

With regard to policy and practice—crime prevention initiatives specifically— if yearly aggregate data are used to identify problematic areas of crime (whether those problematic areas be absolute or relative) any efforts to reduce crime may be doomed to fail. Such crime prevention initiatives would only work if the said initiatives were set up to operate all year round. If, however, yearly aggregated crime data were used to identify crime prevention initiative locations for a specific time of year, it is more likely that the crime prevention initiatives would not work and money from the private or public purse would be wasted. Perhaps worse, researchers and practitioners may be led to believe that the particular crime prevention initiative is not appropriate when it was simply applied in the wrong place at the wrong time.

Directions for future search revolve around investigations of the spatial dimension of the seasonality of crime. First and foremost, this research must be undertaken in other locations to confirm that the results presented here are not simply an artifact of the area under study. And second, a similar analysis needs to be undertaken for a variety of crime types. Assault was used in the current analysis because of the pervasiveness of this crime type in this literature. However, as discussed above, the nature and degree of seasonality varies by crime type and geography.

10 Testing the stability of crime patterns

Implications for theory and policy

Introduction

During the past 180 years, research in spatial criminology has been performed at ever finer spatial resolutions (Weisburd *et al.*, 2009a). Moving from counties to towns to wards and to neighborhoods, we are forced to ask: what is the appropriate scale of analysis for crime? Is it the neighborhood? Or are there relatively few "chronic places" that make an entire neighborhood problematic, much like a small percentage of offenders may cause a significant portion of trouble (Wolfgang *et al.*, 1972). Research in the "crime at places" literature, a term coined by Eck and Weisburd (1995),[1] has emerged which uses microspatial units of analysis. This research has generated an increasing body of evidence which shows that neighborhoods and/or communities are far from being spatially homogeneous with regard to criminal activity.

The first city-wide study known to systematically investigate crime at places (street segments) is Sherman *et al.*'s (1989) analysis of predatory crime in Minneapolis. One of the most significant findings from this study is that 50 percent of calls for police service are generated from 3 percent of street segments. Therefore, even within the highest crime neighborhoods, crime tends to cluster at very few locations within those neighborhoods and other areas are (relatively) crime free. Understanding this is critical, because there is clear evidence that any spatial analysis of crime at the neighborhood level is at high risk of committing the ecological fallacy (Robinson, 1950). Moreover, because these crime places are discrete locations within neighborhoods that are often comprised of transient populations (Sherman *et al.*, 1989), any census-based information regarding the neighborhood may not represent the population at risk at these crime places. This calls any inference based on neighborhood level census information into question.

The second city-wide study of crime at places is Smith *et al.* (2000), investigating the integration of routine activity theory and social disorganization theory. Smith *et al.* (2000) state that the empirical support for the integration of these theories is not strong. However, the reason for this is not because these two theories should not be integrated, but because the spatial units of analysis have been too coarse in attempts to integrate the theories. Using street segments as the spatial unit of analysis, Smith *et al.* (2000) are more successful in this integration than previous research. This is because of the inherent heterogeneity within neighborhoods that may help explain *where* crime occurs.

Most recently, and most relevant to the current analysis, Weisburd *et al.* (2004) and Groff *et al.* (2009) undertook trajectory analyses of crime at places in Seattle. Similar to Sherman *et al.* (1989), Weisburd *et al.* (2004) found that approximately 5 percent of street segments accounted for 50 percent of all criminal incidents, over a 14-year period. In addition, they found that the concentration of crime at crime places remained remarkably stable over time. Through the use of kernel density mapping, Weisburd *et al.* (2004) found some evidence that the geography of crime trajectories is clustered. This was particularly true for street segments that had their trajectories increasing or decreasing.

In a more explicit analysis of the spatial patterns of the trajectories in Seattle, Groff *et al.* (2009) confirmed that street segments with the same trajectory had a tendency to be clustered. In addition, they found significant variation in the trajectory patterns of street segments. As such, even aggregating to an areal unit as small as census blocks would have resulted in Groff *et al.* (2009) losing a tremendous amount of information.[2] And most recently, using a Lorenz plot and Gini coefficients, Johnson and Bowers (2010) demonstrated that crime is more concentrated than expected at the street segment level after considering the distribution of targets.

In this chapter, we contribute to the crime-at-places literature in two ways. First, we analyze crime at the level of the street segment over a span of 10 years in another city. Second, and most significantly, using a newly developed spatial point pattern test, we investigate the changes in the spatial distribution of crime at three levels of aggregation: census tracts, dissemination areas (census blocks), and street segments—all at a local level. We are able to show significant spatial heterogeneity within larger spatial units, and that the actual spatial distribution of crime is far more persistent when street segments are the unit of analysis. Implications for theory and policy are discussed.

Data and testing methodology

All data in the analysis below are for the City of Vancouver, British Columbia, Canada.

Crime data are obtained for 1991, 1996, and 2001 in order to facilitate a comparison of spatial patterns of crime over a 10-year time span. The data used in the analysis are from the Vancouver Police Department (VPD) Calls for Service (CFS) Database generated by its Computer Aided Dispatch (CAD) system, described in Chapter 3. Similar to Chapter 8, offenses consisting of assault, burglary, robbery, sexual assault, theft, theft of vehicle, and theft from vehicle are used in the analysis—homicide is excluded because of its low incidence in Vancouver: 15 to 25 per year over the past 10 years. The data sets include 82,264, 92,481, and 56,878 crimes in 1991, 1996, and 2001, respectively. The counts of each crime type range from a low of 440 (sexual assault, 2001) to 28,941 (theft from vehicle, 1996); aside from robbery that has counts averaging 1,500 in each year, the crime counts for the crime types range from approximately 6,000 to approximately 30,000. It should come as no surprise that theft-related crimes dominate property offenses and simple assault dominates violent offenses in Vancouver. The geocoding procedure used for the current data generated 93, 93, and 94 percent success rates for 1991, 1996, and 2001, respectively.

Spatial units of analysis

Similar to Chapter 8, three spatial units of analysis are used in the analysis below: census tracts, dissemination areas, and street segments (blocks). Figure 10.1 provides a representation of the scales for these three spatial units of analysis: one census tract, nine dissemination areas, and one hundred and fifty-two street segments.

The testing methodology is an application of the spatial point pattern test developed by Andresen (2009a), described in Chapter 8. A number of tests for similarity are performed. For each crime classification and each spatial unit of analysis, indices of similarity are calculated for 1991–1996, 1996–2001, and 1991–2001. These indices are then used to reveal whether or not spatial patterns of crime are stable over time as indicated by previous crime-at-places research, and if the spatial unit of analysis matters for this search for stability.

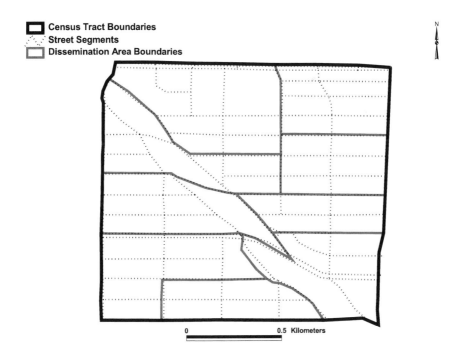

Figure 10.1 Spatial units of analysis.

Table 10.1 Percentage of spatial units accounting for 50 percent of crime

	A			B			C		
	Percentage of street segments accounting for 50% of crime			Percentage of street segments that have any crime			Percentage of street segments with crime that accounts for 50 percent of crime		
	1991	1996	2001	1991	1996	2001	1991	1996	2001
Assault	7.47	1.93	1.62	23.69	23.23	18.75	31.52	8.29	8.64
Burglary	7.85	8.14	7.61	45.51	48.99	39.43	17.25	16.62	19.31
Robbery	0.92	0.84	0.84	6.05	6.97	5.32	15.21	12.00	15.87
Sexual assault	1.63	1.41	1.12	4.50	3.57	2.99	36.17	39.38	37.32
Theft	4.36	3.82	2.58	38.70	39.85	26.79	11.28	9.58	9.64
Theft of vehicle	6.21	6.76	5.97	26.64	32.14	27.11	23.33	21.03	22.01
Theft from vehicle	4.95	2.89	2.64	46.85	45.97	36.00	10.57	6.29	7.34

Results and discussion

Replicating and extending previous results

Before we turn to the results of the spatial point pattern tests of spatial change, we discuss some replication results for Vancouver. As shown in Table 10.1, column *A*, a very small percentage of street segments account for 50 percent of the various crime classifications in Vancouver. There is a fair degree of variation, less than 1 percent (robbery) to 8 percent (burglary), across the seven crime classifications. Regardless, these numbers are in line with Sherman *et al.* (1989) and Weisburd *et al.* (2004). Also worthy of note is that the percentage of streets segments that account for 50 percent of crime is quite stable over time: 1991, 1996, and 2001. If any trend is present, the numbers are decreasing, indicating that the concentration of crime is increasing.

In addition to replicating the results of Sherman *et al.* (1989) and Weisburd *et al.* (2004), we investigated two further concentrations. First is the percentage of streets segments that have *any* crime. As column *B* of Table 10.1 shows, in all cases one-half of Vancouver is free from each of the crime classifications—some street segments may experience none of one crime and some of another. In the cases of robbery and sexual assault, approximately 95 percent of Vancouver is free from these crimes, according to the police data—this may partially be a result of under-reporting, particularly for crimes related to sexual assault. Only crimes such as burglary and theft from vehicle approach the 50-percent mark. But this is only for 1991, as both crime classifications show notable decreases by 2001. When plotted on maps, many of these crime classifications appear to be occurring everywhere, but this is clearly not the case. This only points to the importance of spatial scale in any efforts to understand the spatial distribution of crime.

Lastly, column *C* of Table 10.1 shows the percentage of street segments with any crime that accounts for 50 percent of crime. Consider the case of robbery. Depending upon the year of analysis, robbery occurs in approximately 6 percent of all streets segments of Vancouver. This is a high degree of clustering. Within that 6 percent of street segments, 50 percent of all robberies occurred on 15 percent of street segments. The results are similar for the other crime classifications. Needless to say, the crime classifications under analysis exhibit a high degree of concentration in particular places; and even within those places that have any crime, there is also a high degree of concentration.

An obvious question emerges from this high degree of clustering for all crime classifications: do the different crime classifications cluster in the same places? An analysis using the parametric (Pearson's) and non-parametric (Spearman's) correlations for the different crime classifications, using street segments as the unit of analysis, was used to investigate this possibility. All correlations are statistically significant at the 1 percent level. This is hardly a surprise because of the large number of zero values for each crime classification—the vast majority of street segments have zero criminal incidents. Of particular interest are the correlations between crime classifications with large numbers of incidents: assault, burglary, theft, and theft from vehicle. These crime classifications with large numbers of incidents have the greatest magnitude correlations. This result implies, though does not confirm, that street segments with high volumes of one crime classification have high volumes of other crime classifications.

Upon close inspection of the street segments that comprise 50 percent of all crimes in each classification, there is not a high degree of overlap for *all* crime classifications. As such, there are no "super chronic" street segments that are problematic for all crime classifications. However, the "top ranking chronic" street segments for particular crime classifications do overlap—this set of street segments comprises 50 percent of all criminal incidents for each crime classification as identified in Table 10.1. For example, the top ranking chronic street segments for theft often overlap with the top ranking chronic street segments for theft from vehicle, and similarly for assault and robbery. Incidentally, these particular overlapping street segments correspond to the greatest magnitude correlations. In addition, the top ranking chronic street segments for each crime classification are always clustered in the same general locations: the central business district and Vancouver's skid row, the Downtown Eastside. Therefore, chronic street segments tend to specialize in one or two crime classifications, most often related to opportunity, and they are in close proximity of one another. For example, assaults are highly clustered in areas with large numbers of drinking establishments and theft from vehicles are highly clustered in areas with many parking lots. Both these areas are in or close to the central business district.

Spatial point pattern test results

Turning to the results of the spatial point pattern test for the temporal stability of crime, Table 10.2 shows the Indices of Similarity for census tracts, dissemination

Table 10.2 Indices of Similarity: census tracts, dissemination areas, street segments

	1991–1996	*1996–2001*	*1991–2001*
Census tracts			
Assault	0.346	0.318	0.300
Burglary	0.173	0.218	0.155
Robbery	0.282	0.364	0.327
Sexual assault	0.455	0.409	0.509
Theft	0.199	0.218	0.136
Theft of vehicle	0.282	0.227	0.300
Theft from vehicle	0.091	0.218	0.146
Dissemination areas			
Assault	0.365	0.357	0.335
Burglary	0.284	0.288	0.299
Robbery	0.624	0.675	0.662
Sexual assault	0.715	0.753	0.691
Theft	0.377	0.271	0.237
Theft of vehicle	0.313	0.332	0.332
Theft from vehicle	0.224	0.332	0.261
Street segments			
Assault	0.659	0.659	0.659
Burglary	0.537	0.557	0.567
Robbery	0.866	0.856	0.875
Sexual assault	0.920	0.941	0.919
Theft	0.534	0.559	0.577
Theft of vehicle	0.638	0.577	0.659
Theft from vehicle	0.408	0.445	0.442

areas, and street segments; a value of 1 represents identical spatial patterns and a value of 0 represents completely different spatial patterns. Evident from Table 10.2, none of the crime classifications has stable spatial patterns over time. The highest Index value for the census tracts is 0.509, for sexual assault, and that is only for one of the three tests for stability in the spatial patterns. Even crime classifications that appear to occur everywhere when inspecting mapped point data, i.e. burglary and theft from vehicle, have low degrees of similarity in their spatial patterns over time.

The Indices of Similarity for dissemination areas, have increased in all cases, with a few notable results. According to the census tract results, robbery does not appear to have much stability in its spatial patterns over time—Indices range from 0.282 to 0.364. However, for the dissemination areas, the Indices have increased substantially to approximately 0.65. Therefore, two-thirds of the dissemination areas have the same percentage of robberies year to year and, given the high degree of concentration for robbery (see Table 10.1), this percentage is probably zero. However, the important aspect of this finding is that crimes appear to be far more stable when the spatial scale of analysis becomes smaller. Though little has changed for assault, the other crime classifications have large magnitude increases in their Index values, particularly sexual assault.

The results for street segments show an even greater change in the Index values. Even assault now has an incredibly stable spatial pattern over time—only theft from vehicle is still less than 0.50. The most notable results are those for robbery and sexual assault. It may be the case that this high degree of stability is because of the low numbers of these crimes; there are so many areas without any robbery or sexual assault. In the analysis using census tracts, robbery appeared to have a rather unstable spatial pattern over time; now with the analysis of street segments more than 85 percent of street segments have the same percentages of robberies year to year. As stated above, these street segments are likely always zero. However, what matters is that the spatial pattern of this crime is very stable year to year, unlike the results from the more conventional spatial unit of analysis in spatial criminology, the census tract. The results for sexual assault are similar to those of robbery, but sexual assault did have a more stable spatial pattern in the census tract analysis.

Sensitivity analysis

Though support for the use of micro-spatial units of analysis is compelling, one may argue that the results reported above are an artifact of the data and/or method rather than an artifact of spatial consistency becoming more apparent at smaller scales of analysis. As shown in Table 10.1, the percentage of street segments that have zero crime can be substantial. As such, smaller units of analysis will have greater degrees of similarity due to the presence of all the zeros. Consequently, the greater degree of spatial consistency at smaller units of analysis may not be present if only non-zero units of analysis are used.

In order to address this concern, we undertake the spatial point pattern test at all scales of aggregation, only using non-zero spatial units; a spatial unit is considered non-zero if it has at least one crime in any of the three years of data. The results of this sensitivity analysis are presented in Table 10.3. In the last column of the table, the percentage of spatial units retained is reported. Immediately apparent is that the smaller units of analysis retain far fewer spatial units than the larger units of analysis. In the case of robbery and sexual assault, 12.7 and 9.4 percent, respectively, of street segments are retained for the test. Not surprisingly, this has a significant impact on the street segment results, but the general pattern outlined above (i.e. spatial consistency becomes more apparent at smaller units of analysis) is still present.

The sensitivity analysis results for census tracts show very little change from the initial test results in Table 10.2. The Indices of Similarity do decrease, but because so many of the census tracts are retained in the sensitivity analysis, this comes as no surprise. The sensitivity analysis results for dissemination areas show more change than census tracts when compared with the initial test results, but the same basic pattern remains: the Indices increase (substantially in some cases) when moving to a smaller unit of analysis.

Table 10.3 Indices of Similarity: non-zero census tracts, dissemination areas, street segments

	1991–1996	1996–2001	1991–2001	Percentage spatial units retained
Census tracts				
Assault	0.321	0.264	0.274	96.4
Burglary	0.149	0.224	0.140	97.3
Robbery	0.238	0.343	0.286	95.5
Sexual assault	0.438	0.391	0.476	95.5
Theft	0.194	0.213	0.121	98.2
Theft of vehicle	0.269	0.250	0.287	98.2
Theft from vehicle	0.056	0.222	0.148	98.2
Dissemination areas				
Assault	0.321	0.328	0.294	94.2
Burglary	0.257	0.265	0.279	96.8
Robbery	0.399	0.498	0.458	63.1
Sexual assault	0.509	0.579	0.471	57.6
Theft	0.298	0.253	0.221	96.9
Theft of vehicle	0.291	0.298	0.294	95.7
Theft from vehicle	0.197	0.311	0.239	96.9
Street segments				
Assault	0.340	0.351	0.326	38.2
Burglary	0.327	0.355	0.372	63.8
Robbery	0.387	0.385	0.427	12.7
Sexual assault	0.518	0.516	0.501	9.4
Theft	0.291	0.343	0.354	56.6
Theft of vehicle	0.414	0.325	0.424	49.5
Theft from vehicle	0.206	0.326	0.253	63.9

Turning to the sensitivity analysis results for street segments, the decreases in the Indices are most prominent when compared to the initial test results. However, this should be expected, given that no more than 64 percent of the street segments are ever retained in the sensitivity analysis. Most important is the comparison between the results for non-zero dissemination areas and non-zero street segments. Clearly evident is that the non-zero street segments exhibit more stability (spatial consistency) than non-zero dissemination areas—notably more stability in some cases. Only robbery consistently shows moderately less stability in the non-zero street segment sensitivity analysis. This result is no surprise given that more than 85 percent of the street segments are excluded in this sensitivity analysis.

This sensitivity analysis shows that the results reported above are similar to the results for the non-zero spatial units of analysis: an increase in Indices of Similarity as the spatial unit of analysis becomes smaller. Though the size of the effect in the sensitivity analysis is smaller than in the initial analysis, the overall distribution of Index values are different depending on the spatial unit of analysis employed. Using a Wilcoxon signed ranks test on the paired observations, the Indices are higher for the non-zero street segments than for the non-zero dissemination areas, $p = 0.0173$.

However, it should be noted that the original results would have merit even if the sensitivity analysis did not show the same general pattern. This merit lays in showing the magnitude of the ecological fallacy when using larger spatial units of analysis. Quite clearly, the presence of so many spatial units with zero crime shows that there are "safe places" in "bad areas" (Sherman *et al.,* 1989). Consequently, even if there were no similarity in non-zero street segments, the fact that some street segments are free from particular crime types in upward of 90 percent of cases (sexual assault, for example) has important implications for theory and policy.

Interpretation of the results

Overall, the spatial pattern of crime is rather stable over time when one considers the street segment as the spatial unit of analysis. An obvious question, of course, is: why? This may simply be a case of the modifiable areal unit problem (Openshaw, 1984a) whereby the choice of district boundaries is influencing the results. If this is the case then different boundaries might reveal more similarity across crime types as we find with street segments, although there is no evidence to suggest this would be the case. Or the ecological fallacy (Robinson, 1950; Openshaw, 1984b) might be influencing the results, causing us to make potentially false claims regarding smaller areas within the larger areas. We argue, however, that there is no *problem* with our results. In the first place, if there were no underlying process that needs to be understood, we would not expect the changing results from census tracts to dissemination areas to street segments to be so consistent across crime classifications. Rather, we believe these changing results are a product of using increasingly appropriate spatial units of analysis. Indeed, the results provide evidence that the ecological fallacy *is* present when data are aggregated to the dissemination area and census tract.

It is clear from these results that the choice of the spatial unit of analysis may have substantial implications on the analysis. Moreover, these substantial implications cannot simply be labeled a *problem* resulting from modifying areal units. Rather, the street segments are most often driving the change for the larger spatial units. Specifically, a *small* number of "chronic" street segments dictate the results for the entire dissemination area or census tract, much like a small number of chronic offenders can dictate the results for a larger set of individuals (Wolfgang *et al.*, 1972). In some cases, the results of the street segments are unrelated to that of the larger spatial units. This is precisely the trajectory of spatial criminology over the past 180 years: the move toward smaller units of analysis because new research showed that the ecological fallacy was being committed, explicitly or implicitly, when labeling departments, towns, wards, and neighborhoods. This is clearly problematic in any attempts to understand why crime is high/low or increasing/decreasing in particular areas, or for the formulation of initiatives to deal with crime.

Turning to a city-wide representation of the results to provide context of the change in spatial patterns, the street segments with statistically significant increases and decreases (1991–2001) in robbery are shown in Figure 10.2—robbery is used because of its relatively low frequency which allows for a meaningful

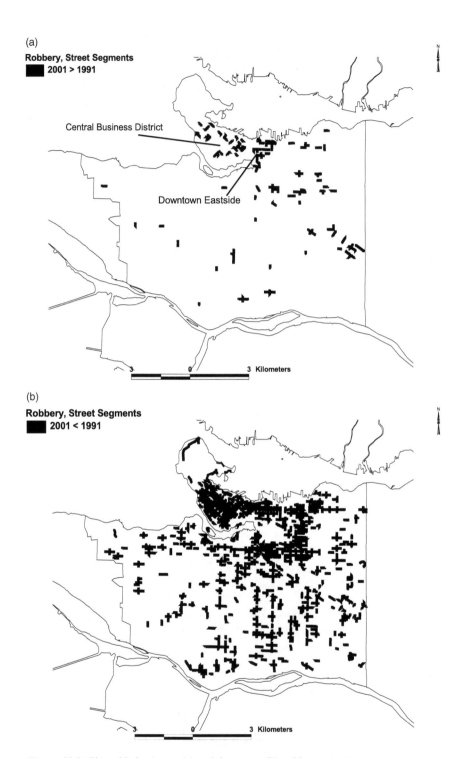

(a)

Robbery, Street Segments
■ 2001 > 1991

Central Business District

Downtown Eastside

3   0   3 Kilometers

(b)

Robbery, Street Segments
■ 2001 < 1991

3   0   3 Kilometers

Figure 10.2 City-wide increases (a) and decreases (b), robbery, street segments.

visualization of the test results at the level of the city. Figure 10.2a shows the street segments with statistically significant increases, whereas Figure 10.2b shows the street segments with statistically significant decreases. It should be clear from Figure 10.2b that most areas of Vancouver are experiencing decreases in robbery. However, as shown in Figure 10.2a, only particular areas within Vancouver are experiencing increases in robbery: the central business district, the Downtown Eastside (Skid Row), and one street (Kingsway) that runs southeast from the Downtown Eastside. With the vast majority of Vancouver maintaining a stable crime pattern (approximately 85 percent) and much of the remainder of the city (approximately 11 percent) exhibiting decreases in crime, what is it about these three areas that is increasing?

Fifty years ago, Calvin Schmid (1960a, 1960b) outlined the importance of understanding a city's structure when considering the spatial distribution of crime. Simply put, the central business district has a lot of crime because of the abundance of people—more offenders and more targets. Indeed, this is the fundamental point of routine activity theory: if there is an increase in the convergence of motivated offenders, suitable targets, and a lack of capable guardianship, crime will increase (Cohen and Felson, 1979; Felson and Cohen, 1980, 1981). In the context of Vancouver, the central business district, the Downtown Eastside (adjacent to the central business district), and Kingsway are all places with high concentrations of people. Therefore, the street segments with statistically significant increases in their share of robbery are located in highly populated areas in Vancouver. Moreover, these are areas that do not necessarily have large residential populations, but do have ambient populations because people are attracted to these locations for the varied land uses present (Andresen, 2006a, 2007).

Implications for theory and policy

Consistent with previous research in the crime-at-places literature, the above analysis has shown that micro-places, such as the street segment, are the driving force behind broader neighborhood change. If micro-places are the appropriate spatial units of analysis in any effort to understand crime, a number of implications are immediately apparent. These implications are best organized along two lines of thought: theory and policy.

The implications for theory may be organized to correspond with the three theoretical perspectives discussed in terms of crime at places (routine activity theory, geometric theory of crime, and rational choice theory) as well as social disorganization theory. Though there is strong support for the use of routine activity theory on individual characteristics (Kennedy and Forde, 1990) to predict criminal victimization, there is a need for further research into the routine activities of places (Felson, 1987; Sherman et al., 1989). With such stable and high concentrations of crime occurring at so few micro-places, an in-depth understanding of these places is in order. Such an understanding is in order because it is the convergence of suitable targets and motivated offenders without capable guardians at (micro-) places that leads to crime.

Consequently, knowing *why* the convergence occurs on *this* street segment and not *that* street segment needs to be incorporated into further understanding of the importance of that convergence. In addition, at the heart of understanding the routine activities of micro-places is a temporal analysis. This is because *changes* in routine activities lead to *corresponding changes* in crime. Though significant insight may be gathered through comparisons of multiple places at the same time, relationships are less likely to be causal when temporal change is not considered.

The geometric theory of crime was highly developed when it first emerged 30 years ago (Brantingham and Brantingham, 1981, 1993b). However, very few tests of this theory (for the purpose of further understanding and refinement) have been performed—see Rengert and Wasilchick (1985) for an exception. The reason for the lack of empirical tests of the geometric theory of crime is that the data requirements for proper testing are very high: not only is detailed crime data necessary (spatially and for individual offenders), but so is information on legitimate and criminal movement patterns of large numbers of people. The data used in this analysis are longitudinal and very precise spatially, but do not have information on individual offenders, let alone their movement patterns. Perhaps it is time for such an analysis to be done.

Rational choice theory has always made the point of stressing the importance of focusing on choices specific to a crime classification (Clarke and Cornish, 1985; Cornish and Clarke, 1986)—the decisions necessary to commit a burglary are different from the decisions necessary to rob a convenience store. These choices were shortly thereafter broken down into what Cornish and Clarke (1987) referred to as choice-structuring properties. Some of these properties include: the accessibility of targets, risks of apprehension/detectability, and the time required to commit the crime. Because of the prevalence of various crime classifications at particular places (Table 10.1, column *A*), criminal choices that involve these factors are easier to make at those particular places: one street segment versus another. As such, the micro-place must be considered one of the many choice-structuring properties for committing a crime.

Lastly, with regard to social disorganization theory, it appears that the neighborhood is no longer appropriate for understanding the spatial distribution of crime. Though this may be an unpopular claim to state, given the widespread use of the neighborhood in crime analysis to this day, we must keep in mind the work of Burgess (1916), Shaw (1929), and Shaw and McKay (1931, 1942), which showed that the previous era of spatial criminology used spatial units of analysis that were too coarse for an appropriate understanding of the spatial distribution of crime: there was significant variation in crime within cities and counties. Similarly, the crime-at-places literature has found a similar result: there is significant variation in crime within neighborhoods—dangerous neighborhoods are generally safe (Sherman *et al.*, 1989). Consequently, social disorganization theory can only matter for crime at places *if and only if* socially disorganized neighborhoods (theoretically predicted to be high in crime) have more dangerous *places* than socially organized places. This, of course, is an empirical question, and is a direction for further research.

Regardless of the theoretical perspective within spatial criminology, the importance of crime at micro-places has practical implications. The incorporation of these very few places that generate the majority of crime across our urban landscapes reinforces that crime is indeed a rare event. The convergences, activity patterns, and choices that lead to crime, all occur in these discrete locations.

With regard to policy, the stability of spatial crime patterns implies that crime prevention through environmental design is an appropriate course of action (Jeffery, 1969, 1971, 1976, 1977). In its most common application, routine activity theory is used to make statements regarding the change of routine activities for victims of crime. However, it is far easier to change and/or regulate places than individuals (Sherman *et al.,* 1989). And because these places are micro-places, the specific crime prevention activity that should be employed is situational crime prevention (Clarke 1980, 1983). This focus on situational crime prevention should occur because it works best when applied to crime- and place-specific problems. Though one may argue that this will simply result in the spatial displacement of crime, the most recent and definitive research on spatial displacement indicates that such will not occur (Weisburd *et al.*, 2006; Guerette and Bowers, 2009); in fact, this research shows that there will likely be the diffusion of benefits to surrounding places.

Because of the stability of the spatial patterns of crime at micro-places, especially for robbery and sexual assault, these micro-places should if possible be disrupted or altered to prevent crime—modifying the conditions for one of the choice-structuring properties of crime. The theoretical justification and empirical support for such a practice is well known. And now, with the growing body of crime-at-places literature, there is theoretical justification and empirical support for the application of crime prevention activities focused on micro-places.

The difficulty with considering micro-places for theory and policy is data availability. Census data are not available for areas smaller than dissemination areas (Canada) and the census block (United States), aside from some microdata that are based on 20 percent sampling—many street segments will, therefore, be missing data. One possible alternative is in-situ fieldwork that could provide context for micro-place theory and policy analysis. Such data collection is not feasible in a city-wide analysis, making it limited for testing theory at the street segment level because of the limited number of observations. However, this type of data would prove useful for situational crime prevention policy because it is locally based. Therefore, with the empirical support for analysis at micro-places, the significance of future research in the crime-and-places literature (in part) depends on supplementary data at the street segment level to better understand crime patterns occurring at micro-places.

11 Spatial heterogeneity in crime analysis

Introduction

The drive for analyses in the geography of crime literature to be undertaken at ever finer spatial scales has led to the discovery of significant heterogeneity within smaller spatial units of analysis: there are safe places within bad neighborhoods and dangerous places within good neighborhoods (Sherman *et al.*, 1989). Spatial heterogeneity is defined as the presence of a large spatial unit of analysis that has smaller spatial units of analysis within it, which do not all exhibit the same properties. Because of this finding, an obvious question to emerge within this geography of crime literature is: what is the appropriate spatial scale of analysis? Indeed, those that advocate for smaller spatial units of analysis state that micro-places are now deemed appropriate, whereas larger spatial units of analysis are not (Andresen and Malleson, 2011). But how much does this issue really matter? Yes, there may be significant spatial heterogeneity, but does this impact the analysis?

A small branch of literature has investigated this question. The results most frequently cited show that the choice of the spatial unit of analysis is irrelevant (Land *et al.*, 1990; Wooldredge, 2002). As a result, much of the literature that followed has used this finding as a justification for only analyzing one type of spatial unit (Schulenberg, 2003; Osgood and Anderson, 2004; Bernasco and Block, 2009; Matthews *et al.*, 2010). But is this a reasonable assumption to be made in all contexts? We argue that it is not.

In this chapter, calls for service and recorded crime data are used from police forces in two municipalities (one in Canada and another in England) and a similarity-based spatial point pattern test. We are able to show that despite similarities in the results of global analyses, the results are significantly different at alternative spatial scales of analysis. Because of the nature of this spatial point pattern test we are able to show how results change when the spatial unit of analysis is changed. Previous research has investigated this phenomenon, but we explicitly show the results using two different spatial units of analysis: census tracts and dissemination areas in Canada and middle-layer super output areas and output areas in England. Specifically, we are able to quantify the spatial heterogeneity within larger units of analysis for multiple crime classifications and in a cross-national comparison: Vancouver, Canada and Leeds, England.

Scale and spatial crime analysis

In geography, scale matters: changing the size or shape of the spatial unit under analysis may lead to unexpected and substantial changes in results (Gehlke and Biehl, 1934; Blalock, 1964; Openshaw, 1984a, 1984b; Fotheringham and Wong, 1991). This is referred to as the modifiable areal unit problem (MAUP). Faced with the MAUP, three possible scenarios may emerge when modifying the spatial units of analysis under study. First, there may be no impact. In other words, the results are identical (or differences are statistically insignificant) at all spatial scales of analysis. This is clearly the ideal situation. Second, there may be a quantitative impact on the results, but the qualitative results are the same. In this situation, the estimated parameters for the variables in an analysis may change (with statistical significance, so bias is present) but those estimated parameters do not change signs (positive to negative, become statistically insignificant, or negative to positive); as such, variables may be thought to have a stronger or weaker relationship with the dependent variable than is actually the case, but the qualitative interpretations are the same. Third, there may be a qualitative impact in the results. If this occurs, the results may lead the researcher to make substantively incorrect statements: rejecting or accepting a theory when they should not, and/or making incorrect statements regarding a policy initiative in an evaluation. This is the worst-case scenario and is the possibility outlined by Fotheringham and Wong (1991).

Another, but related, issue emerges when one makes inference based on an analysis at one spatial scale and applies it to another spatial scale. When the inference is based on a larger spatial unit and applied to a smaller spatial unit it is referred to as the ecological fallacy (what is true of the whole is not necessarily true of its parts); and when the inference is based on a smaller spatial unit of analysis and applied to a larger spatial unit it is referred to as the atomistic fallacy (what is true of the parts is not necessarily true of the whole). Such problems in inference have been long known and are most often occur in the context of assigning neighborhood characteristics/relationships to individuals, the ecological fallacy (Robinson, 1950). Because of the ecological fallacy, change that occurs at a larger spatial scale may be driven by a small number of the smaller spatial scale units within the larger spatial scale unit. Consequently, there may be variations in the spatial patterns at different scales.

Of course, when it comes to the choice of spatial scale there may be limitations in the geography of crime that are beyond the control of the researcher. For example, when using census data, issues of confidentiality may arise that lead to missing data values and preclude the analysis at a particular geography—Andresen (2006b), Chapter 3, was unable to undertake an analysis at a smaller spatial scale because almost 25 percent of the census boundary units were missing data owing to confidentiality issues. There is also the issue of missing data because of under-reporting of crime and/or systemic biases in reporting crime. This may or may not have spatial implications, but we are unaware of any research that addresses this issue. In addition, there may be a number of factors in a decision-making process for research that leads to the use of only one spatial scale. First, data availability may prevent the use of multiple scales of analysis; because of confidentiality concerns, a police department may only provide counts of crime based on one spatial unit. Second, there may be specific spatial scales of interest for those performing the analysis; in such a research context, other spatial scales are simply not of interest or relevant. Third, the researcher may be interested in replicating (being consistent with) previous research that is only concerned with one spatial scale. Though not an exhaustive list, these examples do show that spatial scale is not necessarily being ignored by researchers. Barring situations such as this, we did expect to find the use of multiple scales of analysis in the geography of crime literature in order to investigate the role of the MAUP. However, we found that this is not the case.

For example, Wooldredge (2002), comparing census tracts to administrative neighborhoods, found that the substantive results for different spatial units of analysis are the same. This led Wooldredge (2002: 681) to refer to the "(ir)relevance of aggregation bias" in the context of the MAUP, for the geography of crime.[1] Despite the increasing availability of crime data as points (addresses, street intersections, and x-y coordinates), aggregation will still be a concern as long as those using these data aggregate points in order to analyze crime relative to other data that are only available as area polygons, such as census data. More importantly for this issue, it is not that a small number of studies have found such a relationship, but that these studies, particularly Wooldredge (2002), are used as justification for only using one spatial unit of analysis. The use of Wooldredge (2002) for this purpose was picked up almost immediately (Schulenberg, 2003), and continues in a variety of contexts (see, for example, Osgood and Anderson 2004; Bernasco and Block, 2009; Matthews *et al.*, 2010).

Despite this rapid adoption of Wooldredge's (2002) conclusion, there is another side to this literature. Ouimet (2000) showed that using census tracts versus neighborhoods does impact the results; specifically, the choice of spatial aggregation impacts the theory that is supported by the data. More recently, and similar to Ouimet (2000), Hipp (2007) showed that explanatory variables exhibit different effects on crime and disorder based on the level of aggregation. Consequently, it is curious that Wooldredge (2002) is almost always cited to support the use of only one level of spatial aggregation.

In no way are we being critical of the work done by Wooldredge (2002) and others. In fact, for the case of Vancouver using the crime data described below, we find that the choice of spatial unit of analysis matters little for the substantive results of a spatial regression. Rather, we are asking whether we can simply dispense with multiple spatial units of analysis when studying the geography of crime. In other words, is there any spatial heterogeneity and does it matter? We are unable to find any research that quantifies the degree of spatial heterogeneity, so this is our task in this chapter.

Data and methods

Data for Vancouver, Canada and Leeds, England are used in the analysis below. We use data from these two cities for three reasons. First, these are the police data available to us for analysis. Second, we know these cities and are, therefore, able to make interpretation using local knowledge. Third, and most significantly, the inclusion of data from two different countries aids in our ability to make generalizations rather than relying on one set of data that may produce spurious results. The Vancouver data used in the analysis below are for the years 1991 and 2001, described in a number of previous chapters.

In Vancouver, there has been a notable decrease in the counts of crime, consistent with the international crime drop phenomenon (Tseloni *et al.*, 2010; Farrell *et al.*, 2011). Despite this significant decrease in crime (31 percent drop), the distribution of the different crime classifications has remained rather constant; assault has experienced a decrease, with corresponding increases in theft of vehicle and theft from vehicle. Leeds has experienced an increase in crime from 2001 to 2004, just under 4 percent. However, it should be noted that there was a change in recording practices in Leeds between these time periods. Also, the two data sets for Leeds are only 3 years apart. As such, this increase in crime counts could simply be a result of year-to-year fluctuations. Regardless, aside from the assault classifications, the distribution of the different crime classifications has remained relatively constant, aside from an increase in theft.

Leeds and its data

The Leeds data used in the analysis are for the years 2001 and 2004. Ideally, the same time period would be used for both countries, but data constraints mean that the most reliable crime data in Leeds are only available for these years—reliability refers to the standardization of crime data, discussed below. Leeds is the third largest city in the United Kingdom, after London and Birmingham, with a population estimated to be approximately 812,000 in 2011 (Office for National Statistics, 2010). Spatially, Leeds is the second largest city in the UK, covering an area of approximately 550 square kilometers. As a consequence of hosting two universities, Leeds has a very large student population that has had a strong influence on the development of the city in order to cater for a large number of student migrants. The student population is also highly concentrated into a relatively small area to the north of the universities, which has a substantial effect on crime patterns. Spatially, the Leeds area can be subdivided into 108 medium-level super output areas (MSOAs) and further into 2,440 output areas (OAs). An OA is the smallest 2001 census geography available and contains a minimum of 40 households or 100 people, but the recommended size is approximately 125 households. The MSOA is a larger geographic unit which contains 7,200 people on average and has been designed to fit to the borders of OAs to allow for data aggregation.

In terms of crime, Leeds has generally followed the United Kingdom's national trend and has seen consistent yearly reductions in most types of crime since 1997. Leeds has higher than average crime rates compared to the average for England and Wales, although this is not unexpected given its demographic and socioeconomic characteristics. The most unusual observation is that rates of residential burglary are particularly high: almost double the national average (18.4 crimes per 1,000 people compared to 9.6) and it has not exhibited the decline that the other types of crime have shown. The explanation for this is largely tied in with the effects of the student population who generally suffer a disproportionate number of burglaries.

The crime data used in the analysis below consists of all crimes recorded by the police in the Leeds area. The data cover the time periods 1 April 2000 to 31 March 2001 (hereby abbreviated to "2001") and 1 April 2003 to 31 March 2004 ("2004"). The data are coded by crime type and are stored with a location address that can be geocoded. There are numerous implications for using this type of data in research; namely, not all crime is reported to the police in the first place and, even if a crime is reported, it might not necessarily be *recorded* by the police. In fact, recording practices varied substantially across police forces so to standardize them the National Crime Recording Standard was phased in through 2001 to 2004. The new standard followed a more "victim centered" approach so that a crime should be recorded even if there is no evidence that it has taken place. This led to an apparent increase in some types of crime, particularly violent crimes: assault and, to a lesser extent, sexual assault.

Geocoding

In the United Kingdom, the street system is not regular so it is not possible to estimate a location based on a building number. Instead, a lookup table is used to match an address directly to some spatial coordinates. The Leeds data were then matched directly to the coordinates of the building at which the crime occurred, or they were assigned manually in places where no building was available to provide a link. The data were cleaned considerably (both manually and using computer software) before use so we could be confident that geocoding issues would not influence the analysis.

The Vancouver data used in the current analysis are geocoded to the street network and the Leeds data are geocoded directly to points. Both data are then subsequently aggregated to their respective census boundary units using a spatial join function.[2] We use the same (most recent) street network or address lookup table in each city for geocoding different years of data; this avoids the problem of not being able to find new streets or buildings but has the potential of old roads being closed and old buildings being torn down. No such street closures occurred in Vancouver and, as mentioned above, if no building was present (from a possible tear-down) points were manually assigned to the spatial units of analysis. Though shorter street segments may have a lower probability of having a criminal event, *ceteris paribus*, the randomization process in the spatial point pattern test minimizes the potential for having less scope for change than longer street segments. Lastly, the interpolation issue of geocoding algorithms, whereby a point's position on a street segment might be inaccurate, is not a concern here because no inference is made at a finer scale than the dissemination area (DA) (Vancouver) or the OA (Leeds).

The spatial point pattern test

In order to investigate spatial heterogeneity within larger spatial units of analysis—census tracts (CTs) in Vancouver and MSOAs in Leeds—a testing methodology that identifies changes in spatial crime patterns at multiple scales is necessary. The spatial point pattern test developed by Andresen (2009a), discussed in Chapter 8, serves this purpose well because it can be used to independently identify changes in the spatial patterns of crime at different spatial scales and the output may then be used to quantify spatial heterogeneity. The change for each smaller spatial unit of analysis (DA and OA) can be assigned to its respective larger spatial unit of analysis (CT and MSOA) and then spatial heterogeneity (or homogeneity) can be assessed by counting the number (percentage) of smaller spatial units within their larger units of analysis that have the same classification of change.

A number of tests for similarity are performed. For each crime classification and each spatial unit of analysis, Indices of Similarity are calculated for 1991–2001 (Vancouver) and 2001–2004 (Leeds). These indices are then used to quantify the degree of spatial heterogeneity present with the changes of the spatial point patterns at the different scales of analysis.

Results

Spatial heterogeneity is remarkably similar not only across crime classifications but also across municipalities. In the case of assault (Table 11.1), the number of larger areas with zero smaller areas in Vancouver and Leeds is always zero. This is the expected result. In fact, if (when) this occurs, it is highly problematic; such a situation is further discussed below. However, the number of larger areas with all smaller areas having the same classification is also zero in most cases—all cases in Leeds. When this does occur (2001 < 1991 and insignificant change, in Vancouver), it occurs in very few cases. Overall, the average percentage of smaller areas with the same larger area classification is surprisingly low. The best case scenario, for both Vancouver and Leeds, is that a little more than half of the smaller areas have the same larger area classification. Though this may be viewed positively, it also means that a little less than half do not have the same classification. This is a substantial degree of spatial heterogeneity that must be considered when inference is being made at only one level of analysis. The results for burglary (Table 11.2) are similar to those for assault and require little further discussion. The primary result to note here is that assault and burglary have similar results despite these two crime classifications exhibiting different patterns over time, see Chapter 10: relatively speaking, assault is decreasing in Vancouver and increasing in Leeds, but burglary in both cities is constant. As such, the degree of spatial heterogeneity does not necessarily depend on other changes in a crime's distribution.

The results for robbery (Table 11.3) and sexual assault (Table 11.4) are similar for the average percentage of smaller areas with the same larger area classification, but some of the other results are worthy of note. In both Leeds and Vancouver, robbery and sexual assault have some larger areas with zero smaller areas having

Table 11.1 Spatial heterogeneity, assault

	Vancouver[a]		
	CTs: 2001 > 1991	CTs: 2001 < 1991	CTs: insignificant change
Number (percentage) of CTs with *zero* DAs having same classification	0	0	0
Number (percentage) of CTs with *all* DAs having same classification	0	1 (2.2)	4 (12.1)
Average percentage of DAs with same CT classification	0.35	0.61	0.43
Total number of CTs with this classification	31	46	33
	Leeds[b]		
	MSOAs: 2004 > 2001	MSOAs: 2004 < 2001	MSOAs: insignificant change
Number (percentage) of MSOAs with *zero* OAs having the same classification	0	0	0
Number (percentage) of MSOAs with *all* OAs having the same classification	0	0	0
Average percentage of OAs with same MSOA classification	0.58	0.43	0.27
Total number of MSOAs with this classification	48	35	25

CT, census tract; DA, dissemination area; MSOA, middle-layer super output area; OA, output area.
Notes: [a]total CTs = 110; [b]total MSOAs = 108.

the same classification: 2001 > 1991, for both cases in Vancouver, and insignificant change for both cases in Leeds. Such a result is particularly problematic because the nature of the spatial heterogeneity is such that the smaller spatial units of analysis have nothing in common with the larger spatial units of analysis. A problem emerges here specifically in the context of policy. If policy is being implemented based on global results and the larger area is used as a reference point for policy implementation, the policy may be applied in error. This will lead to a misallocation of resources, at best, or aggravate the original situation that policy-makers are trying to correct, at worst.

Table 11.2 Spatial heterogeneity, burglary

	Vancouver[a]		
	CTs: 2001 > 1991	CTs: 2001 < 1991	CTs: insignificant change
Number (percentage) of CTs with **zero** DAs having same classification	0	0	1 (5.9)
Number (percentage) of CTs with **all** DAs having same classification	1 (2.4)	0	3 (17.6)
Average percentage of DAs with same CT classification	0.50	0.57	0.45
Total number of CTs with this classification	41	52	17
	Leeds[b]		
	MSOAs: 2004 > 2001	MSOAs: 2004 < 2001	MSOAs: insignificant change
Number (percentage) of MSOAs with **zero** OAs having same classification	0	0	0
Number (percentage) of MSOAs with **all** OAs having same classification	0	0	0
Average percentage of OAs with same MSOA classification	0.66	0.49	0.14
Total number of MSOAs with this classification	55	37	16

CT, census tract; DA, dissemination area; MSOA, middle-layer super output area; OA, output area.
Notes: [a]total CTs = 110; [b]total MSOAs = 108.

Turning to the three classifications of theft—theft (Table 11.5), theft of vehicle (Table 11.6), and theft from vehicle (Table 11.7)—the results are more promising in terms of the magnitude of spatial heterogeneity within larger spatial unit. The average percentages of smaller areas with the same larger area classification are of the same magnitude as the other crime classifications. Though theft from vehicle (Leeds) and theft of vehicle (Vancouver) do have a small number of larger areas with zero small areas with the same classification, Vancouver has promising results for the number of larger areas with all corresponding small areas having

Table 11.3 Spatial heterogeneity, robbery

	Vancouver[a]		
	CTs: 2001 > 1991	CTs: 2001 < 1991	CTs: insignificant change
Number (percentage) of CTs with **zero** DAs having same classification	3 (11.1)	0	0
Number (percentage) of CTs with **all** DAs having same classification	0	0	8 (22.2)
Average percentage of DAs with same CT classification	0.21	0.36	0.74
Total number of CTs with this classification	27	47	36
	Leeds[b]		
	MSOAs: 2004 > 2001	MSOAs: 2004 < 2001	MSOAs: insignificant change
Number (percentage) of MSOAs with **zero** OAs having same classification	0	0	2(5.6)
Number (percentage) of MSOAs with **all** OAs having same classification	1 (2.4)	0	0
Average percentage of OAs with same MSOA classification	0.61	0.39	0.35
Total number of MSOAs with this classification	42	30	36

CT, census tract; DA, dissemination area; MSOA, middle-layer super output area; OA, output area.
Notes: [a]total CTs = 110; [b]total MSOAs = 108.

the same classification. The magnitudes of the percentages are not that great, ranging from 2.8 percent (theft of vehicle) to 18.8 percent (theft from vehicle), but this is a definite improvement over the results for the other crime classifications.

Discussion

In this chapter, the phenomenon of spatial heterogeneity has been investigated in the context of spatial point patterns changing over time. Though this is only one dimension of change that may be investigated, the results are strong enough to

Table 11.4 Spatial heterogeneity, sexual assault

	Vancouver[a]		
	CTs: 2001 > 1991	*CTs: 2001 < 1991*	*CTs: insignificant change*
Number (percentage) of CTs with *zero* DAs having same classification	7 (43.8)	0	0
Number (percentage) of CTs with *all* DAs having same classification	0	0	8 (14.3)
Average percentage of DAs with same CT classification	0.11	0.31	0.69
Total number of CTs with this classification	16	38	56
	Leeds[b]		
	MSOAs: 2004 > 2001	*MSOAs: 2004 < 2001*	*MSOAs: insignificant change*
Number (percentage) of MSOAs with *zero* OAs having same classification	0	0	5 (13.9)
Number (percentage) of MSOAs with *all* OAs having same classification	11 (37.9)	0	0
Average percentage of OAs with same MSOA classification	0.53	0.51	0.35
Total number of MSOAs with this classification	29	43	36

CT, census tract; DA, dissemination area; MSOA, middle-layer super output area; OA, output area.
Notes: [a]total CTs = 110; [b]total MSOAs = 108.

cause some concern over the lack of sensitivity analyses in the geography of crime literature—the lack of using multiple spatial scales of analysis. The general result is that, on average, approximately one-half of smaller spatial units of analysis have the same classification as their larger counterparts. Though this may translate into an irrelevant effect when using a global statistical technique, as it does using the data in the current analysis, the magnitude of the spatial heterogeneity cannot be ignored. Therefore, spatial heterogeneity in the presence of an irrelevant effect in a particular context does not mean there are no aggregation biases present, generally speaking. As such we, as researchers, cannot simply assume that aggregation bias is not present and only perform analyses at one

Table 11.5 Spatial heterogeneity, theft

	Vancouver[a]		
	CTs: 2001 > 1991	CTs: 2001 < 1991	CTs: insignificant change
Number (percentage) of CTs with *zero* DAs having same classification	0	0	0
Number (percentage) of CTs with *all* DAs having same classification	2 (8.7)	5 (6.9)	2 (13.3)
Average percentage of DAs with same CT classification	0.46	0.70	0.45
Total number of CTs with this classification	23	72	15
	Leeds[b]		
	MSOAs: 2004 > 2001	MSOAs: 2004 < 2001	MSOAs: insignificant change
Number (percentage) of MSOAs with *zero* OAs having same classification	0	0	0
Number (percentage) of MSOAs with *all* OAs having same classification	0	0	0
Average percentage of OAs with same MSOA classification	0.53	0.36	0.29
Total number of MSOAs with this classification	45	33	30

CT, census tract; DA, dissemination area; MSOA, middle-layer super output area; OA, output area.
Notes: [a]total CTs = 110; [b]total MSOAs = 108.

spatial scale because a small number of research projects have not found evidence for aggregation bias; aggregation is present, it just does not manifest itself in particular contexts using particular techniques.

The case of sexual assault in Vancouver is of particular interest here. Figure 11.1 shows the results from the spatial point pattern test. All four census tracts shown in Figure 11.1 have statistically significant increases, 2001 > 1991. The two middle census tracts are likely representative of the presence of spatial heterogeneity: some DAs exhibit increasing trends, some DAs exhibit decreasing trends, and some DAs exhibit insignificant change. In these cases, a small number of DAs (one in the case of the CT on top of the map) are driving the results for the larger CTs. However, for the CTs on either side of Figure 11.1, there is clearly

Table 11.6 Spatial heterogeneity, theft of vehicle

	Vancouver[a]		
	CTs: *2001 > 1991*	*CTs:* *2001 < 1991*	*CTs:* *insignificant change*
Number (percentage) of CTs with *zero* DAs having same classification	0	0	1 (3.0)
Number (percentage) of CTs with *all* DAs having same classification	1 (2.8)	2 (4.9)	3 (9.1)
Average percentage of DAs with same CT classification	0.42	0.59	0.42
Total number of CTs with this classification	36	41	33
	Leeds[b]		
	MSOAs: *2004 > 2001*	*MSOAs:* *2004 < 2001*	*MSOAs:* *insignificant change*
Number (percentage) of MSOAs with *zero* OAs having same classification	0	0	0
Number (percentage) of MSOAs with *all* OAs having same classification	0	0	0
Average percentage of OAs with same MSOA classification	0.71	0.52	0.11
Total number of MSOAs with this classification	56	41	11

CT, census tract; DA, dissemination area; MSOA, middle-layer super output area; OA, output area.
Notes: [a]total CTs = 110; [b]total MSOAs = 108.

something else going on. In each case, no DAs exhibit increasing trends; rather, most have statistically insignificant change with a small number of decreasing trends. How can this be the case?

As it turns out for the CTs on the sides of Figure 11.1, there are DAs with statistically insignificant changes that have increasing trends. And these increasing trends are close to being statistically significant; if a 90 percent confidence interval had been chosen, for example, the results of those DAs would have been statistically significant and increasing. But the point of this discussion is not in regard to the choice of statistical significance. Rather, the point is that insignificant

Table 11.7 Spatial heterogeneity, theft from vehicle

	Vancouver[a]		
	CTs: 2001 > 1991	CTs: 2001 < 1991	CTs: insignificant change
Number (percentage) of CTs with *zero* DAs having same classification	0	0	0
Number (percentage) of CTs with *all* DAs having same classification	1 (5.0)	3 (4.1)	3 (18.8)
Average percentage of DAs with same CT classification	0.46	0.67	0.43
Total number of CTs with this classification	20	74	16
	Leeds[b]		
	MSOAs: 2004 > 2001	MSOAs: 2004 < 2001	MSOAs: Insignificant change
Number (percentage) of MSOAs with *zero* OAs having same classification	0	1 (2.6)	0
Number (percentage) of MSOAs with *all* OAs having same classification	0	0	0
Average percentage of OAs with same MSOA classification	0.68	0.53	0.24
Total number of MSOAs with this classification	48	38	22

CT, census tract; DA, dissemination area; MSOA, middle-layer super output area; OA, output area.
Notes: [a]total CTs = 110; [b]total MSOAs = 108.

changes at the level of a smaller spatial unit of analysis may become statistically significant with a larger spatial unit of analysis. In other words, there is an aggregation effect.

Comparing the results from Tables 11.1 to 11.7 to the counts of the various crime types, an interesting relationship emerges. The crime classifications that had the most problematic results (robbery and sexual assault) had the lowest counts and percentages for both Vancouver and Leeds, and the crime classifications that had the most promising results (burglary, theft, and theft from vehicle) had the greatest counts and percentages for both Vancouver and Leeds—theft of vehicle also had promising results. Therefore, it would appear that if the event is more common, the results are less problematic. This does not mean that spatial

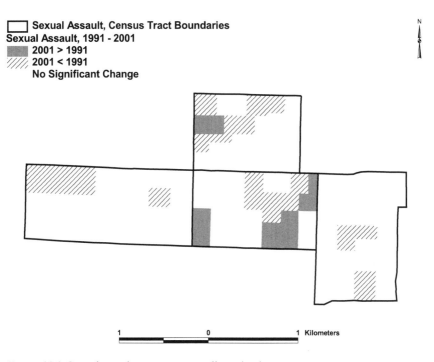

Figure 11.1 Sexual assault, census tract to dissemination area.

heterogeneity is not an issue when there are more crimes, just that the issue does not appear to be as great. This result relates to the discussion above regarding the ecological fallacy. Variations in spatial patterns may be more evident when the count of points in the spatial pattern is less. Such a situation is understood intuitively: a spatial pattern with fewer points is more likely to have zero values in spatial units, leading to more spatial heterogeneity within larger spatial units. This is confirmed in Chapter 10 for Vancouver that has the highest S-Index values for the low-count crime classification of robbery and sexual assault. Therefore, the degree of concern for spatial heterogeneity should be inversely related to the number of points in the spatial pattern. Consequently, if an analysis (for the purposes of pure academic interests, policy, or a combination of both) is restricted to one spatial unit of analysis, results may have to be tempered depending on the number of points under analysis.

There are a number of obvious directions for future research. Though we have performed this analysis in two municipalities that are quite distant from one another, more replication is always preferable. We claim that too often research relies on a small number of other studies which claim aggregation bias is minimal or non-existent as justification for only performing analyses at one spatial scale. Consequently, we wish to be careful with our generalizations. The form of replication needs to be varied as well. Not only should further investigations into spatial heterogeneity be in other urban areas, but suburban and rural areas as well. Because rural areas tend to have less crime than urban areas, the spatial heterogeneity may be more of a problem in rural areas than suburban and urban areas. Similarly, the crime mix probably varies across urban, suburban, and rural areas, so may the issue of spatial heterogeneity. The more context we have regarding spatial heterogeneity, the better choices we can make regarding spatial scale.

Though the current analysis is instructive, the format of quantifying spatial heterogeneity should be performed in different ways. For example, it would be most useful to investigate spatial heterogeneity in the context of standard spatial theories of crime. It may be the case that a small number of small areas (DAs/OAs) are driving the results for their aggregate areas (CTs/MSOAs). Specifically, once we have more information regarding the role of spatial scale and spatial heterogeneity, we may be able to further develop/refine/test spatial theories of crime. Not only may a small number of small areas be driving aggregate results, but the way we think about particular theoretical frameworks may change.

12 Future directions in the science of crime measurement

This book has investigated a number of issues with regard to spatially referenced crime data. The general result of this research is that spatially referenced crime data has a set of rather significant issues that may impact the reliability of inference. This should come as no surprise because all data have their limitations, but some of the most common assumptions we make in the spatial crime analysis literature appear to cause problems within their respective contexts. In short: crime rates are problematic; alternative measures of crime (location quotients) are in use but not widespread; ecological stability may only be present at micro-spatial units of analysis; many of the aggregations we take for granted in research have implications for spatial patterns; and there is still much spatial heterogeneity within the "small" spatial unit of analysis most commonly employed, namely the census tract.

This discussion is not meant to discredit previous research that did not address these issues; we do what we can with the data that are available. Rather, this discussion is meant to point in the direction of where we need to go in spatial criminology. Our theories and our methods are quite simply ahead of our measurement—see Prescott (1986) for a discussion of this issue in the context of macroeconomic theory. With the development of new data and the growth of partnerships between policing agencies and academics (such as the one at the Institute for Canadian Urban Research Studies at Simon Fraser University), this is a very exciting time to work in the field of spatial criminology. Based on the research presented in this book, aside from the need for replication in different contexts, there are three areas of future research in the science of crime measurement which are immediately apparent.

First, the measurement of the population at risk needs further development. As discussed in Part I, Oak Ridge National Laboratory has been working on better quality ambient population data, particularly for the United States. However, technology now allows for quite direct measurement of ambient populations in most areas of the world and at any time of day by means of hand-held mobile devices. Research centers such as the SENSEable City Laboratory, a new research initiative at the Massachusetts Institute of Technology, http://senseable.mit.edu, are investigating the uses of such data. These devices (mobile phones, tablets, etc.) are seemingly omnipresent and would provide excellent predictors of the relative distribution of populations. Many of us are bombarded with messages from mobile applications for Facebook and Twitter that use global positioning systems accounting for time and place. With such data available with highly detailed time information, this combination with calls for service police data with time references would prove to be most instructive. The limitation that must be overcome within the context of these data is privacy. The terms and conditions for most, if not all, of these mobile applications require us to surrender our usage data to the various providers, but the availability of such information is clearly sensitive.

Second, are there other forms of crime measurement that would prove to be instructive? The location quotient is but one of many "specialization" or "entropy" measures. Are there others that share the ease of calculation as with the location quotient? This may lead to the adaptation of old measures for (spatial) crime analysis, or the development of entirely new measures of crime based on the new questions we are forced to ask.

Last, and related to the similarity of spatial patterns of crime, is probably one of the most fundamental issues faced in spatial criminology. Our entire literature almost exclusively relies on police data. Is the pattern of police data the same as actual victimization? Actual victimization data are not available at a scale able to answer this question right now, but some research indicates that police data may have a very different spatial pattern than actual victimization. Research on Vilnius, Lithuania by Ceccato and Lukyte (2011) has found that the spatial pattern of police data differs substantially from victimization data. With the level of aggregation available to these authors nothing definitive can be stated at this point in time. However, such research findings should have the attention of spatial criminologists. The difficulty here is a scientifically sound investigation into this phenomenon. Such an investigation would require a victimization survey with sampling performed at the neighborhood level (or smaller) in order to compare the resulting spatial patterns to police data—replication would also be necessary because of the potential implications from the results. Because of the sampling necessary, this would be a rather expensive endeavor. In the end, if our research is implicitly or explicitly based on the underlying spatial patterns of crime and we use police data, we must assume that the spatial patterns of police data (though a sample) are truly representative of actual spatial patterns of crime. Otherwise, everything we think we know about the spatial patterns of crime using such data may be wrong.

Notes

3 The ambient population and crime analysis

1 Ethnic heterogeneity is measured using an index that ranges in value from zero to 100, with 0 representing no ethnic mix and 100 representing a perfectly even mix of ethnic groups: $\dfrac{-\sum_{i=1}^{n} p_i \ln p_i}{\ln n}$, where p_i is the proportion of ethnic group i and n is the number of ethnic groups.

2 These include employment insurance benefits, old-age security benefits, net federal supplements, Canada and Quebec pension plan benefits, the Canada Child Tax Benefit, provincial government family allowances, the goods and services tax credit, workers' compensation benefits, social assistance, and provincial or territorial refundable tax credits.

3 A completed certificate, diploma, or degree.

4 This is defined as individuals spending 20 percent or more of disposable income than the average private household, on food, shelter, and clothing.

5 This represents the perception of physical disorder and decay.

6 This is a measure of housing affordability, an indicator of socio-economic disadvantage.

7 The use of Rook's contiguity does not alter the results in any meaningful way. Most often, Rook's contiguity only necessitates a higher degree of contiguity to control for spatial autocorrelation. Also, in the present context, areas that may only be considered spatial neighbors at one point (a corner) are still expected to be similar because of the nature of urban landscapes; as such, Queen's contiguity is appropriate.

8 Some may consider a 10 percent significance level too high and prefer a 5 percent significance level. However, for the purposes of this comparative analysis, a more liberal testing methodology is used to err on the side of variable inclusion. If a 5 percent significance level is used in the analysis (Tables 3.3 – 3.7) the qualitative results do not change, but the case for using the ambient population in spatial crime analysis becomes even stronger.

9 It is a relatively easy task to inflate the Pseudo–R^2 by including more variables, such as a lagged dependent variable. This is easily justified in a temporal analysis because of path dependency and a desire to predict crime rates.

6 Crime specialization across the Canadian provinces and Metro Vancouver's municipalities

1 Level 1: simple assault; level 2: assault with a weapon; level 3: aggravated assault. These same levels are used for sexual assault.

8 The (in)appropriateness of aggregating across crime types

1 There are two general forms of spatial point pattern tests: area-based and distance based. See Andresen (2009a) for a discussion of their respective benefits and limitations.
2 An 85 percent sample is based on the minimum acceptable hit rate to maintain spatial patterns, determined by Ratcliffe (2004). Maintaining the spatial pattern of the complete data set is important so we used this as a benchmark for sampling. An 85 percent sample was for the purposes of generating as much variability as possible while maintaining the original spatial pattern. Also note that "replacement" in this context refers to subsequent samples; any one point may only be sampled once per iteration in this procedure to mimic Ratcliffe (2004).
3 The program written to perform the test uses double precision that has at least 14 decimal points when dealing with numbers less than unity. The smallest number that we have to deal with in the current analysis (regardless of scale) is 0.000030498. This is well within the limits of double precision.
4 It should be noted that the role of local spatial analysis has been growing in interest in recent years (Lloyd, 2011).

10 Testing the stability of crime patterns

1 There is other notable research that analyzes small units of analysis. First is the work on crime prevention initiatives, which involves microspatial analysis of crime and the effects of prevention initiatives, and tends to focus on relatively small areas rather than city-wide analyses. See Sherman *et al.* (1989) and Weisburd *et al.* (2004) for reviews of this literature. Second is the work of Brantingham *et al.* (1976) regarding the changes in crime patterns when the spatial unit of analysis is altered. Third is the work of Bowers and Johnson (2004), Johnson and Bowers (2004a, 2004b), and Townsley *et al.* (2000, 2003) with their research on near-repeat victimization.
2 Though not reviewed here or in Weisburd *et al.* (2004), Taylor *et al.* (1995) analyze street segments/blocks but are concerned with physical deterioration, not crime. Also, Weisburd *et al.* (2009b) is a more recent collection of essays that discusses the appropriate unit of analysis in spatial criminology.

11 Spatial heterogeneity in crime analysis

1 Wooldredge (2002) is not the first to make this type of claim (see Land *et al.* 1990, for example), but is the most often cited research on this topic.
2 The street network in Vancouver recognizes to which side of the street a point is geocoded. If that particular street is a boundary for a spatial unit, the point is assigned to the census unit on the appropriate side of the street in the spatial join.

References

Ackerman, W. V. (1998). Socioeconomic correlates of increasing crime rates in smaller communities. *Professional Geographer*, 50(3), 372–387.

Andresen, M. A. (2006a). Crime measures and the spatial analysis of criminal activity. *British Journal of Criminology*, 46(2), 258–285.

Andresen, M. A. (2006b). A spatial analysis of crime in Vancouver, British Columbia: A synthesis of social disorganization and routine activity theory. *Canadian Geographer*, 50(4), 487–502.

Andresen, M. A. (2007). Location quotients, ambient populations, and the spatial analysis of crime in Vancouver, Canada. *Environment and Planning A*, 39(10), 2,423–2,444.

Andresen, M. A. (2009a). Testing for similarity in area-based spatial patterns: A nonparametric Monte Carlo approach. *Applied Geography*, 29(3), 333–345.

Andresen, M. A. (2009b). Crime specialization across the Canadian provinces. *Canadian Journal of Criminology and Criminal Justice*, 51(1), 31–53.

Andresen, M. A. (2010a). Diurnal movements and the ambient population: An application to municipal level crime rate calculations. *Canadian Journal of Criminology and Criminal Justice*, 52(1), 97–109.

Andresen, M. A. (2010b). Canada–United States interregional trade: Quasi-points and spatial change. *Canadian Geographer*, 54(2), 139–157.

Andresen, M. A. and Felson, M. (2010). The impact of co-offending. *British Journal of Criminology*, 50(1), 66–81.

Andresen, M. A. and Felson, M. (2012a). An investigation into the fundamental regularities of co-offending for violent and property crime classifications. *Canadian Journal of Criminology and Criminal Justice*, 54(1), 101–115.

Andresen, M. A. and Felson, M. (2012b). Co-offending and the diversification of crime types. *International Journal of Offender Therapy and Comparative Criminology*, 56(5), 811–829.

Andresen, M. A. and Jenion, G. W. (2008). Crime prevention and the science of where people are. *Criminal Justice Policy Review*, 19(2), 164–180.

Andresen, M. A. and Jenion, G. W. (2010). Ambient populations and the calculation of crime rates and risk. *Security Journal*, 23(2), 114–133.

Andresen, M. A., Jenion, G. W. and Jenion, M. L. (2003). Conventional calculations of homicide rates lead to an inaccurate reflection of Canadian trends. *Canadian Journal of Criminology and Criminal Justice*, 45(1), 1–17.

Andresen, M. A., Jenion, G. W. and Reid, A. A. (2012). An evaluation of ambient population estimates for use in crime analysis. *Crime Mapping: A Journal of Research and Practice*, 4(1), 7–30.

Andresen, M. A. and Malleson, N. (2011). Testing the stability of crime patterns: Implications for theory and policy. *Journal of Research in Crime and Delinquency*, 48(1), 58–82.

Anselin, L. (1988). Spatial econometrics: Methods and models. Dordrecht: Kluwer Academic Publishers.

Anselin, L. (1995). Local indicators of spatial association—LISA. *Geographical Analysis*, 27(2), 93–115.

Anselin, L., Syabri, I. and Kho, Y. (2006). GeoDa: An introduction to spatial data analysis. *Geographical Analysis*, 38(1), 5–22.

Bailey, P. E., Keyes, E. B., Parker, C., Abdullah, M., Kebede, H. and Freedman, L. (2011). Using a GIS to model interventions to strengthen the emergency referral system for maternal and newborn health in Ethiopia. *International Journal of Gynecology and Obstetrics*, 115(3), 300–309.

Bernasco, W. and Block, R. (2009). Where offenders choose to attack: A discrete choice model of robberies in Chicago. *Criminology*, 47(1), 93–130.

Birkin, M., Clarke, G. and Clarke, M. P. (2002). *Retail geography and intelligent network planning*. Chichester: John Wiley & Sons.

Blalock, H. M. (1964). Causal inferences in nonexperimental research. Chapel Hill, NC: University of North Carolina Press.

Block, S., Clarke, R. V., Maxfield, M. G. and Petrossian, G. (2012). Estimating the number of U.S. vehicles stolen for export using crime location quotients. In M. A. Andresen and J. B. Kinney (eds), *Patterns, prevention, and geometry of crime* (pp. 54–68). New York, NY: Routledge.

Boggs, S. L. (1965). Urban crime patterns. *American Sociological Review*, 30(6), 899–908.

Bouchard, M. (2007). A capture–recapture model to estimate the size of criminal populations and the risks of detection in a marijuana cultivation industry. *Journal of Quantitative Criminology*, 23(3), 221–241.

Bowers , K. J. and Johnson, S. D. (2004). Who commits near repeats? A test of the boost explanation. *Western Criminology Review*, 5(3), 12–24.

Brantingham, P. L. and Brantingham, P. J. (1981). Notes of the geometry of crime. In P. J. Brantingham and P. L. Brantingham (eds), *Environmental Criminology* (pp. 27–54). Prospect Heights, IL: Waveland Press.

Brantingham P. J. and Brantingham, P. L. (1984). *Patterns in crime*. New York, NY: Macmillan.

Brantingham, P. J. and Brantingham, P. L. (1991). Introduction: The dimensions of crime. In P. J. Brantingham and P. L. Brantingham (eds), *Environmental criminology* (pp. 7–26). Prospect Heights, IL: Waveland Press.

Brantingham, P. L. and Brantingham, P.J. (1993a). Location quotients and crime hot spots in the city. In C. R. Block and M. Dabdoub (eds), Workshop on crime analysis through computer mapping, *Proceedings* (pp. 175–197). Chicago, IL: Criminal Justice Information Authority.

Brantingham, P. L. and Brantingham, P. J. (1993b). Nodes, paths and edges: Considerations on the complexity of crime and the physical environment. *Journal of Environmental Psychology*, 13(1), 3–28.

Brantingham, P. L. and Brantingham, P. J. (1995). Location quotients and crime hot spots in the city. In C. R. Block, M. Dabdoub and S. Fregly (eds), *Crime analysis through computer mapping* (pp. 129–149). Washington, DC: Police Executive Research Forum.

Brantingham, P. L. and Brantingham, P. J. (1998). Mapping crime for analytic purposes: Location quotients, counts and rates. In D. Weisburd and T. McEwen (eds), *Crime mapping and crime prevention* (pp. 263–288). Monsey, NY: Criminal Justice Press.

Brantingham, P. J., Dyreson. D. A. and Brantingham, P. L. (1976). Crime seen through a cone of resolution. *American Behavioral Scientist*, 20(2), 261–273.

Bulwer, H. L. (1836). France, social, literary, political, volume I, book I: Crime. London, UK: Richard Bentley.

Burgess, E. W. (1916). Juvenile delinquency in a small city. *Journal of the American Institute of Criminal Law and Criminology*, 6(3), 724–728.

Cahill, M. E. and Mulligan, G. F. (2003). The determinants of crime in Tucson, Arizona. *Urban Geography*, 24(7), 582–610.

Carrington, P. J. (2009). Co-offending and the development of the delinquent career. *Criminology*, 47(4), 301–335.

Ceccato, V. (2005). Homicide in San Paulo, Brazil: Assessing spatial-temporal and weather variations. *Journal of Environmental Psychology*, 25(3), 307–321.

Ceccato, V. and Lukyte, N. (2011). Safety and sustainability in a city in transition: The case of Vilnius, Lithuania. *Cities*, 28(1), 83–94.

Clark, L. M. G. and Lewis, D. J. (1977). *Rape: The price of coercive sexuality*. Toronto, ON: Women's Educational Press.

Clarke, R. V. G. (1980). Situational crime prevention: theory and practice. *British Journal of Criminology*, 20(2), 136–147.

Clarke, R. V. G. (1983). Situational crime prevention: Its theoretical basis and practical scope. *Crime and Justice: An Annual Review of Research*, 4, 225–256.

Clarke, R. V. G. (ed.) (1997). Situational crime prevention: Successful case studies. Albany, NY: Harrow and Heston Publishers.

Clarke, R. V. G. and Cornish, D. B. (1985). Modeling offenders' decisions: A framework for research and policy. *Crime and Justice: An Annual Review of Research*, 6, 147–185.

Clarke, R. V. G. and Felson, M. (1993). Introduction: Criminology, routine activity, and rational choice. In R. V. G. Clarke and M. Felson (eds), *Routine activity and rational choice* (pp. 1–14). London, UK: Transaction Publishers.

Cohen, L. E. and Cantor, D. (1980). The determinants of larceny: An empirical and theoretical study. *Journal of Research in Crime and Delinquency*, 17(2), 146–159.

Cohen, L. E. and Felson, M. (1979). Social change and crime rate trends: A routine activity approach. *American Sociological Review*, 44(4), 588–608.

Cohen, L. E, Kaufman, R. L. and Gottfredson, M. R. (1985) Risk-based crime statistics: A forecasting comparison for comparison for burglary and auto theft. *Journal of Criminal Justice*, 13(5), 445–457.

Cohen, L. E., Kluegel, J. R. and Land, K. C. (1981). Social inequality and predatory criminal victimization: An exposition and test of a formal theory. *American Sociological Review*, 46(5), 505–524.

Cohn, E. G. and Rotton, J. (2000). Weather, seasonal trends and property crimes in Minneapolis, 1987–1988: A moderator-variable time-series analysis of routine activities. *Journal of Environmental Psychology*, 20(3), 257–272.

Cornish, D. B. and Clarke, R. V. G. (1986). *The reasoning criminal: Rational choice perspectives on offending*. New York, NY: Springer-Verlag.

Cornish, D. B. and Clarke, R. V. G. (1987). Understanding crime displacement: An application of rational choice theory. *Criminology*, 25(4), 933–947.

Daly, M., Wilson, M. and Vasdev, S. (2001). Income inequality and homicide rates in Canada and the United States. *Canadian Journal of Criminology*, 43(2), 219–236.

Dauvergne, M. and Turner, J. (2010). Police-reported crime statistics in Canada, 2009. Ottawa, ON: Statistics Canada, Canadian Centre for Justice Statistics.

DeKeseredy, W. S. and Ellis, D. (1995). Intimate male violence against women in Canada. In J. I. Ross (ed.), *Violence in Canada: Sociopolitical perspectives* (pp. 97–125). Don Mills, ON: Oxford University Press.

Department of Justice Canada. (1990). Sexual assault legislation in Canada, an evaluation: Overview (Report No. 5). Ottawa, ON: Minister of Supply and Services Canada.

Department of Justice Canada. (1992). *Sexual assault legislation in Canada, an evaluation: A review of the sexual assault case law 1985-1988* (Report No. 6). Ottawa, ON: Minister of Supply and Services Canada.

Dobson, J. E. (2003). Estimating populations at risk. In S. L. Cutter, D. B. Richardson and T. J. Wilbanks (eds), The geographical dimensions of terrorism (pp. 161–167). New York and London: Routledge.

Dobson, J. E. (2004). The GIS revolution in science and society. In S. D. Brunn, S. L. Cutter, and J. W. Harrington, Jr. (eds), *Geography and technology* (pp. 573–587). Dordrecht: Kluwer Academic Publishers.

Dobson, J. E., Bright, E. A., Coleman, P. R. and Bhaduri, B. L. (2003). LandScan: A global population database for estimating populations at risk. In V. Mesev (ed.), *Remotely sensed cities* (pp. 267–279). London and New York: Taylor & Francis.

Dobson, J. E., Bright, E. A., Coleman, P. R., Durfee, R. C. and Worley, B.A. (2000). LandScan: A global population database for estimating populations at risk. *Photogrammetric Engineering and Remote Sensing*, 66(7), 849–857.

Easton, S. T. (2004). Marijuana growth in British Columbia. *Public Policy Forces*, Number 74. Vancouver, BC: The Fraser Institute.

Eck, J. E. and Weisburd, D. (eds) (1995). Crime prevention studies, volume 4, crime and place. Monsey, NY: Criminal Justice Press.

Ellis, L. and Walsh, A. (2000). *Criminology: A global perspective*. Boston, MA: Allyn and Bacon.

Elvidge, C. D., Sutton, P. C., Ghosh, T., Tuttle, B. T., Baugh, K. E., Bhaduri, B. and Bright, E. (2009). A global poverty map derived from satellite data. *Computers and Geosciences*, 35(8), 1652–1660.

Erickson, M. (1971). The group context of delinquent behavior. *Social Problems*, 19(1), 114–129.

Estrich, S. (1986). Rape. *Yale Law Journal*, 95(6), 1087–1184.

Farrell, G. and Pease, K. (1994). Crime seasonality: Domestic disputes and residential burglary in Mereyside 1988-90. *British Journal of Criminology*, 34(4), 487–498.

Farrell, G., Tseloni, A., Mailley, J. and Tilley, N. (2011). The crime drop and the security hypothesis. *Journal of Research in Crime and Delinquency*, 48(2), 147–175.

FBI. (2012). Uniform Crime Reports. Washington, DC: Federal Bureau of Investigation. Available on-line at http://www.fbi.gov/about-us/cjis/ucr/ucr [accessed 24 January 2013].

Felson, M. (1987). Routine activities and crime prevention in the developing metropolis. *Criminology*, 25(4), 911–931.

Felson, M. (2006). *Crime and nature*. Thousand Oaks, CA: Sage Publications.

Felson, M. and Cohen, L. E. (1980). Human ecology and crime: A routine activity approach. *Human Ecology*, 8(4), 398–405.

Felson, M. and Cohen, L. E. (1981). Modeling crime trends: A cumulative opportunity perspective. *Journal of Research in Crime and Delinquency*, 18(1), 138–164.

Field, S. (1992). The effect of temperature on crime. *British Journal of Criminology*, 32(3), 340–351.

Fisher, B. S. and Wilkes, A. R. P. (2003). A tale of two ivory towers: A comparative analysis of victimization rates and risks between university students in the United States and England. *British Journal of Criminology*, 43(3), 526–545.

Fotheringham, A. S. and Wong, D. W. (1991). The modifiable areal unit problem in multivariate statistical analysis. *Environment and Planning A*, 23(7), 1025–1044.

Galvin, J. (1985). Rape: A decade of reform. *Crime and Delinquency*, 31(2), 163–168.

Gannon, M. (2006). *Crime statistics in Canada, 2005*. Ottawa, ON: Statistics Canada, Canadian Centre for Justice Statistics.

Gehlke, C. E. and Biehl, K. (1934). Certain effects of grouping upon the size of the correlation coefficient in census tract material. *Journal of the American Statistical Association Supplement*, 29(185), 169–170.

Getis, A. and Ord, J. K. (1992). The analysis of spatial association by use of distance statistics. *Geographical Analysis*, 24(3), 189–206.

Getis, A. and Ord, J. K. (1996). Spatial analysis: Modelling in a GIS environment. In P. Longley and M. Batty (eds), *Local spatial statistics: An overview* (pp. 261–277). London: Geoinformation International.

Ghosh, T., Elvidge, C. D., Sutton, P. C., Baugh, K. E., Ziskin, D. and Tuttle, B.T. (2010). Creating a global grid of distributed fossil fuel CO_2 emissions from nighttime satellite imagery. *Energies*, 3(12), 1895–1913.

Giffen, P. J. (1965). Rates of crime and delinquency. In W. T. McGrath (ed), *Crime and its treatment in Canada* (pp. 59–90). Toronto, ON: Macmillan.

Giffen, P. J. (1976). Official rates of crime and delinquency. In W .T. McGrath (ed.) *Crime and its treatment in Canada, 2nd edition* (pp. 66–110). Toronto, ON: Macmillan.

Gold, M. (1970). *Delinquent behavior in an American city*. Belmont, CA: Brooks/Cole.

Gold, S. S. (2003). Watch us move: Homeland security requires a new kind of population map. *Popular Science,* January, 40.

Gottfredson, D. C., McNeil III, R. J. and Gottfredson, G. D. (1991). Social area influences on delinquency: A multilevel analysis. *Journal of Research in Crime and Delinquency*, 28(2), 197–226.

Groff, E., Weisburd, D. and Morris, N. A. (2009). Where the action is at places: Examining spatio-temporal patterns of juvenile crime at places using trajectory analysis. In D. Weisburd, W. Bernasco and G. J. N. Bruinsma (eds), *Putting crime in its place: Units of analysis in geographic criminology* (pp. 61–86). New York, NY: Springer.

Guerette, R. T. and Bowers, K. J. (2009). Assessing the extent of crime displacement and diffusion of benefits: A review of situational crime prevention evaluations. *Criminology*, 47(4), 1331–1368.

Guerry, A. M. (1833). *Essai sur la statistique morale de la France*. Paris: Crochard.

Harries, K. D. (1974). *The geography of crime and justice*. New York, NY: McGraw-Hill.

Harries, K. D. (1981). Alternative denominators in conventional crime rates. In P. J. Brantingham and P. L. Brantingham (eds), *Environmental criminology* (pp. 147–165). Beverly Hills, CA: Sage Publications.

Harries, K. D. (1991). Alternative denominators in conventional crime rates. In P. J. Brantingham and P. L. Brantingham (eds), *Environmental criminology* (pp. 147–165). Prospect Heights, IL: Waveland Press.

Harries, K. D. (1995). The ecology of homicide and assault: Baltimore City and Country, 1989–1991. *Studies in Crime and Crime Prevention*, 4(1), 44–60.

Hartnagel, T. F. (1978). The effect of age and sex composition of provincial populations on provincial crime rates. *Canadian Journal of Criminology*, 20(1), 28–33.

Hartnagel, T. F. (1997). Crime among the provinces: The effect of geographic mobility. *Canadian Journal of Criminology*, 39(4), 387–402.

Hawley, A. H. (1944). Ecology and human ecology. *Social Forces*, 22(4), 398–405.

Hawley, A. H. (1950). *Human ecology: A theory of community structure*. New York, NY: Ronald Press.

Hipp, J. R. (2007). Block, tract, and levels of aggregation: Neighborhood structure and crime and disorder as a case in point. *American Sociological Review*, 72(5), 659–680.

Hipp, J. R., Bauer, D. J., Curran, P. J. and Bollen, K. A. (2004). Crime of opportunity or crimes of emotion? Testing two explanations of season change in crime. *Social Forces*, 82(4), 1333–1372.

Hirschfield, A. and Bowers, K. J. (1997). The development of a social, demographic and land use profiler for areas of high crime. *British Journal of Criminology*, 37(1), 103–120.

Hirschi. T. and Gottfredson, M. (1983). Age and the explanation of crime. *American Journal of Sociology*, 89(3), 552–584.

Isard, W., Azis, I. J., Drennan, M. P., Miller, R. E., Saltzman, S. and Thorbecke, E. (1998). *Methods of interregional and regional analysis*. Aldershot, UK: Ashgate Publishing.

Jeffery, C. R. (1969). Crime prevention and control through environmental engineering. *Criminologica*, 7(3), 35–58.

Jeffery, C. R. (1971). Crime prevention through environmental design. Beverly Hills, CA: Sage Publications.

Jeffery, C. R. (1976). Criminal behaviour and the physical environment. *American Behavioral Scientist*, 20(2), 149–174.

Jeffery, C. R. (1977). Crime prevention through environmental design (second edition). Beverly Hills, CA: Sage Publications.

Johnson , S. D. and Bowers, K. J. (2004a). The burglary as clue to the future: The beginnings of prospective hot-spotting. *European Journal of Criminology*, 1(2), 237–255.

Johnson , S. D. and Bowers, K. J. (2004b). The stability of space–time clusters of burglary. *British Journal of Criminology*, 44(1), 55–65.

Johnson , S. D. and Bowers, K. J. (2010). Permeability and burglary risk: Are cul-de-sacs safer? *Journal of Quantitative Criminology*, 26(1), 89–111.

Johnson, H. and Lazarus, G. (1989). The impact of age on victimization rates. *Canadian Journal of Criminology*, 31(3), 309–317.

Kelling, G. and Coles, C. (1998). Fixing broken windows: Restoring order and reducing crime in our communities. New York, NY: Touchstone.

Kennedy, L. W. and Forde, D. R. (1990). Routine activities and crime: An analysis of victimization in Canada. *Criminology*, 28(1), 137–152.

Kennedy, L. W., Silverman, R. A. and Forde, D. R. (1991). Homicide in urban Canada. *Canadian Journal of Sociology*, 16(4), 397–410.

Kennedy, P. (2003). *A guide to econometrics (fifth edition)*. Malden, MA: Blackwell.

Kinney, J. B., Brantingham, P. L., Wuschke, K., Kirk, M. G. and Brantingham, P. J. (2008). Crime attractors, generators and detractors: Land use and urban crime opportunities. *Built Environment*, 34(1), 62–74.

Kong, R. (1997). *Canadian crime statistics, 1996*. Ottawa, ON: Statistics Canada, Canadian Centre for Justice Statistics.

LaFree, G. D. (1989). Rape and criminal justice: The social construction of sexual assault. Belmont, CA: Wadsworth Publishing.

Land, K. C., McCall, P. L. and Cohen, L. E. (1990). Structural covariates of homicide rates: Are there any invariances across time and social space? *American Journal of Sociology*, 95(4), 922–963.

Landau, S. F. and Fridman, D. (1993). The seasonality of violent crime: The case of robbery and homicide in Israel. *Journal of Research in Crime and Delinquency*, 30(2), 163–191.

Lewis, L. T. and Alford, J. J. (1975). The influence of season on assault. *Professional Geographer*, 27(2), 214–217.

Ley, D. (1999). Myths and meanings of immigration and the metropolis. *Canadian Geographer*, 43(1), 2–19.

Ley, D. (2004). Personal communication, 20 October 2004.

Ley, D. and Smith, H. (2000). Relations between deprivation and immigrant groups in large Canadian cities. *Urban Studies*, 37(1), 37–62.

Linsky, A. and Straus, M. (1986). Social stress in the United States: Links to regional patterns in crime and illness. Dover, MA: Auburn House.

Lloyd, C. D. (2011). Local models for spatial analysis (second edition). Boca Raton, FL: CRC Press, Taylor & Francis Group.

Los, M. (1994). The struggle to redefine rape in the early 1980s. In J. V. Roberts and R. M. Mohr (eds), *Confronting sexual assault: A decade of legal and social change* (pp. 20–56). Toronto, ON: University of Toronto Press.

Løvholt, F., Glimsdal, S., Harbitz, C. B., Zamora, N., Nadim, F., Peduzzi, P., Dao, H. and Smebye, H. (2012). Tsunami hazard and exposure on the global scale. *Earth-Science Reviews*, 110(1–4), 58–73.

McCord, E. S. and Ratcliffe, J. H. (2007). A micro-spatial analysis of the demographic and criminogenic environment of drug markets in Philadelphia. *Australian and New Zealand Journal of Criminology*, 40(1), 43–63.

Matthews, S. A., Yang, T-C., Hayslett, K. L., and Ruback, R. B. (2010). Built environment and property crime in Seattle, 1998–2000: a Bayesian analysis. *Environment and Planning A*, 42(6), 1403–1420.

Miethe, T. D., Stafford, M. C. and Long, J. S. (1987). Social differentiation in criminal victimization: a test of routine activities/lifestyle theories. *American Sociological Review*, 52(2), 184–194.

Miller, M. M., Gibson, L. J. and Wright, N. G. (1991). Location quotient: A basic tool for economic development studies. *Economic Development Review*, 9(2), 65–68.

Monmonier, M. S. (1996). *How to lie with maps*. Chicago, IL: University of Chicago Press.

Morenoff, J. D., Sampson, R. J. and Raudenbush, S. W. (2001). *Neighbourhood inequality, collective efficacy and the spatial dynamics of urban violence*. Research Report, no. 00-451. Population Studies Centre. Institute for Social Research. University of Michigan.

Mosher, C. J., Miethe, T. D. and Hart, T. C. (2011). *The mismeasure of crime (second edition)*. Los Angeles, CA: Sage Publications.

Mubareka, S., Ehrlich, D., Bonn, F. and Kayitakire, F. (2008). Settlement location and population density estimation in rugged terrain using information derived from Landsat ETM and SRTM data. *International Journal of Remote Sensing*, 29(8), 2339–2357.

Murray, A. T., McGuffog, I., Western, J. S. and Mullins, P. (2001). Exploratory spatial data analysis techniques for examining urban crime. *British Journal of Criminology*, 41(2), 309–329.

Newman, O. (1971). *Architectural Design for Crime Prevention*. Washington, DC: Law Enforcement Assistance Administration, National Institute of Law Enforcement and Criminal Justice.

O'Brien, R. M. (1989). Relative cohort size and age-specific crime rates: An age-period-relative-cohort-size model. *Criminology*, 27(1), 57–78.

O'Brien, R. M. (2007). A caution regarding rules of thumb for variance inflation factors. *Quality and Quantity*, 41(5), 673–690.

Oak Ridge National Laboratory (2003). LandScan Global Population Database. Oak Ridge, TN: Oak Ridge National Laboratory. Data available on-line at http://www.ornl.gov/gist/ [accessed 30 November 2012].

Office for National Statistics (2010). 2008-based subnational population projections for England. Newport: Office for National Statistics. Report available on-line at http://www.ons.gov.uk/ons/ [accessed July 2011].

Openshaw, S. (1984a). The modifiable areal unit problem. CATMOG (Concepts and Techniques in Modern Geography) 38. Norwich: Geo Books.

Openshaw, S. (1984b). Ecological fallacies and the analysis of areal census data. *Environment and Planning A*, 16(1), 17–31.

Ord, J. K. and Getis, A. (1995). Local spatial autocorrelation statistics: Distributional issues and an application. *Geographical Analysis*, 27(4), 286–306.

Osgood, D. W. and Anderson, A.L. (2004). Unstructured socializing and rates of delinquency. *Criminology*, 42(3), 519–549.

Ouimet, M. (2000). Aggregation bias in ecological research: How social disorganization and criminal opportunities shape the spatial distribution of juvenile delinquency in Montreal. *Canadian Journal of Criminology*, 42(2), 135–156.

Pallone, N. J. (1999). Editor's Notebook: On numerators in search of denominators: On exhortation toward caution in interpreting "reductions" in crime "rates." *Journal of Offender Rehabilitation*, 28(3–4), 145–154.

Patterson, L., Urban, M., Myers, A., Bhaduri, B., Bright, E. and Coleman, P. (2009). The effects of quality control on decreasing error propagation in the LandScan USA population distribution model: A case study of Philadelphia County. *Transactions in GIS*, 13(2), 215–228.

Pease, K. (1998). *Repeat victimisation: Taking stock*. London: Police Research Group, Home Office.

Perreault, S. and Brennan, S. (2010). *Criminal victimization in Canada, 2009*. Ottawa, ON: Statistics Canada.

Pittman, D. J. and Handy, W. F. (1962). Uniform crime reporting: Suggested improvements. *Sociology and Social Research*, 46(2), 135–143.

Platts, P. J., Burgess, N. D., Gereau, R. E., Lovett, J. C., Marshall, A. R., McClean, C. J., Pellikka, P. K. E., Swetnam, R. D. and Marchant, R. (2011). Delimiting tropical mountain ecoregions for conservation. *Environmental Conservation*, 38(3), 312–324.

Plecas, D., Malm, A. and Kinney, B. (2005). *Marihuana growing operations in British Columbia revisited, 1997–2003*. Abbotsford, BC: Department of Criminology and Criminal Justice and International Centre for Urban Research Studies, University College of the Fraser Valley.

Porter, T. M. (1996). Trust in numbers: The pursuit of objectivity in science and public life. Princeton, NJ: Princeton University Press.

Potere, D., Schneider, A., Angel, S. and Civco, D. L. (2009). Mapping urban areas on a global scale: Which of the eight maps now available is more accurate? *International Journal of Remote Sensing*, 30(24), 6531–6558.

Prescott, E. C. (1986). Theory ahead of business cycle measurement. Federal Reserve Bank of Minneapolis, *Quarterly Review*, 10(4), 9–22.

Quetelet, L. A. J. (1831) [1984]. Research on the propensity for crime at different ages. Cincinnati, OH: Anderson Publishing.

Quetelet, L. A. J. (1842). *A treatise on man*. Edinburgh: William and Robert Chambers.

Rain, D. R., Long, J. F. and Ratcliffe, M. R. (2007). Measuring population pressure on the landscape: Comparative GIS studies in China, India, and the United States. *Population and Environment*, 28(6), 321–336.

Ratcliffe, J. H. (2001). On the accuracy of TIGER type geocoded address data in relation to cadastral and census areal units. *International Journal of Geographical Information Science*, 15(5), 473–485.

Ratcliffe, J. H. (2004). Geocoding crime and a first estimate of a minimum acceptable hit rate. *International Journal of Geographical Information Science*, 18(1), 61–72.

Ratcliffe, J. H. and McCullagh, M. J. (2001). Chasing ghosts? Police perception of high crime areas. *British Journal of Criminology*, 41(2), 330–341.

Ratcliffe, J. H. and Rengert, G. F. (2007). Near repeat patterns in Philadelphia shootings. *Security Journal*, 21(1–2), 58–76.

Rengert, G. F. (1996). *The geography of illegal drugs*. Boulder, CO: Westview Press.

Rengert, G. F. and Wasilchick, J. (1985). *Suburban burglary: A time and place for everything*. Springfield, IL: Charles C. Thomas.

Reiss, A. J., Jr. (1988). Co-offending and criminal careers. *Crime and Justice: An Annual Review of Research*, 10, 117–170.

Roberts, J. V. and Grossman, M. G. (1994). Changing definitions of sexual assault: An analysis of police statistics. In J. V. Roberts and R. M. Mohr (eds), *Confronting sexual assault: A decade of legal and social change* (pp. 57–83). Toronto, ON: University of Toronto Press.

Robinson, W. S. (1950). Ecological correlations and the behavior of individuals. *American Sociological Review*, 15(3), 351–357.

Rotton, J. and Cohn, E. G. (2003). Global warming and U.S. crime rates: An application of routine activity theory. *Environment and Behavior*, 35(6), 802–825.

Sacco, V. F. (2000). News that counts: Newspaper images of crime and victimization statistics. *Criminologie*, 33(1), 203–223.

Sacco, V. F. and Kennedy, L. W. (2002). The criminal event: An introduction to criminology in Canada (third edition). Toronto, ON: Thompson and Nelson.

Sampson, R. J. (1997). The embeddedness of child and adolescent development: A community-level perspective on urban violence. In J. McCord (ed.), *Violence and childhood in the inner city* (pp. 31–77). Cambridge, UK: Cambridge University Press.

Sampson, R. J. and Groves, W. B. (1989). Community structure and crime: testing social disorganization theory. *American Journal of Sociology*, 94(4), 774–802.

Sampson, R. J., Raudenbush, S. W. and Earls, F. (1997). Neighbourhoods and violent crime: a multilevel study of collective efficacy. *Science*, 277(5328), 918–924.

Sampson, R. J. and Wooldredge, J. D. (1987). Linking the micro- and macro-level dimensions of lifestyle-routine activity and opportunity models of predatory victimization. *Journal of Quantitative Criminology*, 3(4), 371–393.

Savoie, J. (2002). *Crime statistics in Canada, 2001*. Ottawa. ON: Statistics Canada, Canadian Centre for Justice Statistics.

Schmid, C. F. (1960a). Urban crime areas: Part I. *American Sociological Review*, 25(4), 527–542.

Schmid, C. F. (1960b). Urban crime areas: Part II. *American Sociological Review*, 25(5), 655–678.

Schulenberg, J. L. (2003). The social context of police discretion with young offenders: an ecological analysis. *Canadian Journal of Criminology and Criminal Justice*, 45(2), 127–157.

Semmens, N., Dillane, J. and Ditton, J. (2002). Preliminary findings on seasonality and the fear of crime: A research note. *British Journal of Criminology*, 42(4), 798–806.

Shaw, C. R. (1929). *Delinquency areas*. Chicago, IL: University of Chicago Press.

Shaw, C. R. and McKay, H. D. (1931). *Social factors in juvenile delinquency*. Washington, DC: U.S. Government Printing Office.

Shaw, C. R. and McKay, H. D. (1942). Juvenile delinquency and urban areas: A study of rates of delinquency in relation to differential characteristics of local communities in American cities. Chicago, IL: University of Chicago Press.

Sherman, L. W., Gartin, P. and Buerger, M. E. (1989). Hot spots of predatory crime: Routine activities and the criminology of place. *Criminology*, 27(1), 27–55.

Siljander, M., Clark, B. J. F. and Pellikka, P. K. E. (2011). A predictive modelling technique for human population distribution and abundance estimation using remote-sensing and geospatial data in a rural mountainous area in Kenya. *International Journal of Remote Sensing*, 32(21), 5997–6023.

Silver, W. (2007). *Crime statistics in Canada, 2006*. Ottawa, ON: Statistics Canada, Canadian Centre for Justice Statistics.

Silverman, R. A., Teevan, J. J. and Sacco, V. F. (1996). Measurement of crime and delinquency. In R. A. Silverman, J. J. Teevan and V. F. Sacco (eds), Crime in Canadian society. Toronto, ON: Harcourt Brace.

Simcha-Fagan, O. and Schwartz, J. E. (1986). Neighborhood and delinquency: An assessment of contextual effects. *Criminology*, 24(4), 667–699.

Smith, W. R., Frazee, S. G. and Davison, E. L. (2000). Furthering the integration of routine activity and social disorganization theories: Small units of analysis and the study of street robbery as a diffusion process. *Criminology*, 38(2), 489–523.

Stark, R. (1996). Deviant places: A theory of the ecology of crime. In P. Cordella and L. J. Seigel (eds), *Readings in contemporary criminological theory* (pp. 128–142). Boston: MA: Northeastern University Press.

Statistics Canada (1996). 1996 Census of Population. Ottawa, ON: Statistics Canada.

Statistics Canada (2007a). Canadian Socio-Economic Information Management System. Ottawa, ON: Statistics Canada, Canadian Centre for Justice Statistics.

Statistics Canada (2007b). *2006 community profiles*. Ottawa, ON: Statistics Canada, Canadian Centre for Justice Statistics.

Statistics Canada (2011). 2011 Census of Population. Ottawa, ON: Statistics Canada.

Statistics Canada (2012). Uniform Crime Reporting Survey (UCR). Ottawa, ON: Statistics Canada. Available on-line at http://www23.statcan.gc.ca/imdb-bmdi/pub/indexU-eng. htm [accessed 24 January 2013].

Stolzenberg, L. and D'Alessio, S. J. (2008). Co-offending and the age-crime curve. *Journal of Research in Crime and Delinquency*, 45(1), 65–86.

Tatem, A. J., Campiz, N., Gething, P. W., Snow, R. W. and Linard, C. (2011). The effects of spatial population dataset choice on estimates of population at risk of disease. *Population Health Metrics*, 9, Article Number 4.

Taylor, R. B. (1997). Social order and disorder of street blocks and neighborhoods: ecology, microecology, and the systemic model of social disorganization. *Journal of Research in Crime and Delinquency*, 34(1), 113–155.

Taylor, R. B., Koons, B. A., Kurtz, E. M., Greene, J. R. and Perkins, D. D. (1995). Street blocks with more nonresidential land use have more physical deterioration. *Urban Affairs Review*, 31(1), 120–136.

Townsley, M., Homel, R. and Chaseling, J. (2000). Repeat burglary victimisation: Spatial and temporal patterns. *Australian and New Zealand Journal of Criminology*, 33(1), 37–63.

Townsley, M., Homel, R. and Chaseling, J. (2003). Infectious burglaries: A test of the near repeat hypothesis. *British Journal of Criminology*, 43(3), 615–633.

Tseloni, A., Mailley, J., Farrell, G. and Tilley, N. (2010). Exploring the international decline in crime rates. *European Journal of Criminology*, 7(5), 375–394.

Tseloni, A., Osborn, D. R., Trickett, A. and Pease, K. (2002). Modelling property crime using the British Crime Survey: What have we learnt? *British Journal of Criminology*, 42(1), 109–128.

Tseloni, A., Wittebrood, K., Farrell, G. and Pease, K. (2004). Burglary victimization in England and Wales, the United States and the Netherlands. *British Journal of Criminology*, 44(1), 66–91.

Twain, M. (1906). Chapters from my autobiography. *North American Review*, 183, 321–330.

United States Census Bureau (2006). National Crime Victimization Survey, 2006. Washington, DC: United States Census Bureau.

van Mastrigt, S. B. and Farrington, D. P. (2009). Co-offending, age, gender and crime type: Implications for criminal justice policy. *British Journal of Criminology*, 49(4), 552 – 573.

van Koppen, P. J. and Jansen, R. W. J. (1999). The time to rob: Variations in time of number of commercial robberies. *Journal of Research in Crime and Delinquency*, 36(1), 7–29.

Wallace, M. (2003). *Crime statistics in Canada, 2002*. Ottawa, ON: Statistics Canada, Canadian Centre for Justice Statistics.

Wallace, M. (2004). *Crime statistics in Canada, 2003*. Ottawa, ON: Statistics Canada, Canadian Centre for Justice Statistics.

Weisburd, D., Bushway, S., Lum, C. and Yang, S. (2004). Trajectories of crime at places: A longitudinal study of street segments in the City of Seattle. *Criminology*, 42(2), 283–321.

Weisburd, D., Bruinsma, G. J. N., and Bernasco, W. (2009a). Units of analysis in geographic criminology: Historical development, critical issues, and open questions. In D. Weisburd, W. Bernasco and G. J. N. Bruinsma (eds), *Putting crime in its place: Units of analysis in geographic criminology* (pp. 3–31). New York, NY: Springer.

Weisburd, D., Bernasco, W. and Bruinsma, G. J. N. (2009b). *Putting crime in its place: Units of analysis in geographic criminology*. New York, NY: Springer.

Weisburd, D., Wyckoff, L. A., Ready, J., Eck, J. E., Hinkle, J. C. and Gajewski, F. (2006). Does crime just move around the corner? A controlled study of the spatial displacement and diffusion of crime control benefits. *Criminology*, 44(3), 549–591.

Wikstrom, P. O. H. (1991). Urban crime, criminals and victims: The Swedish experience in an Anglo-American comparative perspective. New York, NY: Springer-Verlag.

Wolfgang, M. E., Figlio, R. M. and Sellin, T. (1972). *Delinquency in a birth cohort*. Chicago, IL: University of Chicago Press.

Wooldredge, J. (2002). Examining the (ir)relevance of aggregation bias for multilevel studies of neighborhoods and crime with an example of comparing census tracts to official neighborhoods in Cincinnati. *Criminology*, 40(3), 681–709.

Xue, J. P., McCurdy, T., Burke, J., Bhaduri, B., Liu, C., Nutaro, J. and Patterson, L. (2010). Analyses of school commuting data for exposure modeling purposes. *Journal of Exposure Science and Environmental Epidemiology*, 20(1), 69–78.

Index

Introductory note

References such as '178–9' indicate (not necessarily continuous) discussion of a topic across a range of pages. Wherever possible in the case of topics with many references, these have either been divided into sub-topics or only the most significant discussions of the topic are listed. Because the entire work is about 'crime measurement', the use of this term (and certain others which occur constantly throughout the book) as an entry point has been restricted. Information will be found under the corresponding detailed topics.

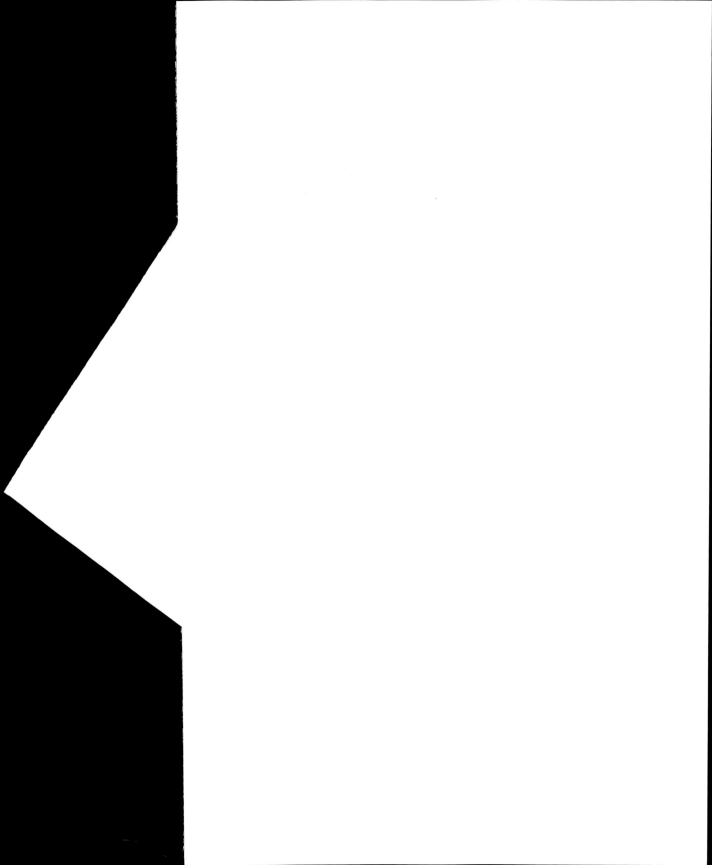

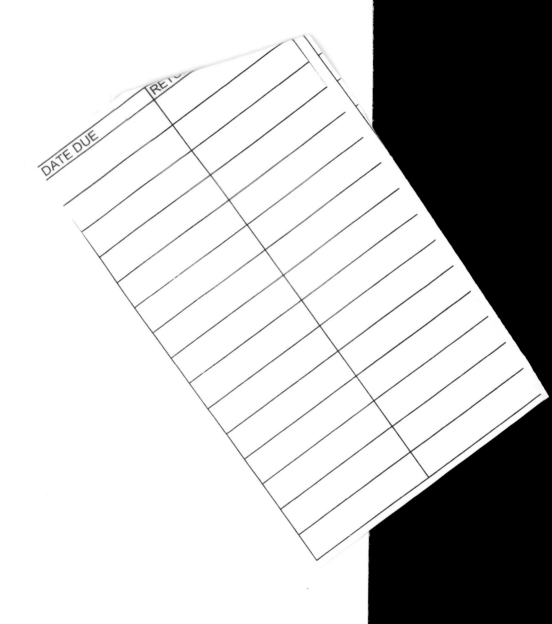

DATE DUE | RETU